THE GENDERED KIWI

THE GENDERED KIWI

Edited by
Caroline Daley and Deborah Montgomerie

AUCKLAND UNIVERSITY PRESS

For the little Gendered Kiwis in our lives, Briony and Caspar.

First published 1999

Auckland University Press
University of Auckland
Private Bag 92019
Auckland
New Zealand
http://www.auckland.ac.nz/aup

© The contributors 1999

ISBN 1 86940 219 7

Publication is assisted by the Historical Branch of the Department of Internal Affairs

Cover design by Christine Hansen
Printed by Publishing Press, Auckland

Contents

Introduction

Caroline Daley and Deborah Montgomerie

Kiwis are hard to sex: to the untrained eye, one small brown bird looks much like another. People, however, are expected to signal whether they are male or female in readily accessible ways. Their gender – the ways their sex is perceived in their everyday lives – matters. This book explores some of the ways that gender has shaped Pakeha lives. It brings together unpublished essays from historians at various stages of their careers, from established scholars through to graduate students. Through the lens of gender, old topics such as the family, demography and war are refocused; newer topics such as fashion, sexual politics and leisure are brought into view.

New Zealand social history is relatively rich in studies of women and of men. Patricia Grimshaw's *Women's Suffrage in New Zealand*, published in 1972, was our first 'second wave' feminist history. She was followed by a substantial group of historians writing about women's lives. This collection of essays is indebted to the work of Grimshaw and other women's historians. With the publication of Jock Phillips's *A Man's Country?* in 1987, women's history was joined by an emerging field of men's history, although it is still more common for women's gender to be recognised and written about. The groundwork has been laid for a gendered history of New Zealand but, as yet, there is no single volume analysing the experiences of women and men in concert. This book is intended to be the first bridge across that gap.

In the last 25 years women have been resolutely written into New Zealand history, a project that has gathered strength as more women entered graduate programmes in history and related disciplines. Writing women into history created a gendered history by default, but one in which women were the only explicitly gendered subjects; the gendering of men remained largely implicit. Books, articles and theses have engaged with the ideas of writers

7

overseas but, unlike the international pattern, there is no strict chronological divide between the different approaches in New Zealand women's history. We have not moved in a simple line from a women-centred approach, recovering and celebrating the women hidden from history, to analysing women's 'agency' and experiences, to then thinking about the construction of 'woman' as a category and then on to questions about the relative power of women and men, and how such relations are constructed, maintained and destabilised. Rather, in New Zealand these approaches have co-existed as different strands of the same rope, all aiming to hang masculinist mainstream studies that ignore, marginalise or trivialise women's past.

Eighteen-ninety three has been the 1066 of New Zealand women's history – in other words, tracing the history of feminism has been central to the creation of the discipline of women's history. Grimshaw's work marked the beginning of that project, but not its end. The masculine domain of party politics and government has continued to fascinate New Zealand women historians, partly, no doubt, because of the relatively early enfranchisement of women in this country.[1] Indeed the centenary of women's suffrage led to a flood of books about politics, many still written in a fairly uncritical, celebratory style.[2]

Alongside this interest in the women's movement has been an interest in individual women. This has manifested itself in a strong biographical tradition. These biographies range from individual portraits such as Judith Devaliant's book-length study of leading suffragist Kate Sheppard, to collections such as *The Book of New Zealand Women* and the essays on women in the various volumes of *The Dictionary of New Zealand Biography*. In some senses, these biographies fit into a celebratory mode of women's history. They recover women's lives in the hope of redressing the masculine bias of other historical studies. Yet at the same time they remind us of women's different pasts and of the battles they fought, whether they won or lost. Although the biographical tradition in New Zealand is still more celebratory than analytical, it nonetheless serves an important purpose.[3]

Just as the individual experiences of women have attracted attention, so have their shared experiences. Carroll Smith-Rosenberg's idea of a female world of love and ritual and a separate female culture has had some impact on the New Zealand historiography, but even more important has been the idea of women's agency and experience.[4] Again, there is no simple linear pattern to this. The idea of women as active agents in the making of their own history can be as attractive in the 1990s as it was in the 1970s. When Charlotte Macdonald wrote about single women immigrants to New Zealand she was interested in both recovering their experiences and understanding the choices they made. The focus was women-centred. So, too, when Barbara Brookes looked at the inquiry into abortion. Rather than the institutional focus of mainstream historical accounts, the central concern was how women experienced their past. More recent publications, such as Sandra Coney's *Standing in the Sunshine*, Anne Else's *Women Together* and Dame Mira Szaszy's *Te Timatanga Tatau Tatau: Early Stories from Founding Members of the Maori Women's Welfare League, Te Ropu Wahine Maori Toko i te Ora*, have all continued with this tradition of focusing on the organisations and worlds women created for themselves.[5]

In contrast to this women-centred approach, other historians have been more concerned with placing women in the established historical narrative, often rethinking that narrative. For example, women have been added to health and welfare history, reshaping understandings of state and male power. Bronwyn Dalley's study of child welfare, Margaret Tennant's work on the charitable aid system and Philippa Mein Smith's book on the medicalisation of childbirth are part of this trend. These histories centre on women as the object of state and medical intervention rather than as the agents of their own destinies. This genre focuses more on women's oppression than on celebrating women's achievements.[6]

One of the more recent trends in the international literature has been to stress differences among women, and to reject the notion of an essential woman. Again the New Zealand literature does not fall neatly into the chronology of the overseas scholarship. New Zealand women's history, like all New Zealand history, has not dealt well with class or ethnicity. But a binary model of respectable versus non-respectable women, stated most emphatically in the title of Anne Summers's *Damned Whores and God's Police,* was adopted.[7] Raewyn Dalziel's much referred-to 1977 essay, 'The Colonial Helpmeet', could be seen as the first attempt to look at the artificiality of respectable womanhood within the New Zealand colonial context.[8] Like the other works discussed above, it contributed to the effort to understand the subordination of women historically, and raised issues about the relative power of men and women.

The notion of men's relative power over women was central to the first monograph on the history of New Zealand men, Jock Phillips's *A Man's Country?*. Phillips wrote from a feminist perspective, influenced by the works of Smith-Rosenberg and others. Women's history had examined the social construction of femininity; this raised questions for Phillips and others about the nature of masculinity.[9] This movement away from questions of agency and towards an effort to understand power as relational led to further questions about how power is gendered. Building on women's history and men's history, gender history emerged.

The trend towards a gendered approach was reinforced by the appearance of two key works in 1988, Joan W. Scott's collection of essays, *Gender and the Politics of History* and Denise Riley's *"Am I That Name?" Feminism and the Category of 'Woman' in History*.[10] Scott's collection included her influential essay 'Gender: A Useful Category of Historical Analysis', and Riley drew attention to the construction of 'woman' in history, pointing out the instability of this notion. Issues of power, of social construction and of the interlocking of masculinities and femininities came to the fore of the debate, though, as with so many 'new' issues in historical debate, they were not entirely new. Feminist historians had long worked from an agenda of identifying men's power over women and fighting that oppression. Back in the 1970s, Joan Kelly-Gadol called for relational studies, pointing out that to understand women you needed to study them in relation to men.[11] The social construction of women had been the key to Barbara Welter's much-cited essay on the cult of true womanhood and Jill Matthews's *Good and Mad Women*.[12] But Scott and Riley gave fresh impetus to the debates. They were influential catalysts, along with the new voices from historians of masculinity. In 1985 Tim Carrigan, Bob Connell and John Lee published their essay 'Toward a New Sociology of Masculinity'.[13] With writers like John Tosh, David Morgan and Jeff Hearn, they have brought into sharper focus issues of power and the ways men are socially constructed. Taking their cue from feminism, many of these historians reject the notion of a unified, essential male past and instead talk about the history of masculinities. Plurality is important.[14]

As with any new term, gender history has taken on a variety of meanings, so it seems important to spell out how we see and use the term in this book. Four aspects of gender history are crucial to its use in this collection: that gender is relational, that women's and men's experiences tend to be different, that power relations are key to understanding those differences, and that rather than being monolithic, there are a plurality of masculinities and femininities. There is no archetypal Mr or Mrs New Zealand.

First, gender as a relational concept. In the overseas literature much has been made of the notion of separate spheres – the idea that women and men should occupy different spaces and perform different duties. Much of the existing New Zealand literature also deals with the separate institutions and sites of either femininity or masculinity; a gendered analysis does not treat femininities and masculinities as discrete phenomena. We need to study their confluences as well as their separate streams. As Michael Kimmel has said, '[m]asculinity and femininity are relational constructs; the definition of either depends on the definition of the other'.[15] Kimmel talks in the singular, but since he wrote many other scholars have pushed for analysis of the plurality and the interrelatedness of different kinds of masculinities and femininities. Indeed we have been forced to consider whether there are more than two genders.[16] Gender analyses the interrelatedness of masculinities and femininities. These relationships are sometimes positive, sometimes negative; sometimes they are between the sexes, sometimes they are within the sexes.[17]

Gender can be explored in situations where women and men act together in everyday situations and events, be that in the family, at work or in play. In the first essay, for example, Charlotte Macdonald revisits the issue of demographic imbalance between men and women in nineteenth-century New Zealand and questions its significance. This demographic theme is picked up by Erik Olssen in his exploration of gender relations within the nineteenth-century family. Both reject the image of New Zealand as a man's country, and advocate a more subtle reading of population statistics. The two essays on leisure also explore the ways gender relations are played out in sex-segregated activities like sport. Caroline Daley examines how the Auckland Domain was a gendered space in the period before the Second World War, while Jock Phillips looks more generally at the changing nature of leisure in the late twentieth century.

The diverse experiences and reactions of women and men are also part of gender history. They can often be perceived most readily in relation to dramatic events, such as economic crisis. Tim Frank's essay discusses shifting attitudes to male breadwinning and female workforce participation in 1930s New Zealand. Waging war is one of the most gendered activities. In her essay on men's and women's involvement in the Second World War, Deborah Montgomerie argues that gender ideology played an important part in reconciling these very different experiences of war. In this, as in all the essays in the collection, the dynamic relations between women and men are linked to wider issues of social power.

The issue of power is central to our understanding of gender. As Joan Scott has maintained, 'gender is a primary way of signifying relationships of power'.[18] This focus on power – on who has it, and how it is dispersed and differentiated – means that gender is not just a descriptive category. We can use gender to tell a story, or use it as a way to revision arenas in which power is conventionally exercised, such as the courts or the world of business. Bronwyn Dalley examines the narrow parameters within which women could defend their actions in the melodramatic narratives of nineteenth-century child murder cases. Both Danielle Sprecher and Frazer Andrewes explore office politics and power dressing. Representations of men in white-collar occupations configured masculine power in modern ways. The suited man embodied power, but he was not the only figure to do so. Daley details the ways men's bodies dominated public space in the Domain, from the entrance gate to the pavilion.

Although part of the power equation is to study situations where men oppress women, that is not the sum total of how power operates in our history. We are also interested in exploring how certain women can participate in men's power, have power over other women or use their femininity as a form of power over men. Dalley analyses how 'respectable' women were avid spectators and participants in the trials of other women, sharing in the power of men. Conversely, Barbara Brookes examines the efforts of feminist men in the 1970s to equalise power in their own households. The ways that power has been contested over the last 150 years is crucial to our understanding of Pakeha gender relations.

The notion that power is dispersed and differentiated leads to the fourth aspect of our use of gender in this book. Gender is about the plurality of experiences. We have no desire to create an essential woman or man in these pages. Macdonald shows the importance of regional variation in the balance of numbers between the sexes. Olssen examines a multitude of experiences under the heading of family. We should not assume that the norms of masculinity were relevant only to men or femininity to women. The fear of appearing masculine constrained many women's actions while men could not adopt feminine norms without transgression. Sprecher provides a number of humorous anecdotes about the way men had to be lured into department stores and affirmed in their masculinity while they were shopping. On the other hand, the women she writes about were expected to provide glamour in the office without appearing frivolous.

Sexuality is part of our understanding and use of gender, be it the sexual politics of the workforce or the home. That said, this collection could be accused of being part of what queer theorists have termed 'heteronormativity', reiterating the centrality of heterosexual gender relations in our history. [19] To some extent we must plead guilty. The absence of essays on homosexuality, lesbianism and trans-sexuality reflects the fact that these issues are only slowly being researched historically. This is true for other types of history too. Histories revolving around class relations remain scant in the New Zealand historiography, as do those on ethnicity. We acknowledge that this is yet another collection of essays in Pakeha historiography. Although this is a cause for concern, it is also inevitable, given that gender history stands on the shoulders of women's history, and women's history in New Zealand has tended to be about Pakeha women. We are not trying to claim here that Pakeha experiences were more important than Maori experiences, or that gender was a more important structure in our society than any other. The question of how we write Maori into New Zealand gender history is one aspect of the larger exercise of understanding the nature of New Zealand's gender relations. We expect that, as research proceeds, the distinctiveness of Maori gender ideology and lived experience will become clearer. At that point it will be possible to draw more conclusions about the relationship between the gendering of Maori and Pakeha.

The essays in this collection are examples of sites and periods in which we can begin gendering the kiwi, but they are not intended as an exhaustive list. While this book cannot be all things to all people, we hope that it will help to reconcile the history of gender and the histories of men and women, and does not ignore the political project encompassed by women's history or the on-going need for men's history. Nor are we reaffirming mainstream history under a 'sexier' label. Rather the aim is to use gender as another way into our history, a way that does not privilege a male or female reading, but problematises both. To this end, we hope that this book both reflects the strengths of past scholarship and indicates avenues for further research. We are not aiming for a cosy orthodoxy. If this collection provokes disagreement and more analysis, she'll be right.

January 1999

1 Pre-1993 publications include Phillida Bunkle, 'The Origins of the Women's Movement in New Zealand: The Women's Christian Temperance Union, 1885-1895', in Phillida Bunkle and Beryl Hughes, eds, *Women in New Zealand Society*, Auckland, 1980; Raewyn Dalziel, 'The Colonial Helpmeet: Women's Role and the Vote in Nineteenth-Century New Zealand', *New Zealand Journal of History (NZJH)*, 11, 2, 1977, pp. 112-23; Patricia Grimshaw, *Women's Suffrage in New Zealand*, 2nd edn, Auckland, 1987; Margaret Lovell-Smith, *The Woman Question: Writings by the Women who Won the Vote*, Auckland, 1992.

2 The suffrage centennial outpourings included Angela Ballara, 'Wahine Rangatira: Maori Women of Rank and their Role in the Women's Kotahitanga Movement of the 1890s', *NZJH*, 27, 2, 1993, pp. 127-39; Arthur Baysting, Dyan Campbell and Margaret Dagg, eds, *Making Policy Not Tea: Women in Parliament*, Auckland, 1993; Helena Catt and Elizabeth McLeay, eds, *Women and*

Politics in New Zealand, Wellington, 1993; Caroline Daley and Melanie Nolan, eds, *Suffrage and Beyond: International Feminist Perspectives*, Auckland, 1994; Jean Garner, 'Sir John Hall and Women's Suffrage', *Historical News*, 67, October 1993, pp. 8-11; Janet McCallum, *Women in the House: Members of Parliament in New Zealand*, Picton, 1993; Charlotte Macdonald, *The Vote, the Pill and the Demon Drink: A History of Feminist Writing in New Zealand, 1869-1993*, Wellington, 1993; Dorothy Page, introduction, *The Suffragists: Women Who Worked for the Vote*, Wellington, 1993; Tania Rei, *Maori Women and The Vote*, Wellington, 1993; Rosemarie Smith, *The Ladies Are At It Again! Gore Debates the Women's Franchise*, Wellington, 1993.

3   Some recent biographical writings include Maureen Birchfield, *She Dared to Speak: Connie Birchfield's Story*, Dunedin, 1998; Annabel Cooper, ed., *The Not So Poor: An Autobiography*, Auckland, 1992; Judith Devaliant, *Kate Sheppard: A Biography*, Auckland, 1992, and *Elizabeth Yates: The First Lady Mayor in the British Empire*, Auckland, 1996; Ruth Fry, *Maud and Amber: A New Zealand Mother and Daughter and the Women's Cause, 1865 to 1981*, Christchurch, 1992; David Gee, *My Dear Girl: a Biography of Elizabeth McCombs, New Zealand's First Woman Member of Parliament, and Her Husband, James McCombs, Member of Parliament for Lyttelton for Twenty Years*, Christchurch, 1993; Betty Gilderdale, *The Seven Lives of Lady Barker: Author of Station Life in New Zealand*, Auckland, 1996; Lynley Hood, *Minnie Dean: Her Life and Crimes*, Auckland, 1994; Margaret Lovell-Smith, *Plain Living, High Thinking: The Family Story of Jennie and Will Lovell-Smith*, Christchurch, 1995; Charlotte Macdonald, Merimeri Penfold and Bridget Williams, eds, *The Book of New Zealand Women, Ko Kui Ma Te Kaupapa*, Wellington, 1991; Jessie Munro, *The Story of Suzanne Aubert*, Auckland, 1996; Frances Porter, *Born to New Zealand: A Biography of Jane Maria Atkinson*, Wellington, 1989; Jane Tolerton, *Ettie: A Life of Ettie Rout*, Auckland, 1992; Fay Hercock, *Alice: The Making of a Woman Doctor, 1914–1974*, Auckland, 1999.

4   Carroll Smith-Rosenberg, 'The Female World of Love and Ritual: Relations Between Women in Nineteenth-Century America', *Signs*, 1, 1, 1975, pp. 1-27.

5   See, for example, Barbara Brookes, 'Housewives' Depression: The Debate over Abortion and Birth Control in the 1930s', *NZJH*, 15, 2, 1981, pp. 115-34; Sandra Coney, *Every Girl: A Social History of Women and the YWCA in Auckland 1885-1985*, Auckland, 1986 and *Standing in the Sunshine: A History of New Zealand Women Since They Won the Vote*, Auckland, 1993; Raewyn Dalziel, *Focus on the Family: The Auckland Home and Family Society 1893-1993*, Auckland, 1993; Anne Else, ed., *Women Together: A History of Women's Organisations in New Zealand, Nga Ropu Wahine o te Motu*, Wellington, 1993; Charlotte Macdonald, *A Woman of Good Character: Single Women as Immigrant Settlers in Nineteenth-century New Zealand*, Wellington, 1990; Dorothy Page, *The National Council of Women: A Centennial History*, Auckland, 1996; Mira Szaszy, *Te Timatanga Tatau Tatau: Early Stories from Founding Members of the Maori Women's Welfare League, Te Ropu Wahine Maori Toko i te Ora*, Wellington, 1993.

6   Bronwyn Dalley, *Family Matters: Child Welfare in Twentieth-Century New Zealand*, Auckland, 1998; Philippa Mein Smith, *Maternity in Dispute, New Zealand 1920-1939*, Wellington, 1986; Margaret Tennant, '"Brazen-faced Beggars of the Female Sex": Women and the Charitable Aid System, 1880-1920', in Barbara Brookes, Charlotte Macdonald and Margaret Tennant, eds, *Women in History: Essays on European Women in New Zealand*, Wellington, 1986, '"Magdalens and Moral Imbeciles": Women's Homes in Nineteenth Century New Zealand', in Barbara Brookes, Charlotte Macdonald and Margaret Tennant, eds, *Women in History 2*, Wellington, 1992, and *Paupers and Providers: Charitable Aid in New Zealand*, Wellington, 1989.

7   For work influenced by this dichotomy see Andrée Lévesque, 'Prescribers and Rebels: Attitudes To European Women's Sexuality in New Zealand, 1860-1916', in Brookes et al, eds, *Women in History*; Tennant, '"Brazen-faced Beggars of the Female Sex"', and '"Magdalens and Moral Imbeciles"'.

8   Dalziel, 'The Colonial Helpmeet', pp. 112-23.

9   Published work on New Zealand men includes James Allan, *Growing Up Gay: New Zealand men tell their stories*, Auckland, 1996; Nigel Gearing, *Emerging Tribe: Gay Culture in New Zealand in the 1990s*, Auckland, 1997; Kai Jensen, *Whole Men: The Masculine Tradition in New Zealand Literature*, Auckland, 1996; Alison Gray, *The Jones Men: 100 New Zealand Men Talk About Their Lives*, Wellington, 1983; Michael King, ed., *One of the Boys? Changing Views of Masculinity in New Zealand*, Auckland, 1988; Jock Phillips, *A Man's Country? The Image of the Pakeha Male –*

   A History, revised edn, Auckland, 1996.
10 Denise Riley, *"Am I That Name?" Feminism and the Category of 'Woman' in History*, Minneapolis, 1988; Joan W. Scott, *Gender and the Politics of History*, New York, 1988.
11 Joan Kelly-Gadol, 'The Social Relation of the Sexes: Methodological Implications of Women's History', *Signs*, 1, 4, 1976, pp. 216-27.
12 Jill Julius Matthews, *Good and Mad Women: The Historical Construction of Femininity in Twentieth-Century Australia*, Sydney, 1984; Barbara Welter, 'The Cult of True Womanhood 1820-1860', *American Quarterly*, 18, 2, Part 1, 1966, pp. 151-74.
13 Tim Carrigan, Bob Connell and John Lee, 'Toward a New Sociology of Masculinity', *Theory and Society*, 14, 1985, pp. 551-604.
14 Some of the more influential literature on masculinities includes Harry Brod, ed., *The Making of Masculinities: The New Men's Studies*, Boston, 1987; Mark C. Carnes and Clyde Griffen, eds, *Meanings For Manhood: Constructions of Masculinity in Victorian America*, Chicago, 1990; Rowena Chapman and Jonathon Rutherford, eds, *Male Order: Unwrapping Masculinity*, London, 1988; R. W. Connell, *Masculinities*, Berkeley, 1995; Jeff Hearn, *Men in the Public Eye: The Construction and Deconstruction of Public Men and Public Patriarchies*, London, 1992; J. A. Mangan and James Walvin, eds, *Manliness and Morality: Middle-class Masculinity in Britain and America 1800-1940*, New York, 1987; David H. J. Morgan, *Discovering Men*, London, 1992; Michael Roper and John Tosh, eds, *Manful Assertions: Masculinities in Britain since 1800*, London, 1991; Lynne Segal, *Slow Motion: Changing Masculinities, Changing Men*, New Brunswick, 1990.
15 Michael Kimmel, 'The Contemporary "Crisis" of Masculinity in Historical Perspective', in Brod, ed., *The Making of Masculinities*, p. 122. Or as Judith Butler puts it, gender marks 'the constitutive asymmetry of sexed positions'. Judith Butler, 'Against Proper Objects', *differences*, 6, 2 and 3, 1994, p. 17.
16 Walter L. Williams, *The Spirit and the Flesh: Sexual Diversity in American Indian Culture*, Boston, 1992, *passim*.
17 Gisela Bock, 'Women's History and Gender History: Aspects of an International Debate', *Gender & History*, 1, 1, 1989, pp. 7-30.
18 Joan W. Scott, 'Gender: A Useful Category of Historical Analysis', in *Gender and the Politics of History*, p. 42.
19 The relationship between gender and sexuality is discussed in Judith Butler, *Bodies That Matter: On the Discursive Limits of 'Sex'*, New York, 1993; Biddy Martin, 'Sexual Practice and Changing Lesbian Identities', in Michèle Barrett and Anne Phillips, eds, *Destabilising Theory: Contemporary Feminist Debates*, Cambridge, 1992; Suzanna Danuta Walters, 'From Here to Queer: Radical Feminism, Postmodernism, and the Lesbian Menace (Or, Why Can't a Woman Be More Like a Fag?)', *Signs*, 21, 4, 1996, pp. 830-67. It is important to note the danger of again privileging sex at the expense of gender and other axes of power. At its best, queer theory points to the blurred lines between sex and gender and their conflicted intimacy: gender norms regulate sexuality, gender is itself sexed.

Far from the image of the crude, beer-swilling 'bush bachelor', these Scandinavian picnickers were going about their Sunday afternoon festivities with a high degree of ritual and formality. The scene is Lowry Bay on Wellington's eastern harbourside, the setting of Katherine Mansfield's childhood story 'At the Bay', 27 December 1896.
Alexander Turnbull Library, National Library of New Zealand, Te Puna Matauranga o Aotearoa, 1/2-05226.

Too Many Men and Too Few Women: Gender's 'Fatal Impact' in Nineteenth-Century Colonies

Charlotte Macdonald

There is a strong Malthusian legacy in historical accounts of Pakeha New Zealand's patterns of gender. Numbers matter. That many more men than women were drawn to New Zealand to settle or to sojourn has long been a commonplace of our colonial history. What that disparity means is much less a matter of consensus. While Malthus's famous 'principle of population' predicted a geometrical increase in population alongside an arithmetic increase in subsistence, with dire consequences for social life, historians of nineteenth-century New Zealand have been equally deterministic – though generally more sanguine – about the effect of an unbalanced 'sex ratio' in the settler population.

Jock Phillips's influential account of New Zealand's masculine culture was based on what he termed 'truth by numbers':[1] the overwhelming male population providing the necessary soil in which a masculine culture first thrived. The consequences were self-evident: 'It does not require a great imagination to see what a difference such an imbalance must have made to colonial society or to the experience of Pakeha males in particular'.[2] In the absence of women, men 'naturally looked to other men for support and company'.[3] It was this demographic base, Phillips claims, which 'turned Pakeha New Zealand into a man's country'.[4] In advancing the argument of New Zealand settler society as an ideal society subverted, characterised primarily by atomisation, 'the masculinity variable' (ratio of adult males to adult females) features prominently as one of Miles Fairburn's three key explanatory factors.[5] In general histories of nineteenth-century New Zealand, too, the predominance of European males in the settling population is held to infuse the society with a rude vigour. The abundance of men had a roughening effect on the incipient culture and on the men themselves. Drunkenness, drifting, an admiration for strength of muscle rather than mind were the costs of such lives; what was won was a rugged, stoic individualism forged in an unforgiving terrain.

Social historians argue that the imbalance of the sexes made mid-Victorian aspirations of social order based on gendered boundaries between work and home, family and stranger, domestic and public, less easy to achieve.[6] For colonial men, sharing a table with other men was a more common experience than sharing one where a woman presided over teapot and breadboard. At its most expansive, the abundance of men forms part of a national narrative that takes up the story of Aotearoa/New Zealand from the point of European exploration, through the drama of early encounters, muskets, speculation, ambitious schemes of colonisation, warfare, gold, the conversion of wilderness into cultivation, and then, with the century coming to a close, the onset of a moderating state intervention exemplified by Richard Seddon's 1898 old age pensions (some of the first recipients being 'old-timers' reaching the end of their lives without the support of families).

On the other side of the gender equation, it has been suggested that the relative scarcity of women, especially those of young adult years, provided women with a fulcrum from which they were able to extract some advantage in economic power, legal rights, political status and social position — both individually and collectively. Raewyn Dalziel's now almost iconic article about the colonial helpmeet took the disparity in numbers of adult men and women as a key element in the argument depicting the nineteenth-century suffrage campaign as a conservative victory: the winning of the vote in 1893 heralded the triumph of domesticity and a reward for dutiful womanhood. [7] The sex ratio, part of Dalziel's delineation of the 'special circumstances' of colonial New Zealand, worked 'in favour of women' by improving opportunities for marriage. The 'demand' for women as marriage partners 'put a premium on women as wives'.[8] For Judith Elphick, the position of scarcity made colonial New Zealand 'a seller's market' for women, whether selling their labour as servants, or searching for a spouse. In addition, high birth rates and relatively low infant mortality amounted to 'a life of real advantage and opportunity'.[9] In James Belich's more recent work, New Zealand is depicted as 'a brides' paradise' for much the same reasons.[10]

In stressing the power of scarcity, historians looking at the position of women have been inclined to view gender relations as a matter of supply and demand in a market where the successful exchange was marriage. Elsewhere such patterns have not been read as optimistically. Commenting on colonial Australia, Gordon Carmichael notes: 'The sheer excess of men and the corollary that many would be unable to lead normal family existences ensured that the colonies would be daunting places for women'.[11] Whether scarcity is interpreted as a position of leverage depends on how relationships of power between women and men are understood, and how relationships between individuals (especially marriage) are explicated in terms of social generalities.

In New Zealand, the New World or 'the frontier' as a metaphor for unbounded opportunity has operated powerfully over understandings of the experiences of women and the shaping of colonial femininity. European women's presence in an uncultivated and, to European eyes, under-occupied land, in lesser numbers than their male compatriots, has been read as constituting a field of expansive possibility. From the greater likelihood of marrying and marrying 'well' in the early decades of settlement, to the physical freedom of bush, mountain, tussock, the satisfactions of independent householding, and their success in winning the vote, New Zealand offered women and femininity scope far beyond what was possible where they had come from.[12]

Historians of women have generally been more preoccupied with establishing and exploring the dimensions of the female *presence* in history, rather than the meanings or significance of the female *absence*. Studies such as my own *A Woman of Good Character*, Sheryl Goldsbury's work on women missionaries, Sandra Quick's on women on the goldfields, are just a few of the large number that have focused attention on groups of women previously at the edges rather than the centre of historical attention.[13] The substantial body of biographical work over the last decade has also added considerably to what is known about women.[14] Together with the thematic studies, they have brought the question of gender more to the forefront of historical studies generally. The combination of the underlying influence of the 'opportunity' metaphor, with this concentration on establishing women as significant and active historical subjects, has resulted in a reinforcement of the impression of New Zealand as a favourable place for women. The advantage to be derived from 'scarcity' has been less central to more recent studies but their conclusions have done little to overturn the notion that being a minority might have had benefits rather than the costs pointed to by Carmichael.

By contrast, the unbalanced sex ratio presents a more difficult interpretive puzzle for historians attentive to the shaping of an antipodean masculinity. The effects on men have been more ambivalently portrayed. On the one hand, the surfeit of men in the founding decades of Pakeha New Zealand has served to help explain how gender has been a major axis of inequality: the incontrovertible nature of numerical predominance provides an unambiguous base for other manifestations of dominance. Moreover, the sex imbalance was a very obvious point of contrast between the new and old worlds. The idea of a rough physical life close to nature is in accordance with the Sinclairian generation of histories which saw the shape of New Zealand society and culture arising from the local environment and the conditions that the predominantly male settling population encountered on the ground, rather than the characteristics of the inherited fragment and the lingering cultural ties to the British societies of origin.[15] Late-nineteenth-century New Zealand emerged as a society forged by the typically vigorous young men in an untrammelled place, in contrast with the crowded, constrained, domesticated and overmannered female-abundant British Isles. Youth and age, male and female were (and are) associated with the young colony and the old country – the language of the two places is contoured by age and gender.[16]

A more benign, perhaps more popular, legacy, which can be traced to the decades when men outnumbered women, is the strong cultural presence of 'the man on the land'. Too many men and too few women gave rise to a society in which bush bachelorism became the formative cultural milieu for men and an intense, but highly utilitarian, domesticity the cultural milieu for women. Although many men did spend their lives harpooning whales, hacking down trees, mustering in the foothills, and so on, these activities were certainly not the only expression of masculinity, and from the 1880s were less and less the common experience of most New Zealand males. Pioneer man increasingly became legend rather than reality.[17] Yet this image of masculinity has persisted and continues to command a central place in popular and literary culture in figures as disparate as John Mulgan's *Man Alone*, Barry Crump's *Good, Keen Man* and beer brewer Speight's', 'Southern Man'.[18]

So, an array of meanings is offered about the way in which colonial New Zealand reshaped gender relations. They may not coalesce but they all agree in attributing an enduring social force to circumstances in which a larger population of men came into 'fatal impact' with a smaller population of women. The results are portrayed as the 'natural' effect of population gender asymmetry: a benign variation of the idea of the 'fatal impact' wrought by Europeans in their colonial encounters with indigenous peoples.[19] Demographic profiles have been adopted unproblematically as *dynamics* of gender. If gender analysis means an understanding of the social organisation of sexual difference, then numbers alone are not enough. To understand the nature of gender relations in New Zealand we need to reconsider the links between population structure and the meanings of gender, between demography and the dynamics of gender.

A necessary first step is to examine further the magnitude and character of the gendered structure of the colonial population, including a consideration of its comparative profile. A general pattern of sex disproportion prevailed in most settler societies. Was New Zealand more or less a masculine society than similar settler societies that comprised the main destination areas for the European, and especially the British, diaspora? The exploration of the histories of women, masculinity and the operation of gender have taken place in the last 20 years largely within the parameters of a New Zealand national history. While drawing on an international literature, studies have focused on local subjects. In few areas is national uniqueness explicitly claimed, but there has been a tendency to build a national history of gender by default. Jock Phillips's history of masculinity is a case in point. Although it first appeared as a history of Pakeha masculinity in a particular society, the response and subsequent work by scholars beyond New Zealand have resulted in findings that emphasise the similarities between masculinities, thereby diminishing the original work's claim to account for a specific national culture (but broadening the originality and influence of the work).[20] Insofar as the sex imbalance has been part of an explanation of a national history, there is a danger that it has come to be seen as something unique rather than a feature shared by most settler societies in the nineteenth century.

Questions about the impact of the disparity in numbers of men and women also deserve reconsideration in the light of the gender dynamic in Maori-Pakeha interactions. To a large extent, the unbalanced sex ratio has been discussed solely in relation to the settler population. What is the basis for such a discussion in isolation? Can we look at consequences of the sex ratio without considering gender and 'race' worlds in the nineteenth century? By the 1890s, the population of Aotearoa/New Zealand was a product of 130 years or more of encounters between the two groups which had their beginning in the 1760s.

The changing tides of population numbers reveal very starkly a shifting balance of power between the two racial groups, and the growth of a people tracing their descent from Maori and European parents. In the late 1850s, the numbers of Maori and Pakeha were roughly equivalent but from this time the geographical distribution and numerical balance of the two populations grew more and more distinct. Settler communities, especially in the South Island, grew up having very little contact with Maori, and in the North Island, the aftermath of the conflicts of the 1860s concentrated Maori populations in the central, eastern coastal and northern regions with relatively limited contact with Europeans. Social experiences and milieu became more distinct. The period in which European numbers really began to grow rapidly, and when the sex ratio was most extreme, was also the time when the two populations were beginning to diverge. From the 1860s onwards, as Maori came to represent a decreasing proportion of the country's total inhabitants, devastated by the impacts of disease and dispossession, the greatest disparities in gender became those between European males and females. The earlier history of interactions shaped by largely male European minorities forming liaisons with Maori women continued in pockets of the country but overall they came to constitute a much less significant aspect of the total distribution of the population. The way in which gender shaped interactions between Maori and Pakeha remains relatively under-investigated and deserves further analysis. As far as the broader picture is concerned, a bringing together of questions concerning gender and 'race' is needed. As will be argued below, such a history requires a careful attention to specificity of place and time, given the vastly different circumstances and timing of settlement and interactions across nineteenth-century New Zealand.

Historians would do well, then, to revisit the way in which they have they have understood the sex imbalance in the population. Are existing arguments about the impact of the sex ratio sufficiently robust to support the edifices built on them? This chapter proposes that there is merit in casting a more sceptical eye on these matters. Specifically, it asks: have historians exaggerated the degree to which colonial New Zealand was a numerically male dominant society? Has the demographic pattern been taken to define a uniquely national pattern of gender relations when the same demographic features can be traced in most other colonial settler societies? To what extent did a male surplus/female deficit population structure reconfigure gender relations? Has the male abundant colonial period as a heroic era of 'men alone' endured far beyond what is justified in demographic terms, and in the face of evidence that many men sought out a domestic existence?

What is the basis for claiming that New Zealand's colonial society was a highly gender-imbalanced society? Table 1 sets out the sex ratios (males per 100 females) for the census years 1851–1901.

Table 1: Sex ratios (males per 100 females) non-Maori, all ages, 1851–1901

1851	128	1878	125
1858	131	1881	122
1861	160	1886	117
1864	162	1891	109
1867	152	1896	111
1871	141	1901	110
1874	135		

(Source: *Census of New Zealand*, 1851–1901)

Fig 1. Sex ratios, 1851–1901, non-Maori

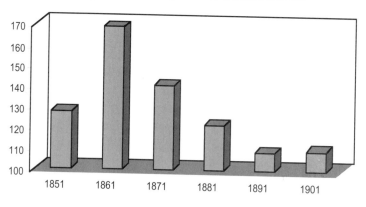

Throughout the second half of the nineteenth century the sex ratio was 'high', exceeding the parity measure of 100; this confirms overall claims about the predominance of males in the settler community. But also evident is the sudden rise and more gradual fall in the measure. Only in one decade did the ratio exceed 150, and that peak of imbalance was relatively short-lived. By the 1890s, the imbalance was quite modest and continued to decline, reaching a level of 104.6 in 1921, very close to that in the Australian, Canadian and white American populations at the same time (it did not reach 100 until 1951).[21] The closing gap between male and female populations towards the end of the century is generally cited as indicating the colony's maturation. 'Frontier' conditions had faded, more people were living in towns and cities in households where income came principally from wage or salary earnings.[22] Even more dramatic was the sharp drop in size of families. As the demographer C. J. Gibson notes, the remarkable

23

feature of New Zealand's nineteenth-century European population was not so much its rapid growth, as its transition, within a very short time, from being a population characterised by exceptionally high rates of natural increase to one of comparatively low rates.[23] If this was the process by which the sex ratio 'normalised' at the end of the century, how had it reached such extremes in earlier decades?

The European settler population grew erratically, and in a very regionally idiosyncratic pattern. Until the mid-1870s, the main population growth came from immigration; thereafter natural increase formed the primary contributor (but in turn fell rapidly).[24] The ratios in Table 1 are derived from populations of very different sizes and spatial distributions. In 1840, when systematic colonisation by Europeans began, the Pakeha population was estimated to total just 2000 throughout the country.[25] By the time of the first national census in 1851, it had reached just 26,707 and by 1874, the last time the ratio exceeded 130, the non-Maori population numbered 299,514.[26] In 1901, the total European population had reached 772,719: more than double that of just two decades earlier. The single most rapid decade of population growth for the European population was the 1870s, when the sex ratio had already dropped from its peak.

Reference to colony-wide patterns in regard to population, economy, politics and social conditions before the 1870s is not very illuminating. The national figures shown in Table 1 must be interpreted with a high degree of qualification. Recognising the highly localised timing, circumstances and patterns of settlement in the different parts of the country, Table 2 presents gender ratios by province.

The contrasts are striking, serving to highlight the degree to which the national aggregates do little to represent the actual demographic shape of any one settlement, but rather present a notional pattern. The most dramatic patterns are those associated with gold – the single most masculinising factor in settler history. By far the most extreme disparity between the sexes is evident at the height of the Otago goldrush in the early 1860s, when the sex ratio for the province's adult population reached a staggering 438.[27] The masculinising force of gold was intensified in the early 1860s by the outbreak of war bringing troops into the north – Auckland, Waikato and Taranaki. 'Gold fever' on the West Coast (from 1865), Nelson/Marlborough (Wakamarina-Canvastown, 1864) and at Thames/Hauraki (from 1867 to 1868) attracted similar swarms of fortune seekers over the next decade.[28]

Table 2: Sex ratio by province 1861–1901, with non-Maori population numbers

	1861 [Pop.]	1871	1881	1891	1901
Auckland	123	132	119	110	111
	24,420	62,335	99,451	133,178	175,946
Taranaki	133	134	134	114	118
	2044	4480	14,858	22,065	37,855
Hawke's Bay	176	146	126	123	113
	2611	6059	17,367	28,506	35,424
Wellington	111	121	114	115	110
	12,566	24,001	61,371	97,725	141,354
Marlborough	188	161	129	124	115
	2299	5235	9300	12,767	13,326
Nelson	115	172	131	126	119
	9952	22,501	26,075	34,770	37,915
Westland		213	152	139	126
		15,357	15,010	15,887	14,506
Canterbury	125	122	117	106	103
	16,040	46,801	112,424	128,663	143,248
Otago	352	153	125	112	109
	27,163	60,722	107,481	116,088	125,341
Southland	154	127			
	1,820	8,769			
NEW ZEALAND	160	141	122	109	110
	106,209	256,393	489,933	626,658	772,719

(Source: *Census of New Zealand*, 1861–1901)

In these places the characteristic configuration of population was for large numbers of men to converge on a highly specific locality, set up temporary camps or bases and become wholly preoccupied in the pursuit of gold. Such populations were highly mobile; the phenomenon of whole towns created and abandoned within very short spaces of time was remarkable even to contemporaries. The almost pathological nature of such behaviour was also recognised, causing simultaneous excitement and alarm.[29] The very high sex ratio evident in these places is, in large part, derived from the same population moving from place to place. The transient gold seekers, most of them men travelling alone, whether married or single, were presumably counted in each goldfield at successive censuses (1861, 1864, 1867, 1871, 1874).

As the first and largest field, the Otago rush was the most remarkable. The discoveries at Gabriel's Gully in 1861 brought the first great influx of men, most of them coming from the fading Victorian diggings. The huge flood overwhelmed the small and relatively well-ordered town of Dunedin, tipping the population of Otago as a whole sharply towards the masculine pole. But the provincial administration acted quickly in an effort to counterbalance the moleskin invasion. In a bold and what some feared would prove a risky undertaking, the province's Edinburgh and London agents were instructed to stop recruiting all but single women as new migrants. It is another reminder of the high drama surrounding gold and one of the biggest experiments in 'social engineering' that took place in nineteenth-century New Zealand. Alongside the hundreds of men disembarking at Port Chalmers in 1862, dead set on cutting a path to the goldfields, were over 1300 young women who had sailed directly from Scotland (and some from England) – fruits of the province's swift about-turn in immigrant recruitment. Such an enterprise was bound to generate some sparks, and they ignited in the tragi-comic events in the Dunedin Immigration Barracks over the summer of 1862–63 where, at one time, over 150 young women, newly arrived, were housed cheek by jowl with members of the constabulary fresh from Victoria and charged with keeping order in the excitable, volatile communities of gold seekers.[30] Amid allegations of improper conduct, prostitution, drunkenness and dissolute behaviour – all swirling around elections for the superintendency – the province's reputation briefly endured infamy in the columns of *The Times* for outbreaks of behaviour previously associated only with the rough Australian migrant trade.

Outside Otago, however, the registrar-general could reassure the General Assembly in 1861 that the population showed signs of 'social progress': the proportion of females to males had increased, yielding a sex ratio of 124, an improvement on 1858.[31] In the 1860s, the European population grew rapidly in the South Island and rather less so in the North, where the outbreak of war in Taranaki led to the dispersal of some local settlers, and the inflow of troops from Australia and other parts of the British Empire. The expansion of government immigration in the 1870s under the ambitious

Vogel scheme and the recovery from economic recession in the late 1860s, in combination with the cessation of large-scale hostilities in the north, brought renewed European immigration in these years.

What is the connection between these statistical profiles and the circumstances in which people were living out their lives? Does the asymmetry evident in such tables translate into unique dynamics of gender at the local level? To get closer to the actual social settings within which people lived, we need to break down these categories further.

Consider, for example, the provincial disaggregations contained in Table 2. Useful contrasts can be drawn between the earlier decades of smaller and more volatile population concentrations, and later decades where, in some areas, a large and more balanced settler population was consolidating. In other areas 'late frontier' conditions prevailed. In the decades 1861–81, two groups of settlements emerge for consideration from the statistics in Table 2, setting aside the aberrations of Otago's gold-skewed population distribution. The three most populous provinces after Otago were Auckland, Wellington and Canterbury, all of which had a commercial centre and a large surrounding rural area of settlement. Over the period 1861–81 these three provinces accounted for around three-quarters of the colony's population outside Otago (Figure 2). What was happening in these regions represents the social conditions in which the larger part of the European population was living. In size of population, if not in land area, Taranaki, Hawke's Bay and Marlborough encompassed less than 20 per cent of the total settler population (no more than 12.5 per cent of the total population beyond Otago). Two of these provinces were pastoral; the third remained small in population through a combination of warring conflict and a terrain that made close settlement difficult.

Figure 2: New Zealand population distribution, 1861 and 1881, non-Maori

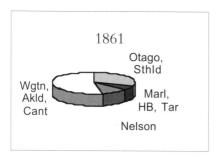 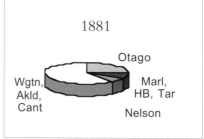

Sex ratios in the major provinces (Auckland, Wellington and Canterbury) ranged from 130 in 1858 to the high of 145 in the mid-1860s but by 1871 were back to 126. The majority of the population, therefore, lived in communities where there were more males than females, but this disparity was not extreme. Taking into account differences between rural and urban populations, further refinement is possible. In 1881, the sex ratio in the urban populations of Auckland and Wellington cities, together with Christchurch, was just 103.[32] In the pastoral districts of Hawke's Bay and Marlborough, and the tiny settler population in Taranaki, the disparity was more marked but formed the social setting for a relatively small proportion of the settler population.

In the last two decades of the nineteenth century, marked shifts in the population structure are evident. Sex ratios for 1891 and 1901 are much lower than in preceding years *and* there is a convergence between the older major settlements, the minor provinces and the anomalous 'gold' regions. The places with the highest sex ratios (over 120 in Westland, Marlborough and Hawke's Bay in 1891) are those with the smallest populations. Nelson is the exception. This suggests that the number of settlers who experienced life in a highly unbalanced population was relatively small, and that such experience was relatively short-lived. All this indicates, first, that generalisations about the sex ratio cannot be applied in a blanket fashion and, second, that the *extent* and *magnitude* of highly unbalanced populations was limited in both place and period, and arose chiefly from extraordinary circumstances such as gold discoveries.

How do these patterns compare with those in the Australian colonies? Was New Zealand more or less 'a man's country' than its trans-Tasman neighbours?

In 1861, the Australian colonies as a whole had a greater surfeit of males than New Zealand beyond Otago (see Table 3). Again, the national sex ratio of 138 encompasses a range of highly variable local conditions. Victoria was still showing the effects of gold with a ratio of 155 but it was only in the older settlements of Tasmania and the Wakefieldian-colonised South Australia that the sex ratio fell below the non-Otago New Zealand figure of 124 (at 123 and 105 respectively).[33] By the end of the century there was a great deal of convergence between the sex ratios on both sides of the Tasman, with exactly the same figure being reached in 1901 (110).

**Table 3: Sex ratio by Australian colony 1861–1901,
with population numbers**

	1861	1871	1881	1891	1901
	[Pop.]				
New South Wales	130	121	121	118	110
	350,860	503,981	751,468	1,123,954	1,354,846
Victoria	155	121	110	109	101
	538,628	731,528	862,346	1,130,463	1,201,885
Queensland	152	149	142	132	126
	30,059	120,104	213,525	393,718	503,266
South Australia	105	106	112	106	102
	126,830	185,425	276,414	315,533	358,508
Tasmania	123	114	112	112	108
	89,977	99,328	115,705	146,667	172,475
Western Australia	171	148	135	149	158
	15,593	23,315	29,708	49,782	184,124
Northern Territory		593	3218	1349	558
		201	3,451	4,989	4,509
AUSTRALIAN COLONIES	138	121	117	116	110
	1,151,947	1,663,882	2,252,617	3,165,015	3,779,613

(Source: Wray Vamplew, ed., *Australians: Historical Statistics*, Sydney, 1987)

Below the national aggregates, however, distinct patterns can be discerned across the Australian colonies and, even more than in New Zealand, the contrasts in *size* of populations mean that in measuring the effect of gender imbalances care must be taken to evaluate social impact. Weighing the relative magnitude of the populations *living* in situations of imbalance, there is a stark comparison in Australia. Throughout the second half of the nineteenth century, the great majority of Australia's white population was spread around the south-eastern edge of the continent. Between the 1860s and 1890s, over 80 per cent of people lived in New South Wales, Victoria and South Australia, with the ascendancy of 'the big three' dropping only slightly below that level in 1901 (to 77 per cent). It was in these places that the effects of a particular population structure would predominantly influence lives. The sex ratio was lowest in South Australia, never exceeding 106, while in New South Wales and Victoria it was highest in 1861 at 130 and 155 respectively. The Victorian figure was high because of the influx of men to the goldfields in the late 1850s, but this highly masculine influence ebbed quite fast, the sex ratio dropping to 110 in 1881. In the same year, New South Wales's ratio was significantly higher at 121. A rough parallel can be drawn between these older, established populous settlements and the first group of larger provinces in New Zealand (Auckland, Wellington and Canterbury).

Those colonies in which settlement came later, and where the urban port focus was the centre for a very much larger surrounding area – in Western Australia and Queensland – the sex ratio is higher, and stays higher over a longer period. In the Swan River colony of Western Australia, the sex ratio in the small 1861 population of just 15,593 was 171; by 1901, the comparative figures were 184,124 and 158. The discovery of gold on the Kalgoorlie fields in the 1890s lifted the male population at the end of the period. In Queensland the 1861 sex ratio was 152; in 1881 it had dropped to 142 and by 1901 to 126. The total numbers of people living in these places characterised by larger disparities in numbers of women and men were relatively small. The parallel here is with the second group of New Zealand provinces: Taranaki, Marlborough and Hawke's Bay. Again, this reiterates the danger of making broadly generalised predictions of the impact of the sex ratio from phenomena of limited duration and limited magnitude.

**Fig 3. Sex ratios, most populated settlements
Australia and New Zealand, 1861–1901**

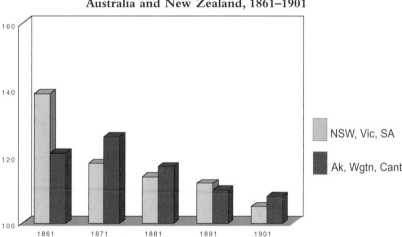

Reaching across to the other side of the Pacific, comparisons can also be made with settler societies in the North American West. In California, of course, gold brought men to the western coast in hordes from 1848. When the territory joined the Union in 1850, with the rush still in full flow, the population was enumerated as comprising 86,000 males and 7000 females, almost all of whom were between the ages of 15 and 44. By 1880 the population had increased almost ten-fold and although the disparity was much less extreme the sex ratio was still 149.[34] In the Yukon (Klondike) at the end of the century the same extreme pattern is evident. As in Australasia, it was gold that most severely tipped communities towards male concentrations. Further into the continent, the great westward movement of people in nineteenth-century America saw the settlement of vast tracts of land west of the Mississippi by predominantly white migrants from the east and from Europe, in what became the prairie states of Illinois, Indiana, Iowa, Minnesota and Missouri, and on the plains in Kansas, Montana, Nebraska, North Dakota, Oklahoma, South Dakota and Wyoming. North of the border in British Columbia and across the prairies to Manitoba, the extension of the railroad opened up the possibility of European settlement beyond the coastal strip from the 1870s. There are broad parallels with New Zealand's nineteenth-century history in the displacement of indigenous people and economies based on extractive, agrarian and pastoral enterprises. Comparisons between the resulting societies are worthy of further examination.

Aside from convict transportation to certain parts of Australia, both the American West and the colonies of Australasia were perceived as places offering opportunity for individual advancement. They served as destinations for a largely voluntary migration with permanent settlement as the long-term ambition. Single people made up the greater portion of the migrating stream but the establishment of familial communities was the goal. Nineteenth-century immigrant societies tended to be dominated by men. Migration is rarely evenly undertaken by men and women alike and the nineteenth-century European diaspora was no exception: it was a population exodus in which more men than women left their countries of origin to test their fate in the New World. It is a circumstance in which the forces that draw women and men together in intimate, reproductive, familial, sexual and economic encounters can be seen to operate within larger imperatives that work to draw them apart. Settler societies, therefore, are characterised by population imbalance – in gender, age, occupation and social status. Those features are most prominent and experienced most sharply by the initial generation. Thereafter they rapidly recede.

As well as being 'products' of the European and British diaspora, these societies share other features that make them of particular interest to historians of gender. Both 'frontiers' – the Australasian and the western North American – were places where strong temperance movements led by women flourished, and where parallel campaigns for women's political rights won early success. The unlikely conjunction of an apparent sympathy towards women's political emancipation with a masculinist society has long been a historical puzzle. Successive historical solutions to the riddle illustrate the malleability of arguments based on the population gender imbalance. One set of answers stresses the innovative and improvising character of these 'new' societies. The disparity between numbers of men and women resulted in more permeable gender boundaries.[35] A diametrically opposed argument stresses the intensification of gender distinctions and the enhanced value of the feminine in a situation where gender divisions were made more conspicuous by the relative scarcity of women. This is the interpretation behind 'the colonial helpmeet'.[36] The debate on this question will continue. The analysis here, however, indicates that the answers are less and less likely to be found in a simple extrapolation of political or social consequences from numerical disparities between women and men.

The conclusion, then, is not to deny the existence of the population imbalance but to give it greater specificity, and to question the degree to which it can be used as an unproblematic dynamic of gender. Numbers alone are not enough. In themselves they contain only weak explanatory power. Gender analysis is not primarily a counting exercise. To date, much of the focus of New Zealand historians has been on the simple *dimensions* of gender rather than on the more powerful tool of a gender analysis that encompasses the social organisation of sexual difference.

The comparative perspective adopted here encourages reconsideration of the dimension and severity of the New Zealand imbalance. The nature of the imbalance between males and females varied considerably over time and place, and reached extreme proportions only for a brief period, largely in the extraordinary circumstances associated with the discovery of gold. Placing New Zealand within a spectrum of settler societies all populated more by men than women but some more masculinist than others, indicates that New Zealand was not exceptional. Even compared with the Australian colonies, New Zealand was more masculinist for only a very short period: largely those years coinciding with gold. It is easy to exaggerate or claim a uniquely national pattern of gender relations; this analysis would suggest there are greater elements of similarity than difference. If there was a gender 'fatal impact' in colonial New Zealand, it was short-lived and occurred in pockets rather than in a general fashion. As with the 'fatal impact' of race, the 'fatal impact' of gender deserves reconsideration.

Further explorations in the study of nineteenth-century masculinity will yield other perspectives on what it means to identify New Zealand as 'a man's country'. Population features will play a part but will need to be further interrogated as to the dynamics of male surfeit. Historians of masculinity will need to look beyond a simple equating of numerical dominance with political or social systems in which power corresponded more often than not with men. Elsewhere, historians of masculinity have emphasised the *varieties* of masculinity, especially at the end of the nineteenth century.[37] Equally, historians of women and femininity must resist the temptation to fall back on arguments based on numerical scarcity.

The unbalanced sex ratio cannot be overlooked in understanding the nature of gender in New Zealand history, but it must be considered with care and cannot be assumed to have led, inevitably, to a single set of social effects or manifestations. The assumption that populations in which gender is in balance are normal and/or optimal needs to be more fully critiqued. Specific social settings are commonly not ones in which males and females exist in equal numbers. Yet the historical focus on the meanings of the surplus of men and deficit of women in colonial settler societies suggests that the late twentieth century has not entirely shaken free from the statistical preoccupations of mid-nineteenth-century England and the anxieties caused by systematic population enumeration. Perhaps it is time to step out of the shadow cast by the figure of Malthus.

Research assistance provided by the Internal Grants Committee, Victoria University of Wellington, is gratefully acknowledged.

1   Jock Phillips, *A Man's Country? The Image of the Pakeha Male – A History*, revised edn, Auckland, 1996, p. 4.
2   *Ibid.*, p. 9.
3   *Ibid.*
4   *Ibid.*, p. 6.
5   Miles Fairburn, *The Ideal Society and its Enemies: The Foundations of Modern New Zealand Society 1850-1900*, Auckland, 1989, Ch. 7, see especially Fig. 7.4, p. 214.
6   See, for example, Jeanine Graham, 'Settler Society', in Geoffrey W. Rice, ed., *The Oxford History of New Zealand*, 2nd edn, Auckland, 1992, pp. 112-40; Jeanine Graham, 'The Pioneers (1840-1870)', in Keith Sinclair, ed., *The Oxford Illustrated History of New Zealand*, Auckland, 1990, pp. 49-74; Erik Olssen and Marcia Stenson, *A Century of Change, 1800-1900*, Auckland, 1989; Laurie Barber, *New Zealand: A Short History*, Auckland, 1989; Duncan Mackay, *Frontier*

New Zealand: The Search for Eldorado 1800-1920, Auckland, 1992; and the two defining histories for the writing of 'modern' New Zealand history: Keith Sinclair, *A History of New Zealand*, first published Harmondsworth, 1959, and W. H. Oliver, *The Story of New Zealand*, London, 1960.

7 Raewyn Dalziel, 'The Colonial Helpmeet: Women's Role and the Vote in Nineteenth-Century New Zealand', *New Zealand Journal of History (NZJH)*, 11, 2, 1977, pp. 112-23.

8 *Ibid.*, pp. 113, 114.

9 Judith Elphick, 'What's Wrong with Emma? The Feminist Debate in Colonial Auckland', *NZJH*, 9, 2, 1975, pp. 129, 130.

10 James Belich, *Making Peoples: A History of the New Zealanders From Polynesian Settlement to the End of the Nineteenth Century*, Auckland, 1996, p. 306.

11 Gordon A. Carmichael, 'Colonial and Post-Colonial Demographic Patterns', in Raymond Evans and Kay Saunders, eds, *Gender Relations in Australia: Domination and Negotiation*, Sydney, 1992, p. 107.

12 See Patricia Grimshaw, *Women's Suffrage in New Zealand*, Auckland, 1972; Frances Porter, *Born to New Zealand: A Biography of Jane Maria Atkinson*, Wellington, 1989; Mary Ann Barker, *Station Life in New Zealand*, first published London, 1870, and in print almost continuously since; Fiona Kidman, 'Lady Barker', in Charlotte Macdonald, Merimeri Penfold and Bridget Williams, eds, *The Book of New Zealand Women/Ko Kui Ma Te Kaupapa*, Wellington, 1991, pp. 47-9; Cherry Hankin, 'Barker, Mary Anne', in *The Dictionary of New Zealand Biography, Vol. One, 1769-1869*, Wellington, 1990, pp. 15-16; Judith Binney, Judith Bassett and Erik Olssen, *The People and the Land: Te Tangata me Te Whenua. An Illustrated History of New Zealand 1820-1920*, Wellington, 1990, *passim*, but for particular points see pp. 171, 246.

13 Charlotte Macdonald, *A Woman of Good Character. Single Women as Immigrant Settlers in Nineteenth-Century New Zealand*, Wellington, 1990; S. J. Goldsbury, 'Behind the Picket Fence: The Lives of Missionary Wives in Pre-colonial New Zealand', MA thesis, University of Auckland, 1986; Sandra Quick, '"The Colonial Helpmeet Takes a Dram": Women Participants in the Central Otago Goldfields Industry 1861-1901', MA thesis, University of Otago, 1997.

14 The biographical work is extensive and includes: Macdonald et al, eds, *The Book of New Zealand Women; The Dictionary of New Zealand Biography*, Volumes One-Four, 1990, 1993, 1996, 1998; Porter, *Born to New Zealand*; Shirley Tunnicliff, ed., *The Selected Letters of Mary Hobhouse*, Wellington, 1992; Lynley Hood, *Minnie Dean: Her Life and Crimes*, Auckland, 1994; Jessie Munro, *The Story of Suzanne Aubert*, Auckland, 1996; *The Suffragists: Women Who Worked for the Vote*, Wellington, 1993; Judith Binney, *Nga Morehu*, Auckland, 1986. See also the list of further reading in Barbara Brookes, Charlotte Macdonald and Margaret Tennant, eds, *Women in History 2*, Wellington, 1992, pp. 300-09.

15 Sinclair, *A History of New Zealand*, *passim*. See also K. A. Pickens, 'The Writing of New Zealand History: A Kuhnian Perspective', *Historical Studies*, 68, April 1977, pp. 384-98; Erik Olssen, 'Mr Wakefield and New Zealand as an Experiment in Post-Enlightenment Experimental Practice', *NZJH*, 31, 2, 1997, pp. 197-218.

16 For a more extended discussion of this point see Dominic David Alessio, 'Domesticating "the Heart of the Wild": Female Personifications of the Colonies, 1886-1940', *Women's History Review*, 6, 2, 1997, pp. 239-69.

17 Phillips, *A Man's Country*, Ch. 1.

18 John Mulgan, *Man Alone*, Hamilton, 1949; Barry Crump, *A Good Keen Man*, first published Wellington, 1960; Robin Law, 'Masculinity, Place, and Beer Advertising in New Zealand: The Southern Man Campaign', *New Zealand Geographer*, 53, 2, 1997, pp. 22-8.

19 The term 'fatal impact' refers to the idea that the encounter between European and indigenous cultures was so uneven that the only possible result was the crippling devastation, if not extinction, of indigenous societies. Current within evangelical circles in the nineteenth century, it also came to characterise a generation of post-war histories in the Pacific, Australia and New Zealand. Alan Moorehead's *The Fatal Impact: An Account of the Invasion of the South Pacific*, Harmondsworth, 1966, was probably the most popularly read work shaped by the idea. The idea of fatal impact has been thoroughly critiqued by a subsequent generation of interpreters who emphasise the resilience, active resistance and agency of indigenous people in the face of

the European presence and colonial imposition.

20 Phillips, *A Man's Country*, p. viii.

21 C. J. Gibson, 'Demographic History of New Zealand', PhD thesis, University of California, Berkeley, 1971, Tables 28 and 29, pp. 94-5, 100. Sex ratios for Australia and Canada in 1921 were 103.4 and 106.4 respectively; for the white American population in 1920 it was 104.4.

22 Erik Olssen, 'Towards a New Society', in Rice, ed., *The Oxford History of New Zealand*, pp. 254-84.

23 Gibson, 'Demographic History of New Zealand', Ch. 7.

24 *Ibid.*, pp. 22-3.

25 J. M. R. Owens, 'New Zealand Before Annexation', in Rice, ed., *The Oxford History of New Zealand*, p. 50.

26 *Census of New Zealand*, 1874.

27 Fifteen–54-year-olds, *Census of New Zealand*, 1861. Even then, the figure does not include an estimated 3000 miners 'in tents in different gullies and on the roads', *Appendices to the Journal of the House of Representatives*, 1862, D-9, p. 5.

28 Malcolm McKinnon, ed., *New Zealand Historical Atlas*, Auckland, 1997, Plate 44: Gold Rushes and Goldfields.

29 See David Goodman, *Gold Seeking: Victoria and California in the 1850s*, Sydney, 1994, for a superbly refreshing argument about goldfields in the contemporary mind.

30 For further discussion of this episode see Macdonald, *A Woman of Good Character*, pp. 27-32. See also A. H. McLintock, *The History of Otago*, Dunedin, 1949, pp. 492-3; Olive Trotter, *The Maid Servants Scandal: A Page from Otago's Early History*, Dunedin, 1993.

31 *Statistics of New Zealand*, 1861, p. vi.

32 *Census of New Zealand*, 1881.

33 Wray Vamplew, ed., *Australians: Historical Statistics*, Sydney, 1987, POP 266-274, p. 39.

34 United States Bureau of the Census, *Historical Statistics of the United States, Colonial Times to 1970*, Washington, 1975, Part I, Series A 195-209, p. 25.

35 This interpretation is most fully developed and most closely associated with Grimshaw's *Women's Suffrage in New Zealand*.

36 See especially Dalziel, 'The Colonial Helpmeet', also Phillida Bunkle, 'The Origins of the Women's Movement in New Zealand: The Women's Christian Temperance Union 1885-1895', in Phillida Bunkle and Beryl Hughes, eds, *Women in New Zealand Society*, Auckland, 1980, pp. 52-76.

37 See, for example, Mark Carnes and Clyde Griffen, eds, *Meanings for Manhood*, Chicago and London, 1990.

The autonomous nuclear family became the ideal in nineteenth-century New Zealand. As this photograph of a group outside one of McCallum & Co.'s sawmill houses shows, natural increase soon helped to even out the preponderance of males in the colony.
Alexander Turnbull Library, National Library of New Zealand, Te Puna Matauranga o Aotearoa, 1/2-066205.

Families and the Gendering of European New Zealand in the Colonial Period, 1840–80

Erik Olssen

In 1978 I wrote the essay, 'Towards a History of the European Family in New Zealand',[1] in the belief that 'the history of the family provides the missing link . . . between the study of culture and the study of social structure, production and power'.[2] I organised that brief history around the idea that a single-family type existed in the Victorian era, centred on the idea of separate spheres, but that it later fragmented to the point where 'there no longer is such an institution as "the New Zealand family", but a variety of family types'.[3] In one sense that was true but in another, perhaps more fundamental sense, the work done on women's history and family history over the past 20 years indicates that the colonial family was more complex than my earlier account allowed. In the mid-nineteenth century a variety of family types existed and the idea of separate spheres was more honoured in the breach than the observance.[4] In the last decade, as the editors have remarked, 'gender' and 'gendering' have increasingly supplanted 'women' and 'family' on the research agenda. By and large, the history of the family has not benefited from the new focus. It might be expected that the family, as a primary site where gender is constructed, would have become of greater interest. That has not been the case. Hence this chapter synthesises the work of the last 20 years on the colonial family and speculates about its significance for the gendering of New Zealand.[5]

'At the core of the unique European family system . . . was the single-family household established by monogamous marriage.'[6] As a result, couples married only when they could afford to establish their own households. This usually occurred quite late in life, generally when they were in their late twenties or early thirties. Mutual consent was central to the relationship, as the church had long insisted, and a high proportion of people never married.[7] Compared with other civilisations, Western Europe conceded greater equality to married women and even more to widows. In the eighteenth century, as literate élites constructed a new topography of public and private in Western Europe and began to define the two sexes as opposites, several influential philosophers concluded that women played a central role in the socio-cultural evolution of human society. While the reconfiguration of sexual difference into binary oppositions created the possibility that women might be asexual, their civilising role now made their status an issue of public policy. At the same time, childhood came to be defined as a natural stage in the human life cycle and one which required a nurturing family to flourish.[8] Because of these new ideas during the nineteenth century, at least in Britain, a new ideal family was imagined: 'the word "family" ceased to mean all the members of a household, unrelated as well as related, and came to signify only the nuclear unit'.[9] Increasingly, the conjugal family, sometimes known as the autonomous nuclear family – a mother, father and their children – shared a dwelling until the children left home.[10] This, then, was the background to the European colonisation of New Zealand.

In the mid-nineteenth century, however, the way in which Britons thought of family still varied considerably according to ethnicity, region or nation, class and religion. The great majority of families in Britain were still enmeshed in production. Wives usually helped in family-based production, besides running the household and providing for apprentices, servants and visitors. Children also contributed to household production. The male heads of household were also much about the house (the precise pattern varied, depending on occupation). Families on the periphery – crofters, those in quarrying and mining districts, fishermen and sailors – had their own distinctive variants of marriage and the domestic division of labour. High levels of illiteracy or ignorance of English often acted as a prophylactic against new ideas. In many regions marriage was still based on consent alone. In rural Scotland, for instance, 'if any two unmarried people of lawful age . . . wished to get married, if they were physically capable of marriage and not within the prohibited degrees of kinship, and they both freely expressed this wish and freely accepted each other in marriage, then they were married. Consent made a marriage – not the clergy, nor the civil official – but the consent of two people wishing to marry.'[11] Married women often enjoyed considerable autonomy in these more 'traditional' communities and could end the marriage if the man had not fulfilled his part of the contract. The community, not the family, policed behaviour with such devices as charivari. In general, as Leonore Davidoff remarks, families and households were not distinguished and still blurred 'their boundaries with categories such as friend and cousin'.[12] Yet the new rituals of family life – what Gillis means by 'family time' – began to influence broader sectors of British society. Christmas, birthdays and christenings had become popular family celebrations for the urban middle class in England by the 1840s and the family dinner was becoming a major weekly ritual.[13] These new fashions quickly proved popular, especially among emigrants.

The European whalers, sealers and traders who settled in New Zealand before 1840 were often drawn from peripheral British communities. They discovered among Maori that 'partnerships recognised as marriages existed' although no marriage ceremony existed as such. Often the couple signified their intention by being discovered, usually after a night together (a practice still common in parts of Britain at that time). Among those of rank, the man asked the woman's senior male relations and if consent was obtained 'carries his "intended" off by force, she resisting with all her strength'. If she escaped the marriage was off. As a rule, Augustus Earle concluded, 'women have a decided aversion to marriage' because they gave up their freedom for servitude.[14] Polygamy existed, however, and men would take as wives the women of defeated hapu. The number of wives may have signified male rank. Several chiefs explained to Samuel Marsden, founder of the first mission, that they needed many wives because nobody else would work for them.[15] Be that as it may, hapu frequently arranged marriages, particularly for persons of rank, in order to create alliances and advance their mana (such practices still occurred among wealthy and aristocratic European families). The wider network of kin relations was paramount, however, and the organisation of Maori society meant 'that marriage partnerships formed neither the primary social nor economic unit, as they did in European society'.[16] Many hapu were keen to provide traders and shore whalers with wives as a means of creating reciprocal obligations and access to trade; men alone needed protection and all European men needed somebody to manage their household.[17]

The blurring of conjugal relationships within broader horizontal kin networks so that, for example, matua signified mother, aunts and even unrelated women of the same cohort, marked a central difference between Maori and middle-class European notions of family. So, too, did the role of marriage in integrating the partner into the complex reciprocal obligations that existed within a hapu and between related hapu, and the fact that, for each partner, especially the woman, the wider kin group remained more important than the spouse and maintained a general interest in the well-being of their relation. Between 1800 and 1850 many European men and Maori women, by marrying, had to negotiate these differences.[17] Middle-class English notions of family were not pervasive throughout Britain and many immigrants, especially from the Gaelic periphery, thought of marriage and family in not dissimilar ways.[19] The Maori wives, however, almost always lived in European-style houses and took responsibility for managing them, whereas the European husbands almost always ended up as part of the Maori world of mutual obligation until, as sometimes happened, they moved on.[20] Later it was less common, but not unknown, for Maori men to marry European women: 'By the end of the century a sizeable portion of New Zealand's population traced a mixed ancestry' and in some regions, notably Southland, a very large proportion of people living in Pakeha-style marriages were of mixed descent.[21] To what extent these mixed marriages created a distinctive New Zealand family remains an unstudied issue. As the influx of Europeans swelled, however, a growing proportion of colonists lived in European-style families, although the different frontiers in the North Island continued to provide socio-geographical spaces where intermarriage continued to occur.[22]

Both the missionaries and the systematic colonisers considered family central to New Zealand's future. Both groups, despite their considerable differences, accepted the Evangelical idealisation of the family that became the Victorian orthodoxy. The missionaries attacked polygamy and preached the spiritual and moral equality of women and men. The Protestant missionary societies sent only married couples to the field, who promptly built homes for their own families, architectural statements of their belief in the conjugal family and Western ideas of public and private. Although many systematic colonisers, led by Edward Gibbon Wakefield, were sceptical about religion, they, too, accepted the centrality of the conjugal family to a civilised society. They also believed in patriarchal authority, a view strengthened by the Evangelical view of the family as a microcosm of the true church.[23] More to the point, at least in the first instance, Wakefield considered the family central to systematic colonisation. In his well-known *Letter from Sydney* (1829), he spelt out the idea that the ideal emigrants would be young married couples who had not yet had any children. By the time he wrote *England and America* (1833), however, he had concluded that a great excess of single young men made frontier societies pathological. He now recognised that the division of labour between married men and their wives enhanced the efficiency and value of men's work and he predicted that the success of his scientific scheme would make 'The colony . . . an immense

40

nursery'. In *A View of the Art of Colonization*, published in 1849, Wakefield emphasised the importance of women's moral authority to the transplantation of civilisation. The importance of a wife to male colonists and of women to the dream of establishing a happy colony remained a recurring theme throughout the nineteenth century. This emphasis would make New Zealand different from other colonies.[24]

The New Zealand Company's advertising campaign placed great emphasis on Wakefield's themes and attracted many young couples from the 'uneasy class'.[25] This vision of a model colony chose those who believed that a right state of society must be centred on the family. The New Zealand Company enticed more than 11,000 emigrants to New Zealand, most of them young married couples or young and single. Few were recruited from Britain's most impoverished classes. The company's agents and sub-agents enjoyed particular success in London, its adjacent counties and in Cornwall and Devon. Later the Otago Association recruited most heavily from Edinburgh and its surrounding counties and among Scots living in or near London, while the Canterbury Association recruited from London and the surrounding counties, from Yorkshire and Lancashire, from Ulster and from the south and west of Ireland.[26] Many, it seems, were from pre-industrial areas where, as Wakefield remarked of Ireland, 'the cottier system . . . turns . . . [many labourers] into something between capitalists and workmen'.[27] As Miles Fairburn has shown, such people dreamed of a familial arcadia where they could achieve independence, abundance and freedom. Many of those from the Home Counties, by contrast, may have dreamed of recreating pre-industrial England, a common criticism of the Canterbury scheme.[28] A large number, however, shared a desire to resist or reverse the separation of home and work and to maintain the family, under the husband-father's authority, as a productive economic enterprise. Men's fear that their moral authority as husbands and fathers would be undermined by the new forms of labour and machinery, not to mention the ignominy of being dependent on wage-earning wives and children, resounds from the 1830s until the 1890s.[29]

The six colonies established between 1840 and 1850 were small and largely isolated from each other. In Otago, established in 1848 by Free Church Presbyterians from Scotland, the first minister, the Reverend Thomas Burns, visited each family, regardless of its church affiliation, in order to maintain a broad surveillance. Even without such pastoral care, the smallness of the settlements and the strong resolve to maintain their valued institutions meant that family largely fulfilled its Wakefieldian role. In order to understand the importance of the family in the new colony, however, we need a precise geography of where migrants came from and the particular meanings of family in those areas. Unfortunately, except for New Plymouth and Waipu, the latter a small colony of peripatetic Highland Scots, we lack good studies of the demographic characteristics of those who settled here between 1840 and 1860. In New Plymouth, however, Raewyn Dalziel discovered that '[m]igration with family members, as expected and encouraged by the [New Zealand] Company, was the norm'. She found that of the steerage passengers 59 per cent belonged to conjugal families, 37 per cent belonged to extended families, and only 4 per cent on the first six ships had no kin already in Taranaki. Cabin passengers, by contrast, were more likely to migrate without kin but 77 per cent of this small group belonged either to conjugal or extended families. Nor were young couples with one or two children, or yet to start their families, the only type of family to migrate. Of 57 couples who had married between 1825 and 1834 – almost 34 per cent of the married – the great majority had more than four children before their arrival. Many of these children, British born, married within a decade of arrival. 'Three generational families became quite common in the 1840s and 1850s.' The fact that adult siblings also often migrated together rendered the kin networks even more dense.[30] Friends and neighbours also often migrated together and were not necessarily distinguished from kin.[31]

Many men and women of the 'uneasy class' confidently sought greater opportunities and a simpler life, secure in the knowledge that the family would be strengthened rather than weakened. Material abundance freed the migrants not only from fear of marriage but also from the fear of having more children than they could afford. It was, indeed, something akin to orgasmic release, aided by a protein explosion. Meat, freely available, was often eaten three times a day. Within 10 years, most of Wakefield's settlements could boast that almost half the population was younger than 12 years old and two-thirds had not yet reached 21. Many couples had between seven and 12 children and a sizeable minority had more. The really keen, like the Cargills, had 19.[32] Charlotte Godley's letters for the period 1850–53, when she lived in Wellington and then Canterbury, suggest an astonishing enthusiasm for the rituals of courtship and heterosexual engagement, at least among the 'uneasy class'.[33] Social life throughout the colony remained a constant whirl of balls, picnics, and excursions. In the 1840s, high rates of fertility were largely produced by marrying at much younger ages than people did in Britain. In New Plymouth, over half the brides were under 20 years old and they averaged 10.4 children each.[34]

Although almost all families expected children to contribute work to the household, they also enjoyed a degree of freedom that often startled visitors from Britain. Colonial freedom fostered greater independence and weakened British beliefs about gender. Girls and boys rode to school or walked, often barefoot; they fished and hunted; built huts and adventured. The children were the first colonists to make themselves fully at home, the first to take full advantage of physical freedom. Edward Wakefield, a stripling on arrival, dismissed the common criticism that colonial children lacked respect for their elders: 'They learn from a very early age to think for themselves and to do a great many things for themselves which their parents would do for them in old countries'.[35] The freedom enjoyed by children, a freedom that shaped the way they dealt with adults, was enhanced because the settlement of New Zealand occurred at about the time when the idea that children were 'natural', but needed improvement, was giving way to the idea that children were born innocent.[36] Such ideas made it appropriate for parents to regard childhood as a special state and to permit considerable freedom and independence. Many families migrated to provide their children with greater freedom and opportunity, of course, but not a few worried about the consequences of 'spoiling'.[37]

Women of the 'uneasy class' adapted British ideas of feminine behaviour to enjoy the new freedoms, the endless tasks and the law of colonial necessity – in a crisis, the first one there copes. Lady Barker's best-selling account of her outdoor pursuits, from pig hunting to picnics, showed that feminine grace and refinement could accommodate quite unladylike pursuits.[38] Few married women enjoyed Lady Barker's leisure and freedom but the link between womanhood and hysteria did not easily survive the voyage and the new land (even if we define hysteria as anything women did which men could not explain). Any woman with hysterical tendencies was as unfitted for the New World as a man who refused to become a jack of all trades. Neither frontier nor farm provided space for neurasthenia and anorexia nervosa (the 'fasting disease'), fashionable disorders among young women in the United States and Britain.[39] If colonial daughters did betray the symptoms of such disorders, parents doubtless dealt them with strictly. Thanks to the systematic colonisers, New Zealand was now constructed as a society of family farms, an antidote to industrialisation and urbanisation as well as to the frontier. Abundant food, especially meat, almost certainly made iron deficiency less common than in Britain. The privations, the endless toil and the isolation from friends, family and familiar places, however, depressed many women migrants.[40]

Marriage instituted a marked difference in the relationship between men and women, for the wife's legal identity was subsumed within her husband's. It went without saying that a wife followed her husband and ran his home. The better the husband's income, the more the wife's role was likely to be modelled on middle-class English practice, at least in the main towns. Women who married according to Christian rites, of course, promised obedience in return for protection (although this did not mean submissiveness, as many husbands complained).[41] For wives alone in households without other women, life could be hard. Some obtained a certain solace from writing and receiving letters, and the colonists were great correspondents.[42] Yet most women had some daughters and many obtained considerable satisfaction from managing their own households.

Many from the 'uneasy class' positively delighted in their freedom from the ornamental role of the Victorian wife. They enjoyed the challenge of mastering the arts of household production and management and often scorned the 'little dolls of women [in England] who do nothing'.[43] Many households needed a maid or servant but, as a rule, the mistress worked alongside and often had to train the servant. Servants were hard to find and harder to keep, often independent to the point of impertinence and usually destined to soon become the mistress of their own households. Wet-nursing was uncommon, except for sisters or close friends, but women developed their own support networks. The idea of the good neighbour, widely noted by visitors, was sustained by female solidarity and children were often lent. In Waipu, Molloy found that almost 50 per cent of all children grew up in the households of non-kin.[44] Households were both the domain and the work of married women (although they often included a kitchen garden, poultry and even a cow); for married men, households were either the place of work or the home base from which they went to work. Few men went into service. The evidence suggests that men and women accepted the gendered division of labour, although many educated wives felt irritated by their subordinate status and limited role.[45]

As pastoralism expanded in the 1850s, the proportion of the colonists living in relative isolation grew and so did the demand for male labour. With the discovery of one goldfield after another in the South Island, the Wakefieldian nightmare came true. In 1861–63 some 50,000 footloose young men swarmed into Central Otago. Otago's population grew from about 12,600 in 1860 to over 67,000 in 1864, which increased the number of Europeans in New Zealand by 25 per cent. Farming and pastoralism expanded dramatically.

The Otago diggings declined in 1864 but fresh discoveries on the West Coast and in Nelson meant that the influx of immigrants continued to grow. The number of Europeans doubled during the decade, most of the growth being concentrated in the South Island, but many came and left so that the population totals understate the size of the flows. In the North Island, at the same time, the wars stalled colonisation but the size of the army grew. Maori remained about one-third of the population. Shortly after the British government withdrew its regiments, gold was discovered at Thames and a rush occurred, although fear of Maori power constrained prospectors.

To the dismay of many, men now decisively outnumbered women.[46] On the Otago diggings, in the most unbalanced year, there were only 30 women for every 100 men, most of them in the hospitality or entertainment industries. As Charlotte Macdonald has argued in the previous chapter, this extreme imbalance lasted only briefly. The sex ratio never became as unbalanced as it had been in the Australian penal colonies from 1789 until the 1840s, where women often constituted no more than 5 per cent of the population. Nor was the situation on the goldfields comparable to the American frontier (on the Californian diggings it had been 7:86 in 1850).[47] In neither the United States nor Australia was anyone much concerned, but here the imbalance immediately prompted action. The New Zealand experiment presupposed equal numbers of young women and men. The vigorous efforts of Otago and Canterbury to redress the imbalance enjoyed some success and organisations in Britain, where an excess of women existed, co-operated to supply the shortfall. Charlotte Macdonald has fully investigated the Canterbury scheme, and the fate of the single women immigrants, most of whom married within three years of arrival.[48]

The influx of young men caused drunkenness and prostitution to become more common and violent deaths soared to become 10 per cent of the total during the 1860s.[49] Not that the authorities happily tolerated such signs of degeneration. Otago outlawed dancing girls in hotels and tried to suppress sly-grog shops. Offenders faced a fine of £20 for the first offence and £50 for the second, plus loss of licence. Detailed regulations also governed the working conditions of women in hotels and boarding houses.[50] The governments and their officials also made vigorous efforts to establish the rule of law on the goldfields.[51] Prominent citizens established institutions for the unwanted children bequeathed by the miners and homes for the rehabilitation of prostitutes (such institutions were seen as providing surrogate homes and families).[52]

To the concern of many, an excess of men continued to exist. Vogel's great scheme for public works and immigration saw the central government take control of immigration in 1871 but the sex ratio among immigrants did not change greatly. The reason for this was simple enough. The public works programme, like the pastoral and gold industries, required large numbers of able-bodied young men, most not yet of marriageable age. When peace arrived in the North Island, the process of colonisation again got under way but felling bush to break in the land also needed large numbers of strong young men. During the 1870s, the European population of New Zealand again doubled but only 74 females arrived for every 100 males. By 1881 there were just over 81 females for every 100 males (the sex ratio varied from province to province and was most unbalanced in frontier rural districts). As a result, the proportion of eligible women who married became very high, but the proportion of men who never married also rose. There were simply not enough women. Despite the imbalance, dances remained popular.[53]

Although in the 1860s and 1870s it was less common for conjugal families to migrate together, there is evidence to suggest that kin continued to structure migration. This is especially apparent in the way that the Irish used the immigration system.[54] The Irish began arriving in large numbers during the goldrushes and constituted almost 30 per cent of all immigrants in the 1870s. Many used various government schemes to relocate extended kin groups around the world. Because they used a system of chain migration, some 60 per cent of Irish immigrants were single compared with 33 per cent of the Scots and 25 per cent of the English. Few couples migrated. Usually one or two sons came first, then more sons and a daughter to manage the household, and finally parents and sometimes grandparents.[55] The planned group colonies of the 1860s, like the Scandinavians who were brought in by the government to clear the Great Bush in the early 1870s, often relocated entire families, but most ethnic minorities, even when unable to take advantage of the nominated scheme, used the same method as the Irish. This was especially true of the small Jewish influx and, later in the century, those from Dalmatia and Syria. The Chinese, by contrast, mainly sent able-bodied men to earn money to repatriate to their families back in China.[56] For religious-ethnic minorities, including Irish Catholics, ethnicity could now do the work of kinship. By contrast, many English and Lowland Scots came alone. James Bodell, who volunteered in Melbourne for service in the Waikato campaign, had long since left his family to seek adventure and opportunity.[57] Yet much evidence indicates that kinship was of ongoing importance to many English and Lowland Scots. Rosalind

McClean's study of Scottish emigration to New Zealand between 1840 and 1880 concluded that the decision to emigrate was almost always made by a family. Many Scottish families, it seems, deliberately established an overseas branch.[58] Every biography of a nineteenth-century woman demonstrates the continuing importance of kin networks. If this was the case with the well-to-do, we can imagine that it was still more important for those with fewer resources.[59]

The presence of a sizeable itinerant population of young single men saw New Zealand take on more of the complexion of a frontier society. Although drunken and feckless husbands doubtless existed in the period 1840-60, the opportunities for anti-social behaviour greatly increased in the 1860s and 1870s. Despite the central importance still attached to family, many husbands proved irresponsible and wayward, incapable of performing their primary duty of providing for their families. Strong drink proved to be a popular refuge and lubricated violence. In this period, violence and the threat of violence were widely accepted as a normal part of life and marriage, although attitudes doubtless varied between religious, class and regional subcultures. Many men settled their disputes by dint of strength and they did not change this behaviour because they were at home. Indeed, some subcultures enjoyed fighting.[60] Some men became compulsively violent towards their wives, however, and this was widely deemed unacceptable.[61] Contemporaries noted the increase in violence during the 1860s. In 1867, Parliament enacted an Offences Against the Person Act, which made rape, attempted rape, indecent assault and carnal knowledge illegal. Over the next seven years, Parliament progressively increased the punishments. G. M. Waterhouse sadly observed in 1876 that 'Fifteen or twenty years ago [we] scarcely heard of such cases; now [we] hear of them continually'.[62]

The unbalanced sex ratio also created a market for prostitution, as Wakefield had predicted, and prostitutes and their clients contributed to the number of illegitimate births and the incidence of venereal disease. For many colonists, prostitution and syphilis represented the most degraded Old World ills from which they had fled. The moral quality of single young women immigrants became a matter of public concern almost as the first schemes to recruit them were launched. Maria Rye, who founded the Female Middle Class Emigration Society in 1862, contributed to this concern when she declared that the upper attics in the Otago immigration barracks were 'occupied by a body of women known only to night and evil deeds'.[63] A terrific kerfuffle followed. Although a select committee investigated and dismissed the charge, the suspicion remained that many prostitutes had come at the colonists' expense to ply their trade. In 1864 J. G. S. Grant, the Dunedin iconoclast, claimed that the city could boast 200 full-time prostitutes.[64] In Christchurch, the Reverend Henry Torlesse, a nephew of Wakefield, claimed that '22 unfortunate women' had been reduced to prostitution. By the mid-1860s most sizeable towns had a 'red light' district.[65] The 1869 Contagious Diseases Act allowed provinces to act and Canterbury and Auckland took advantage of the law, but only for brief periods. Macdonald has argued that this law signified the colony's acceptance of the sexual double standard but the fact that only two provinces took advantage of it, and neither with much vigour, indicates that the colonists were ambivalent about this Old World norm. Auckland, indeed, wanted to reassure the Royal Navy that its men were safe here.[66]

Until the end of the century, the quality of women immigrants, and the extent of prostitution and its associated evils, illegitimacy and venereal infection, continued to prompt debate, often tinged with hysteria, but those debates helped to embed a consensus about the central importance of the family to New Zealand society.[67] Settled families came to represent the ideal society; footloose itinerant men and prostitutes its evil shadow. By the 1890s, unmarried itinerants had become the targets of a public policy to turn tramps into taxpayers.[68] As Jock Phillips has argued, that tension, internalised, also helped to define colonial masculinity, while sexual desire in women was increasingly identified with transgression.[69]

The great social disruptions of the 1860s and 1870s only made most colonists place more emphasis on the importance of the family and fret about the dangers of family breakdown. Yet the distinctive features of marriage in the colony survived this disruption and characterise the decades 1840–80.[70]

Throughout the colonial period, youths enjoyed great freedom in choosing their spouses and single immigrants without kin enjoyed unprecedented freedom. All parents hoped that their daughters would marry good providers and that their sons would choose wives who could manage the household and produce healthy children. The reproductive contract was a bit of a lottery, for some couples proved infertile (about 20 per cent of all marriages in pre-modern society were infertile).[71] As the colony flourished and the main towns became larger, parents of wealth and status made an effort to ensure that their children married from within their own social class. Those with money had a potent instrument for securing compliance but more usually, parental control over the social lives of their children ensured that they mixed only with approved potential spouses. Even William Mathew and Rachel Hodgkins, of modest income and falling status, successfully organised the social lives of their daughters, the future artists, Frances Hodgkins and Isabel Field.[72] For wealthier families, the sojourn to Europe and finishing school ensured that their daughters did not meet ineligible young men. In the 1860s and 1870s, it was not unusual for the daughters of well-to-do families to marry their father's business partners or associates, despite the considerable age difference, for such men had already established themselves. Before Parliament enacted the Married Women's Property Act of 1884, 'the rights which the common law gave a husband over the real and personal property of his wife . . . were so extensive that no wealthy father would willingly allow any part of his property to pass to a married daughter under the common law if he could possibly prevent it'.[73]

Most young men and women wanted to marry because marriage gave admission to the adult world. How they went about it depended greatly on their class and region of origin. Among the middle classes, young men and women prepared for their future status in distinct worlds although life in the colony made the worlds less separate than they would have been in Britain. To young men and women of this class the other sex was often an alien species. 'The world of courtship . . . was uncertain, puzzling and, to late twentieth-century eyes, an impossibly nuanced and circuitous one'.[74] By the 1860s, engagements were fashionable and weddings had become major family occasions, increasingly performed in churches. Engagements often lasted for years, however, and even shorter ones did not always survive. A particularly aggrieved fiancée, left 'on the shelf' after years of engagement, could sue for breach of promise. Such cases were rare, doubtless for fear of the attendant publicity, but when they reached the courts they attracted considerable interest and women were conspicuously present as spectators in the courtroom.[75] Throughout the century, however, migrants continued to arrive from regions in Britain where neither engagements nor church ceremonies were yet the custom. Young men and women mixed freely in their peer groups, which resisted any tendency to premature pairing. When a choice had finally been made, and the couple was in a position to establish their own household, they signified their commitment by 'stepping out', then 'keeping company'. The wedding was of no importance. As late as the 1880s, the old Scottish practice still often prevailed although, since the 1854 Marriage Act, the colony required registration. Perhaps, as Annabel Cooper noted, this explains the 'frank representations of feisty wives' in the writing of Mary Lee, mother of the future novelist and Labour MP, John A. Lee. Mary Lee's 'irregular' marriage conformed to Scottish custom.[76] 'Long-term de facto relationships may have been more common in this period than historians have noted', at least among the working classes.[77]

Regardless of how young couples behaved when courting, they all believed, as the churches had long taught, that a wife and husband ought to love each other. Falling in love did not justify marriage; love grew from affection and friendship. Even after marriage, educated men, such as administrator and politician Donald McLean, 'continued to use the language of affection, friendship and duty'.[78] Most people did not go this far but financial advantage alone was now considered quite inadequate, although the requirement that a married couple establish their own household meant that prudential considerations could not be ignored (weighing motives and reasons allowed considerable opportunity for argument and gossip).[79] People also paid attention to common values and a shared nationality and faith. In the end, however, the final consideration of importance was a mutual desire to marry. Although nobody thought sexual compatibility or personal fulfillment a reason for marrying, everyone hoped that the newly-weds would be happy together. The definition of happiness remained modest: that he would be a good provider, she a good manager, and that they would have some healthy children who outlived them. Most no doubt hoped to be 'the best loved of one I loved very much', as Annie Hill confessed, and the importance attached to romantic love as a reason for marriage appears to have increased between 1840 and 1900, at least for the novel-reading public. Some of these issues were aired in 1867 when Parliament passed a Divorce Act and in the late 1860s dissenting voices, often Spiritualists or Freethinkers, began arguing that love was the only legitimate basis for marriage.[80]

Two studies allow us a more precise picture of marriage. Charlotte Macdonald identified more than 2000 marriages from her population of 4028 single-women emigrants who arrived in Canterbury in the 1860s, over 1800 of them the first marriage for both partners. She found that a very high proportion of women emigrants married compared with their sisters in Britain; that women emigrants married for the first time at younger ages, again compared with Britain; and that the age difference between wives and husbands was about twice the British average, four years on average as against two. Although British averages are often suspect, for they disguise large regional differences, the broad trends are fairly clear: 'Those [women] marrying for a first time did so most commonly in their twenty-second year; just over three-quarters did so by the age of twenty-six'. Only 11.3 per cent married before the age of 20.[81] Keith Pickens, who studied a sample of over 2000 marriages in Canterbury between 1851 and 1877, reached very similar conclusions, although his longer period of study allowed him to show that the mean age at first marriage increased over time, for both women and men.[82] A study of couples who married in a church and lived in Devonport, on Auckland's North Shore, found small differences in the age of first marriage between the Protestant denominations and a larger difference between Protestants and Irish Catholics. Irish Catholics were more likely to be younger, they were more likely to conceive before or out of wedlock, their first birth was earlier and births were spaced more closely together. Protestants appear to have managed their fertility more instrumentally. From the 1850s on, however, the Protestant-Catholic difference was substantially less than the difference between Protestants and Catholics in Britain.[83] Whether this was also true of testamentary practice remains to be seen, for Irish husbands 'seem to have been remarkably reluctant to appoint their widows executors of their estates'. Most entrusted the duty to brothers or Irish Catholic friends.[84]

Given the availability of men, Pickens thought it 'surprising that the age at which women married for a first time was not lower'.[85] He attributed this to the potency of Old World custom. Macdonald disagreed, arguing that the caution with which women in the colony married reflected the same desire for independence that persuaded them to migrate. The steady rise in the mean age of first marriage suggests that in the colony, as in Britain, couples did not marry until they could afford to establish their own households. The first arrivals had the best chance of success, and as opportunities shrank, couples waited longer (the mean age continued to rise until the 1920s). The relative scarcity of women in the colony, by contrast, largely explains the increased age gap between spouses compared with Britain, although that gap survived long after an equal sex ratio emerged in the towns. The fluidity of colonial society, both in terms of social mobility and geographical movement, probably gave marriage a more random pattern than it had in Britain. The trend for people to choose spouses from the same class increased, being 'most pronounced at the top and bottom of the social scale', but the children of farmers, white-collar men and manual workers chose partners without much regard for those broad occupational distinctions.[86] In the 1850s and 1860s, national difference constrained choice in Canterbury, especially for the Irish and English, but 'colonial Canterbury [became] . . . a crucible wherein differences between groups, as well as those within groups, tended to melt away'. The number of Catholic-Protestant marriages certainly upset the Catholic bishops in the 1870s.[87] Racial difference now created a stronger barrier, however, and in the 1870s Pakeha rarely married Maori or Chinese.[88]

Although by the 1860s a smaller proportion of women married before their twentieth birthday, fertility remained very high. In Waipu, for instance, couples averaged 'seven to eight children' in the 1860s and 1870s.[89] The single-women immigrants who arrived in Canterbury in the 1860s, usually had between six and 12 children (the average was 9.3 children per woman).[90] In 1871 some 40 per cent of the non-Maori population were under the age of 15. The proportion of extramarital births – then known as illegitimate – was low by Australasian standards, and remained low throughout the century.[91] Not all wives survived the stresses of life in a new society, the constant pregnancies, not to mention 'the ailments & labour of maternity'.[92] High fertility and domestic privations, especially in the disordered society of the 1860s and 1870s, saw mental breakdown become so common that all provinces built asylums. Although most of those committed to asylums in this period were single men, the increasing proportion of women admitted had responded to the stresses of life in the colony by neglecting their children or their housework; an increasing proportion of men were also married and had either refused to work or wasted their money on extravagances.[93] Perhaps for this reason, as R. E. N. Twopeny remarked, 'In the old world palaces are built for kings; in the new, for idiots.'[94] All understood an inability to cope; none could afford to tolerate it.[95]

Despite the ongoing enthusiasm for marriage and the growing numbers of New Zealand-born children, the unbalanced sex ratio continued to amplify anxiety about the dangers of family breakdown. By the 1870s, moralists got almost as agitated about desertion as prostitution. Both topics may have been a Protestant code for bewailing the increased number of Irish Catholic immigrants and the failure of Maori to adopt European family norms.[96] Although the conditions of colonial life allowed men more easily to desert their families, it is not clear how common desertion was. Usually there were more married men in the colony than married women because, from the 1860s on, husbands often came first and sent for their families only when they decided to settle.[97] Much work was also seasonal and when unemployment rose during the winter months many men took off in search of jobs. Nineteenth-century marriages often accommodated quite lengthy separations and even infidelity, although the latter was usually kept secret from the other spouse. Desertions probably peaked during periods when opportunities became abundant elsewhere, as they first did in the 1850s thanks to the Victorian goldrush. The word desertion suggests intention, however, and it is not clear that many men left, determined never to return. Given the informality of marriage in those regions of Britain from which New Zealand disproportionately recruited, desertion may have had different meanings for different groups. As noted earlier, de facto relationships may have been more common than we realise and their termination may have been widely accepted.[98]

For all that, desertions occurred and the community disliked them, not least because the wives were left with many children but few ways of earning an income. Thanks to the numbers of men who left for the Australian goldrushes, the cost of supporting deserted families was such that Parliament enacted a law as early as 1860 to limit husbands' authority over property. Men who had deserted could no longer return and claim ownership of property accumulated by their wives. Precisely when absence could be construed as desertion was unclear, although the husband's failure to send money home was often taken as prima facie evidence that his wife had been deserted. In 1870 Parliament extended the grounds for providing protection.[99] By now many believed that the family was under considerable stress. Although desertion, drunkenness, illegitimacy, prostitution and violence undoubtedly occurred, there is no evidence to suggest that they were typical or especially common. The anxious lamentations of moralists and public authorities may have been designed largely 'to make plain through negative definition that the proper norm was [familial] self reliance'.[100] The Destitute Persons Ordinance, the law since 1846 and the colony's principal provision for welfare, made family responsible for the indigent and the sick. Each amendment extended the range of kin responsible, although it was only in 1877 that magistrates received power to compel deserting husbands to make a financial contribution to their families.[101]

Despite the attention that scholars and contemporaries gave to desertion, marriages were most commonly ended by death. As a rule, men were about four years older than their wives – although in some 10 per cent of marriages the wife was older – and had a lower life expectancy, so that widows constituted a growing proportion of the population as the founding generations aged. In Waipu, some 40 per cent of all marriages were ended by the death of one or other spouse before the youngest child turned 15. Some 54 per cent of widowers remarried but widows were much less likely to marry again; only 23 per cent did so. Later studies suggest that this pattern survived into the twentieth century and widows often comprised around 10 per cent of all heads of household. Many ran farms and businesses. Widows with dependent children faced a grim future unless they found another husband. Widowers, however, needed a wife to cook, mend, bake, wash, clean and run their household. Widowers with dependent children either gave them to the deceased wife's sister or mother or, like William Larnach, remarried, often with a speed that others found unseemly. He married his sister-in-law, who had lived with the family for many years. Parliament made such marriages legal in 1880 but it took another 20 years before all churches did so.[102] If the oldest son were old enough to take over his deceased father's work, he often did so, although the widow was the legal owner and effective manager of the property. In many farming families, as in Waipu, it may have been customary for the oldest children to leave the nest entirely, whereas the youngest son and daughter remained to look after their parents and run the property and household. In that case, they did not marry until after the last parent died.[103] This discussion of death's role in ending marriage and disrupting the conjugal family must not obscure the fact that Pakeha life expectancy was one of the highest in the world, and constantly increasing. Pakeha couples and families had, on average, longer together than was possible in almost any other society in the world, then or previously.[104]

The 1880s marked the start of rapid changes in the colonial family. Pakeha fertility began to fall. Women who first married in 1880 averaged 6.9 children; by 1891 this had fallen to 5.2; by 1921 it was just over three.[105] Women also began demanding greater equality. A small group of Protestant activists spelt out a new vision of an alcohol-free society from which the sexual double standard had been eradicated. As part of the new emphasis on purity, the home was elevated into an article of religious faith and Mother was reinvented as its guardian angel. The conjugal family became *the* family. New standards of mothering and fathering were articulated, adults began 'taming the playground', and even the state began involving itself in protecting children and defining new standards of family life.[106] Although the new ideals were rapidly diffused, the colonial pattern was not quickly eradicated. In 1900 most colonists still lived on farms or in small townships, the four main towns remained small and most people lived in single-unit dwellings. In the towns, as in the country, most men worked in their own homes or close by, many of those who went into town to work came home for midday dinner, and children were expected to contribute. The concept of separate spheres may have governed the lives of well-to-do families but, for most, marriage was defined by interdependence. Familial independence remained a potent dream and state policy.

Many feared that the 'Long Depression' (1879–96) had ended the age of colonial innocence and freedom, but their fears lied. Two influences deserve special note: first, the availability of land allowed a high proportion of families to achieve a considerable independence, whether on their own farm on in their own home; second, the young could still enjoy a generous degree of physical and social freedom. Although we lack studies of the Europeans born in New Zealand or the extent of Maori-Pakeha intermarriage, not to mention the reciprocal influences that operated, it is much clearer now than it was 20 years ago that the idea of family was central not merely to the rhetorical invention of New Zealand as a New World society but also to socio-cultural practice.[107] The evidence, though often fragmentary, allows us to disentangle dream and reality, prescription and practice, to identify that curious discursive gesture where words that seem to signify a social reality actually functioned – and were intended to function – as warnings and exhortations. The preoccupation with the sex ratio, the constant emphasis on the centrality of family, the growing obsession with prostitution and its attendant evils, the quality of immigrants and transgressions against Victorian sexual propriety reflect the widespread belief that the family was the only basis for a happy, prosperous and civilised society. At a very general level we can agree with Joan Scott that gender was 'a constitutive element of social relationships ... and ... a primary way of signifying relationships of power', but the evidence now available suggests two tentative conclusions: first, that gender was reworked in the colony and, second, that many colonists wished to preserve the family as an economic partnership.[108]

Annabel Cooper has read and criticised several drafts of this essay, as have the editors, and I am grateful. I am also grateful to Barbara Brookes, who read an early version.

1   Andrée Lévesque, the co-author, produced the figures and tables and read the draft; see Erik Olssen and Andrée Lévesque, 'Towards a History of the European Family in New Zealand', in Peggy Koopman-Boyden, ed., *Families in New Zealand Society*, Wellington, 1978, pp. 1-26. This was the first of several essays I wrote in order to introduce the 'new social history' and American 'social-science history' into the practice of New Zealand history.

2   Christopher Lasch, 'The Family and History', *New York Review of Books*, 13 November 1975, p. 33.

3   Olssen and Lévesque, 'Towards a History of the European Family in New Zealand', p. 20.

4   Linda Colley, *Britons: Forging the Nation, 1707-1837*, New Haven and London, 1992, pp. 162-3, 250, 281 convincingly contests the orthodox view that the idea of separate spheres restricted women to the private sphere more than ever before.

5   The colonial period provides my focus, however, for the new work does not invalidate the periodisation outlined in my 1978 essay. The rapid decline in fertility, which began in 1879-80 and continued until the 1920s, marked a distinct phase in the New Zealand family's history, just as the 'Long Depression' of 1879-96 led to a reconceptualisation of the family and the role of the wife/mother and home, a view that had its origins in Britain and the United States in the first half of the nineteenth century.

6   John R. Gillis, *A World of Their Own Making: Myth, Ritual and the Quest for Family Values*, Cambridge,

Mass., 1997, p. 7.

7 Gillis, *A World of Their Own Making*, p. 7 and Patricia Crone, *Pre-Industrial Societies*, Oxford, 1989, pp. 152-5.

8 See Thomas Laqueur, *Making Sex: Body and Gender from the Greeks to Freud*, Cambridge, Mass., 1990, Ch. 5; Roy Porter, '"The Secrets of Generation Display'd": *Aristotle's Master-piece* in Eighteenth-Century England', in Robert Purks Maccubbin, ed., *'Tis Nature's Fault: Unauthorized Sexuality during the Enlightenment*, Cambridge, 1987, pp. 1-21; and Colley, *Britons*, Ch. 6, for a discussion of women's changing role. See also Richard Sennett, *The Fall of Public Man*, New York, 1977, and Jürgen Habermas, *The Structural Transformation of the Public Sphere: An Inquiry into a Category of Bourgeois Society*, Cambridge, 1989 (first published in German in 1962).

9 John R. Gillis, 'Making Time for Family: The Invention of Family Time(s) and the Reinvention of Family History', *Journal of Family History*, 21, 1, 1996, p. 13 and H. R. Jackson, *Churches & People in Australia and New Zealand 1860-1930*, Wellington, 1987, p. 160. P. H. Curson, 'Household Structure in Nineteenth-Century Auckland', *New Zealand Geographer*, 32, 1976, pp. 177-93, demonstrates the ongoing importance of household in the 1840s.

10 For the British background I have relied on Leonore Davidoff, 'The Family in Britain', in F. M. L. Thompson, ed., *The Cambridge Social History of Britain 1750-1950, Volume 2, People and Their Environment*, Cambridge, 1990, pp. 71-129.

11 T. C. Smout, 'Scottish Marriage Regular and Irregular 1500-1940', in R. B. Outhwaite, ed., *Studies in the Social History of Marriage*, London, 1980, p. 206. John R. Gillis, 'Married but not Churched: Plebeian Sexual Relations and Marital Nonconformity in Eighteenth-Century Britain', in Maccubbin, *'Tis Nature's Fault*, pp. 31-42, points out that a similar situation prevailed in much of England because of resistance to the efforts of the state and the established church, from the Marriage Act of 1753 to the New Poor Law of 1834, to mandate that valid marriages had to be celebrated at established churches.

12 Davidoff, 'The Family in Britain', p. 80 and Gillis, *A World of Their Own Making*, pp. 9-15, 63-5, 74. Claire Wood, '"Bastardy Made Easy"? Unmarried Mothers and Illegitimate Children on Charitable Aid – Dunedin 1890-1910', research essay, University of Otago, 1990, p. 44, first noted the likely importance of such areas to New Zealand.

13 Davidoff, 'The Family in Britain', pp. 79-80, 99.

14 Augustus Earle, *A Narrative of a Nine Months' Residence in New Zealand*, E. H. McCormick, ed., Oxford, 1966, p. 180.

15 *The Letters and Journals of Samuel Marsden, 1765-1838*, J. R. Elder, ed., Dunedin, 1932, pp. 208-9.

16 Frances Porter and Charlotte Macdonald, eds, *'My Hand Will Write What My Heart Dictates': The unsettled lives of women in nineteenth-century New Zealand as revealed to sisters, family and friends*, Auckland, 1996, p. 253. The fullest discussion remains Bruce Biggs, *Maori Marriage: An Essay in Reconstruction*, Wellington, 1960, especially Chs 3 and 4.

17 E. J. Wakefield, *Adventure in New Zealand*, Vol. 1, London, 1845, pp. 323-5 provides the fullest contemporary account. See also Harry Morton, *The Whale's Wake*, Dunedin, 1982, pp. 213-14, 250-3, 257-63 and Kate Riddell, 'A "Marriage" of the Races? Aspects of Intermarriage, Ideology and Reproduction on the New Zealand Frontier', MA thesis, Victoria University, 1996, pp. 6-7.

18 Such marriages might last a very short time or a lifetime but need to be distinguished from prostitution, which usually involved only a single act of sexual intercourse. See Riddell, '"Marriage" of the Races?', Chs 2 and 3.

19 Maureen Molloy, *Those Who Speak to the Heart: The Nova Scotian Scots at Waipu 1854-1920*, Palmerston North, 1991, pp. 78-84 for sibling-sibling and cousin marriages. Biggs, *Maori Marriage*, pp. 23-4, found first-cousin marriages so rare that he inferred a prohibition.

20 Wakefield, *Adventure in New Zealand*, Vol. 1, p. 323 reported that even men who came only for the whaling season would be provided with a wife or 'helpmate'.

21 Atholl Anderson, *Race Against Time*, Dunedin, 1991, p. 31, points out that from the 1820s these families 'were mainly patrilocal'.

22 Riddell, '"Marriage" of the Races?', Chs 2 and 3.

23 Jackson, *Churches & People*, pp. 147-53. Gerda Lerner, *The Creation of Patriarchy*, Oxford, 1986, establishes that patriarchy began with the origins of civilisation.

24 This became a common justification for men to marry before emigrating; see Eileen L. Soper,

The Otago of Our Mothers, Dunedin, 1948, p. 6. For Wakefield's developing thought see Raewyn Dalziel, 'Men, Women and Wakefield', in *Edward Gibbon Wakefield and the Colonial Dream: A Reconsideration*, Wellington, 1997, pp. 77-88. For the quotation see *England and America*, in M. F. Lloyd Prichard, ed., *The Collected Works of Edward Gibbon Wakefield*, Auckland, 1969, p. 567.

25 In *England and America*, Note III, Wakefield anatomises the 'Uneasiness of the Middle Class' and used the phrase 'the middle or uneasy class' to mean 'those who, not being labourers, suffer from agricultural distress, manufacturing distress, commercial distress . . . and many more kinds of distress', *Collected Works*, p. 355. The definition included tradesmen and farmers.

26 For the campaign see Judith A. Johnston, 'Information and Emigration: The Image Making Process', *New Zealand Geographer*, 33, 2, 1977, pp. 60-7. The best study of immigration is K. A. Pickens, 'The Origins of the Population of Nineteenth-century Canterbury', *New Zealand Geographer*, 33, 2, 1977, pp. 69-75. It should be borne in mind that many of the migrants recruited in London were immigrants to that city, not natives.

27 *England and America*, in *Collected Works*, p. 338.

28 Miles Fairburn, *The Ideal Society and its Enemies: The Foundations of Modern New Zealand Society 1850-1900*, Auckland, 1989, Ch. 1 and for criticisms of Canterbury see Coral Lansbury, *Arcady in Australia: The Evocation of Australia in Nineteenth-Century English Literature*, Melbourne, 1970, pp. 61-8.

29 See Davidoff, 'The Family in Britain', p.96 and on 'boy labour' in the 1890s see Erik Olssen, *Building the New World: work, politics and society in Caversham 1880s-1920s*, Auckland, 1995, pp. 196-8.

30 Raewyn Dalziel, 'Emigration and Kinship: Migrants to New Plymouth 1840-1843', *New Zealand Journal of History* (*NZJH*), 25, 2, 1991, pp. 122-7, discusses the role of kinship and pp. 115-22 the areas from which the migrants came (the great majority of the migrants to New Plymouth were drawn from a relatively small number of towns and villages). Rosalind McClean, 'Class, Family and Church: A Case Study of Interpretation', research essay, University of Otago, 1980, while not addressing the role of kin in emigration, provides considerable evidence in Chs 2 and 3 which indicate its centrality in the settlement of Otago.

31 Even at Waipu, settled by three large kin networks, Molloy found that friendship could do the work of kinship and notes that kin addressed each other as 'Friend'; see *Those Who Speak to the Heart*, p. 84. On the same point see also McClean, 'Class, Family and Church', pp. 77-8 and Gillis, *A World of Their Own Making*, p. 15.

32 Soper, *Otago of Our Mothers*, p. 51 (she estimated that pioneering families often had between nine and 11 children).

33 Charlotte Godley, *Letters from Early New Zealand 1850-1853*, Christchurch, 1951.

34 Raewyn Dalziel, 'Marriage and Reproduction in a Colonial Community: Migrant Mothers and Colonial Daughters', paper given to the New Zealand Historical Association Conference, Dunedin, 1991. I am grateful to Professor Dalziel for permission to quote from this paper.

35 Edward Wakefield, *New Zealand After Fifty Years*, New York, 1889, p. 51. Those who did not want their children infected with colonial habits, like the Selwyns, sent them back to England for their schooling and sometimes did not see them again for more than 15 years. For a small proportion of the educated middle class this remained the practice well into the twentieth century. Mothers, especially, often felt quite bereft: 'I felt ... bewildered and stunned by the grief of leaving my treasures', cited Betty Gilderdale, *The Seven Lives of Lady Barker: Author of Station Life in New Zealand*, Auckland, 1996, p. 49.

36 Karin Calvert, *Children in the House: The Material Culture of Early Childhood, 1600-1900*, Boston, 1992. Although Calvert's conclusion was based on American evidence, scholars working on New Zealand evidence have identified a similar shift occurring in the 1850s and 1860s. See David Keen, 'Feeding the Lambs: The Influence of Sunday Schools on the Socialisation of Children in Otago and Southland, 1848-1902', PhD thesis, University of Otago, 1999.

37 Following the death of his first wife, William Larnach, for instance, remarked that Gladys, his youngest daughter, 'will have her own way in everything and, under the sadness of our circumstances, I must admit that she gets it. So should she grow up a spoilt child there are many excuses to be urged', cited Fleur Snedden, *King of the Castle: A Biography of William Larnach*, Auckland, 1997, p. 143.

38 Lady Barker, *Station Life in New Zealand*, London, 1870 and *Station Amusements in New Zealand*, London, 1873.

39 See Joan Jacobs Brumberg, *Fasting Girls: the emergence of anorexia nervosa as a modern disease*, Cambridge, Mass., 1988.

40 Jane Oates's letters home to her family in the 1850s, held by the Alexander Turnbull Library, poignantly illustrate one woman's sense of privation and homesickness. I am grateful to Frances Porter for suggesting I read them. Rosalind McClean, 'Scottish Emigrants to New Zealand, 1840-1880: Motives, Means and Background', PhD thesis, University of Edinburgh, 1990, p. 370, notes that wives were often reluctant to emigrate and suffered badly from homesickness.

41 Raewyn Dalziel, '"Making us one": courtship and marriage in colonial New Zealand', *Turnbull Library Record*, 19, 1, 1986, pp. 7-26 summarises one couple's expectations of each other (although this marriage was tragically ended by death in childbirth).

42 Keith Sinclair, *A Destiny Apart: New Zealand's Search for National Identity*, Wellington, 1986, p. 96, reported that in 1866 some 220,000 colonists sent a million letters to Britain. On the importance of letters in maintaining family ties see David Fitzpatrick, ed., *Oceans of Consolation: Personal Accounts of Irish Migration to Australia*, Ithaca, New York, 1994, Ch. 17.

43 For the quotation see Frances Porter, *Born to New Zealand: A Biography of Jane Maria Atkinson*, Wellington, 1989, p. 62. Raewyn Dalziel's important article, 'The Colonial Helpmeet: Women's Role and the Vote in Nineteenth-century New Zealand', *NZJH*, 11, 2, 1977, pp. 112-23, has been very influential, although some historians now prefer to use partner rather than helpmeet, e.g. Rollo Arnold, *Settler Kaponga 1881-1914: A Frontier Fragment of the Western World*, Wellington, 1997, p. 311.

44 Molloy, *Those Who Speak to the Heart*, pp. 89-98, 103. See also Porter, *Born to New Zealand*, p. 225 and *passim*; McClean, 'Class, Family and Church', pp. 59-60.

45 See Maria Atkinson, for instance: Porter, *Born to New Zealand*, pp. 261-2.

46 As a consequence, of course, areas such as the Shetlands, which contributed disproportionately to the flow of emigration, had a considerable excess of women; see Brian Heenan, 'Living Arrangements among Elderly Shetlanders in the Parishes of Lerwick, Yell and Unst between 1851 and 1891', in Andrew H. Dawson, ed., *Scottish Geographical Essays*, Dundee and St Andrews, 1993, pp. 218-28.

47 For the Australian colonies see J. C. Caldwell, 'Population' in Wray Vamplew, ed., *Australians: Historical Statistics*, Sydney, 1987, pp. 23-8 and the United States Bureau of the Census, *The Statistical History of the United States from Colonial Times to 1970*, Washington DC, 1975, p. 25.

48 Charlotte Macdonald, *A Woman of Good Character: Single Women as Immigrant Settlers in Nineteenth-Century New Zealand*, Wellington, 1990, pp. 19-28, provides an overview of the various provincial schemes and Ch. 5 analyses the experience of 2293 of the women whose marriages she identified.

49 David Victor Madle, 'Patterns of Death by Accident, Suicide and Homicide in New Zealand 1860-1960: Interpretations and Comparisons', PhD thesis, Victoria University, 1996, pp. 21-3, 153-5.

50 Sandra Quick, '"The Colonial Helpmeet Takes a Dram": Women Participants in the Central Otago Goldfields' Liquor Industry 1861-1901', MA thesis, University of Otago, 1997, Ch. 3.

51 Richard S. Hill, *The History of Policing in New Zealand, Vol. 1: Policing the Colonial Frontier: The Theory and Practice of Coercive Social and Racial Control in New Zealand, 1767-1867*, Part II, Wellington, 1986, Chs 7 and 8.

52 Erik Olssen, *A History of Otago*, Dunedin, 1984, pp. 56-66 for the rushes and pp. 85-8 for problems and responses. For the West Coast see Philip Ross May, *The West Coast Gold Rushes*, 2nd edn, Christchurch, 1967, Ch. 11.

53 In one mining town in 1873 'The dancing … was kept up for three or four hours by some thirty males and two females, [and] struggles for the possession of the fair demoiselles were the source of fun not included in the programme', cited Jock Phillips, *A Man's Country? The Image of the Pakeha Male—A History*, revised edn, Auckland, 1996, p. 7. On sheep stations young men often organised 'what they called a "servants' ball". In vain I protested that the housekeeper was <u>never</u> expected to dance. "Oh yes!" laughed Capt. George, "I've often danced with a housekeeper, and very jolly it was too"', cited Gilderdale, *The Seven Lives of Lady Barker*,

p. 115.

54 Besides Vogel's free passages, instituted in 1873, most provinces and the government-assisted immigrants who had been nominated by somebody already in the colony. There are many monographs that focus on an aspect of migration or a particular group but we lack any overview for the 1860s and 1870s. For a brief account of policy and numbers see W. D. Borrie, *Immigration to New Zealand 1854-1938*, Canberra, 1991, Ch. 5 (for the 1860s), Ch. 9 (for 1871-76), and Ch. 11 (for 1877-80). The fullest study, which emphasises the centrality of families in the migration of the 1870s, is Rollo Arnold, *The Farthest Promised Land: English Villagers, New Zealand Immigrants of the 1870s*, Wellington, 1981.

55 Macdonald, *A Woman of Good Character*, pp. 61-4.

56 See, for instance, K. W. Thomson and A. D. Trlin, eds, *Immigrants in New Zealand*, Palmerston North, 1970; and James Ng, *Windows on a Chinese Past, Vol. 1, How the Cantonese goldseekers and their heirs settled in New Zealand*, Dunedin, 1993. For an overview of planned group settlements see Borrie, *Immigration to New Zealand*, Part III.

57 *A Soldier's View of Empire: The Reminiscences of James Bodell 1831-92*, Keith Sinclair, ed., London, 1982, pp. 125-6.

58 See McClean, 'Scottish Emigrants to New Zealand', pp. 151, 303, 433 and Chs 6.3.1 and 7 *passim*, for an analysis of emigration as a family strategy.

59 Barry Reay, 'Kinship and the Neighbourhood in Nineteenth-Century Rural England: The Myth of the Autonomous Nuclear Family', *Journal of Family History*, 21, 1, 1996, pp. 87-104, demonstrates the importance of 'dense' kin networks in the first half of the century.

60 Whalers fought each other for pleasure with such fury that their Maori wives actively intervened to stop them; see Edward Jerningham Wakefield, *Adventure in New Zealand From 1839 to 1844*, Vol. 1, London, 1845, p. 324. Fairburn, *The Ideal Society*, pp. 146-8, 206-25, discusses the rise of anti-social behaviour.

61 In his analysis of nineteenth-century divorce petitions in Auckland, Roderick Phillips details several instances; *Divorce in New Zealand: a social history*, Auckland, 1981, pp. 117-19.

62 For this law and the quotation see Stevan Eldred-Grigg, *Pleasures of the Flesh: Sex & Drugs in Colonial New Zealand 1840-1915*, Wellington, 1984, p. 55.

63 Cited Macdonald, *A Woman of Good Character*, p. 175.

64 Olssen, *A History of Otago*, p. 74. For Grant see P. J. Gibbons, 'Grant, James Gordon Stuart' in *The Dictionary of New Zealand Biography, Vol. One, 1769-1860*, Wellington, 1990, pp. 157-8.

65 Eldred-Grigg, *Pleasures of the Flesh*, pp. 36-43, provides the fullest discussion.

66 Macdonald, *A Woman of Good Character*, Ch. 7 for a full discussion. Macdonald concluded (p. 186) that 'women who earned their living from prostitution probably comprised a more distinctive subculture and were ostracised to a greater extent than their equivalents in Britain'. See also Eldred-Grigg, *Pleasures of the Flesh*, pp. 33-5 and Macdonald, 'The "Social Evil": Prostitution and the Passage of the Contagious Diseases Act (1869)', in Barbara Brookes, Charlotte Macdonald and Margaret Tennant, eds, *Women in History: Essays on European Women in New Zealand*, Wellington, 1986, pp. 13-33.

67 It is interesting, but unremarked, that contemporary Pakeha explanations for Maori population decline were articulated in terms of the link between sexual freedom/promiscuity, prostitution, venereal infection, and low fertility/fecundity; see Riddell, '"Marriage" of the Races?', Ch. 4.

68 H. D. Lloyd, *Newest England: Notes of a Democratic Traveller in New Zealand, with some Australian Comparisons*, New York, 1900, Ch. 9.

69 Phillips, *A Man's Country?*, p. 80 and Ch. 2 *passim*. If a distinctive male culture emerged, as Phillips argued, it was localised and widely viewed with ambivalence. According to the census, even in 1866-71 over 83 per cent of all men aged 50-54 were married and the proportion rose to 90 per cent by 1900. This is much the same as the British figure. For the association of sexuality with prostitution see Andrée Lévesque, 'Prescribers and Rebels: Attitudes to European Women's Sexuality in New Zealand, 1860-1916', in Brookes, Macdonald and Tennant, *Women in History*, pp. 4-12.

70 Macdonald, *A Woman of Good Character*, Ch. 5 provides the fullest account of marriage in the colony in this period. See also Porter and Macdonald, '*My Hand Will Write*', Chs 5 and 6 and especially pp. 185-92, 252-63.

71 See Jack Goody, *The East in the West*, Cambridge, 1996, pp. 154-5. Many couples would suffer the death of at least one of their children before the age of five and older children were at risk from the colonial scourges of dysentry, diarrhoea and scarlet fever.

72 E. H. McCormick, *The Expatriate: a study of Frances Hodgkins and New Zealand*, Wellington, 1954, pp. 18-49.

73 G. R. Y. Radcliffe and G. Cross, *The English Legal System*, 5th edn, London, 1971, pp. 136-7. For a full discussion of the 1884 act and its predecessors see Bettina Bradbury, 'From Civil Death to Separate Property: Changes in the Legal Rights of Married Women in Nineteenth-Century New Zealand', *NZJH*, 29, 1, 1995, pp. 40-66. Although we now know a lot about the changing law, little is known yet about the social reality. Colley, *Britons*, pp. 239-50, discusses the dangers of inferring social practice from the law.

74 Porter and Macdonald, *'My Hand Will Write'*, p. 187. For a rare study of a courtship and engagement see Dalziel, '"Making us one"', pp. 7-26.

75 Maureen Hickey, 'Breach of Promise of Marriage', research essay, University of Otago, 1992, pp. 9-16 and 18-24. For the British background to breach of promise see Ginger S. Frost, *Promises Broken: Courtship, Class, and Gender in Victorian England*, Charlottesville, 1995.

76 Annabel Cooper, 'Introduction' to Mary Isabella Lee, *The Not So Poor: An Autobiography*, Auckland, 1992, pp. 25-7. For the Marriage Act, which only governed marriages in the colony, see G. A. Wood, 'Church and State in New Zealand in the 1850s', *Journal of Religious History*, 8, 1975, pp. 255-64.

77 Wood, '"Bastardy Made Easy"', p. 42 and Ch. 2 *passim*. Some women had a succession of illegitimate children to the same man, with whom they lived, and officials referred to the women as Mrs but classified the children as illegitimate.

78 For McLean see Dalziel, '"Making us one"', p. 13.

79 See Porter, *Born to New Zealand*, pp. 326-7.

80 Cited by Porter and Macdonald, *'My Hand Will Write'*, p. 186; for the 1867 act see Phillips, *Divorce in New Zealand*, pp. 18-22; and Shaun Broadley, 'Spiritualism in Nineteenth-Century Otago', draft MA thesis, University of Otago, 1998.

81 Macdonald, *A Woman of Good Character*, pp. 135-8. Macdonald's population of domestic servants, however, probably married younger than women or men of higher socio-economic standing; see McClean, 'Class, Family and Church', pp. 42-3 and Shaun Ryan, 'Registry Marriages, 1893-1920', p. 6, in author's possession.

82 K. A. Pickens, 'Marriage Patterns in a Nineteenth-Century British Colonial Population', *Journal of Family History*, 5, 2, 1980, pp. 180-96. The mean age at first marriage for women was 22.3 in the 1850s and 23 in the next two decades, while that for men moved from 26.8 in the 1850s to 27.9 in the 1870s.

83 Susan Sheehan, 'A Social and Demographic Study of Devonport, 1850-1920', research essay, University of Auckland, 1980, Ch. 3. The famine in Ireland, of course, dramatically changed the nature of marriage and family. Whereas couples had married younger than anywhere else in Europe, and almost all had married, thus creating very high fertility rates, after the famine couples married later than elsewhere in Europe, a very high proportion never married and the fertility rate dropped sharply.

84 Lyndon Fraser, '"The Ties that Bind": Irish Catholic Testamentary Evidence from Christchurch, 1876-1915', *NZJH*, 29, 1, 1995, p. 71 and pp. 67-82 *passim*.

85 The law allowed girls to marry at 12 and boys at 14. Those younger than 21 needed parental consent, although the 1854 Marriage Act empowered a magistrate to overrule a parental veto.

86 David Pearson, 'Marriage and Mobility in Wellington 1881-1980', *NZJH*, 22, 2, 1988, pp. 143-5.

87 On Catholic-Protestant marriages in the colonial period see Pickens, 'Marriage Patterns', pp. 189-90, and for the attitude of the Catholic church Jackson, *Churches & People*, pp. 34-5 and 89-91. Analysis of 344 Registry Office marriages in Caversham suggests that Englishmen rarely married Irish women. In Waipu, by contrast, endogamy was the norm until the 1880s; Molloy, *Those Who Speak to the Heart*, p. 107.

88 The construction of race as a biological category, imputing clear differences in intellectual capacity, occurred in the 1860s and 1870s and may have impacted on popular attitudes; see George W.

Stocking, *VictorianAnthropology*, London and NewYork, 1987, Chs 6 and 7. Of course, intermarriage declined proportionately because the European population increased rapidly while Maori numbers fell and, after the wars, many iwi withdrew from contact with Pakeha.

89 Molloy, *Those Who Speak to the Heart*, p. 107.

90 Macdonald, *A Woman of Good Character*, p. 159 and Ch.6 *passim*.

91 Macdonald, *A Woman of Good Character*, Ch. 6, concluded that in the 1860s a high proportion of women whose first child was illegitimate were under 20 years old when they became pregnant, they were largely of working-class background and, intriguingly, mainly New Zealand born. Davidoff, 'The Family in Britain', p. 91, states that 38 per cent of all brides were pregnant when they married. If Macdonald's figure is sustained by further research, it will underline just how different the emigrants to New Zealand were compared with Britons generally. For unwed mothers see Wood, "'Bastardy Made Easy'", pp. 30-5. Figures for the European population may not fully capture the extent of extra-nuptial birth, however, for they ignore the possibility that Maori communities carried the burden of raising the illegitimate children of Pakeha men.

92 Maria Atkinson, cited by Porter, *Born to New Zealand*, p. 244.

93 Jeremy Bloomfield, 'Dunedin Lunatic Asylum, 1863-1876', research essay, University of Otago, 1979; Caroline Hubbard, 'Lunatic Asylums in Otago, 1882-1911', research essay, University of Otago, 1977; Bronwyn Labrum, 'Gender and Lunacy: A Study of Women Patients at the Auckland Lunatic Asylum 1870-1910', MA thesis, Massey University, 1990; M. S. Primrose, 'Society and the Insane. A Study of Mental Illness in New Zealand, 1867-1926 with Special Reference to Auckland Mental Hospital', MA thesis, University of Auckland, 1968; Alan Somerville, 'Ashburn Hall and its Place in Society 1882-1904', MA thesis, University of Otago, 1996.

94 R. E. N. Twopeny, 'Dunedin', in *Pictorial New Zealand. With Preface by Sir W. B. Perceval*, London, Paris and Melbourne, 1895, p. 189.

95 Interestingly enough, the 1898 divorce law made habitual drunkenness a justification for divorce where the husband's drinking 'habitually left his wife without means of support' or when the wife's drinking meant she 'habitually neglected her domestic duties'. See Phillips, *Divorce in New Zealand,* p. 23.

96 R. P. Davis, *Irish Issues in New Zealand Politics, 1868-1922*, Dunedin, 1974, was the first discussion of anti-Irish sentiment, which flourished in the 1870s, and remains the best.

97 During prolonged periods of economic depression, such as the late 1880s and early 1890s, married women outnumbered married men for the only time during the nineteenth century; see *Population Census, Vol. 4, Conjugal Condition*, Wellington, 1928, p. 1. See also McClean, 'Scottish Emigrants', pp. 371–2 for husbands going ahead to reconnoitre.

98 McClean, 'Class, Family and Church', pp. 38-9, notes how quickly 'deserted' wives moved in with another man and combined the various children into a new household. See also Wood, "'Bastardy Made Easy'", pp. 45-6.

99 Married Women's Property Protection Act, 1860, *Statutes of New Zealand 1860-1862*, pp. 35-7. It is not clear how successful this measure was but an attempt to strengthen it in 1870, which Porter considers unsuccessful, suggests that the first measure failed; *Born to New Zealand*, p. 286. For a more positive assessment see Bradbury, 'From Civil Death to Separate Property', pp. 50-3.

100 Fairburn, *The Ideal Society and its Enemies*, pp. 56-7, 198-200. For the quotation see p. 199. As Jackson pointed out in *Churches & People*, p. 161, 'The mistake made by those who talked about the decay of the colonial family was to equate a strong family with tight discipline and submissive children.'

101 On the Destitute Persons Ordinance see David Thomson, *A World Without Welfare: New Zealand's Colonial Experiment*, Auckland, 1998, pp. 22-7.

102 Snedden, *King of the Castle*, pp. 149-52.

103 Molloy, *Those Who Speak to the Heart*, pp. 114-15. See also McClean, 'Class, Family and Church', p. 39; and Sheehan, 'Devonport', p. 62.

104 Ian Pool, *Te Iwi Maori: A New Zealand Population Past, Present and Projected*, Auckland, 1991, p. 77.

105 Miriam Gilson Vosburgh, *The New Zealand Family and Social Change: A Trend Analysis*, Wellington, 1978, p. 55a (the figures are for married women with issue, not all married women).

106 Olssen and Lévesque, 'Towards a History of the European Family in New Zealand', pp. 6-12; Brian Sutton-Smith, 'The Games of New Zealand Children', in *The Folkgames of Children*, Austin, 1972; and Jeanine Graham, 'Child Employment in New Zealand', *NZJH*, 21, 1, 1987, pp. 62-78 discusses the background to the regulation of child labour.

107 Riddell's work on the census suggests that little can be learned from that source ('"Marriage" of the Races?', Ch. 4 and Table 2, p. 94). We still need to know about changes within Maori domestic life and the extent to which Europeans born in New Zealand had distinctive attitudes because of cultural interaction. The old anthropological model of acculturation posited that all influence moved in one direction, from European to Maori, but it is noteworthy that many European observers of the 1830s and 1840s remarked upon the independence and sexual freedom of unmarried men and women in Maori society, the degree of autonomy enjoyed by Maori wives in monogamous marriages, and the importance of kin.

108 For the quotation from Scott, see Joan Wallach Scott, *Gender and the Politics of History*, New York, 1988, p. 42.

Criminal Conversations: Infanticide, Gender and Sexuality in Nineteenth-Century New Zealand

Bronwyn Dalley

Nineteenth-century New Zealand was a dangerous place. Contemporaries saw danger, especially of the moral kind, in many places and in many guises. Alcohol, prostitution, venereal disease, gambling, intemperance, and desecration of the Sabbath headed a list that seemingly proved colonial replication of Old World ills. As in the Old World, most peril lurked in New Zealand's burgeoning towns and cities – at street corners, along darkened alleys, on the stage and in public houses. Discourses of danger abounded, heightening and reproducing a pervasive sense of moral danger that focused on sexuality and gender relations.

Far from indicating wowserism or 'puritanism', such a preoccupation with moral and sexual danger suggests instead a society intensely interested in things sexual. The image of the 'monotonous nights of the Victorian bourgeoisie', as Michel Foucault has argued, is one of modern convenience which bears little resemblance to the writings and actions of nineteenth-century people.[1] Sex, like danger, was everywhere in the nineteenth century. It was both the 'supreme secret' and the 'general substratum' of society:[2] written about, analysed, pathologised, viewed, practised, celebrated and condemned.

If sexual discourses were everywhere, then they sometimes displayed a subtle ubiquity, appearing as coded messages shrouded in euphemism or reticence. Even silence over sexual matters, however, could testify to their acceptability and their 'everyday-ness'.[3] Sexuality could also be extracted from issues and events not 'obviously' sexual in nature. Historian of popular culture, Peter Bailey, has coined the term 'parasexuality' to describe this 'middle ground' where sexuality is 'deployed but contained, carefully channelled rather than fully discharged'.[4] In this chapter I use a 'sexually charged' topic – child

The Christchurch Supreme Court, scene of the sensational 1891 trial in which Anna and Sarah Flanagan were tried for murder, watched by expectant crowds.
Burton Brothers photograph, Canterbury Museum, 3460.

murder – to examine how nineteenth-century New Zealanders constructed perceptions of a morally and sexually dangerous time and place.

Kali Israel has described divorce and murder trials as vibrant social spaces for the re-enactment of access to the secrets of sex.[5] Israel's contention captures the tenor of a new social history of crime and the judicial process. In recent years, historians have used infamous or forgotten sexual scandals and murder cases to delineate dramas of private life, and to read outwards from the discrete events to chart pathways through the social, cultural and political meanings in which the cases are embedded. I adopt this microhistorical approach in two cases of child murder to explore the intersections of sexuality, crime and gender relations.[6]

The accused, counsel and police in these child murder trials told stories that explored sexual behaviour, single parenthood, gender relations and urban life. Criminal narratives are inseparable from the sites of their telling, and courts lent a weighty import to trials, influencing what stories were told, and how they were rendered.[7] As many historians have pointed out, nineteenth-century criminal courts were structured for drama, and criminal stories replayed this drama in particularly melodramatic fashion.[8] The retelling of criminal stories in the press shaped accounts even further, as the new journalistic genre of sensationalist crime reporting structured criminal stories as the spectacular. This interweaving of stories in child murder cases afforded an opportunity for contemporaries to draw meanings about sexuality, gender relations and the dangers of urban life, and to turn chaotic and gruesome domestic affairs into powerful moral tales.

Phoebe Veitch had three children by three different men before she had turned 20.[9] Her first child, a boy, born when Phoebe was 14 years of age, was, she stated, the result of a 'misfortune' in Nelson. Her eldest daughter was born in Feilding, 12 months before her marriage to Robert Veitch, the girl's father. Three months after the marriage, Phoebe gave birth to another daughter. Named Phoebe, but known as Flossie, the child was not Robert's. Phoebe had known Flossie's father in Nelson, where he had worked as a cook in her uncle's hotel; Frank or Sam Timaru, also known as 'Darky Sam' on account of his mixed racial heritage, had followed her to Feilding and, for £5, Phoebe visited his room one evening and 'fell in the family way'.[10] Her husband Robert never enquired after, and Phoebe never told him, the name of Flossie's father.

Deserted by her husband within two years of marriage, Phoebe worked as a domestic servant, took in washing and needlework and tended to her blind mother. Phoebe was battling illness herself, and had been diagnosed with a cancer or lupus which destroyed part of her nose and impaired her speech. Pregnant again, Phoebe moved to Wanganui from Feilding in early 1883, hoping to gain regular employment – and perhaps anonymity – in the larger township. She obtained a little laundry work, but seems to have supported herself and her family through prostitution. With a fourth child on the way, her face disfigured, hard of hearing and with speech made difficult by her disease, Phoebe had few friends in Wanganui. Newspapers referred sternly to her 'utter depravity', the 'weakness of her moral understanding' and her 'life of abandoned profligacy'.[11]

At the end of February 1883, Wanganui experienced a major flood. Parts of the river bank and wharves were washed away, a section of the town was under water and, for days, local residents saw debris and logs wash up on the beach. Given the conditions, no one seemed unduly surprised when the body of a little girl also washed up, her head bruised by the bobbing logs. After all, death by drowning was a frequent enough occurrence in nineteenth-century New Zealand, and one newspaper that carried the story about the little girl's body also recounted deaths by drowning of men in Auckland and Christchurch in the same week.[12] The child's complexion suggested mixed-race parentage and, hearing of her description, locals identified her father as a Pakeha man living with Maori up the Whanganui River. The physician who examined the child's body ventured that she was the offspring 'probably of a Chinaman and a European'.[13] The question of the child's racial origins and the identity of her father remained mysteries in the events that unfolded.

Police identified the child as three- or four-year-old Flossie, daughter of the 23-year-old Phoebe Veitch. Phoebe had told neighbours and employers that she was sending Flossie away to a 'dark lady' and would never see her again. When questioned by police, she denied knowledge of the child's whereabouts; later she said Flossie had fallen in the river; later still, Phoebe claimed that the child's father, 'Darky Sam', had thrown her into the water during an argument. 'Darky Sam' was Fijian perhaps, Anglo-Indian, Chinese, or Scottish – Phoebe was not sure which – and the police could not find him, or evidence that he had been in Wanganui.[14] Phoebe stood trial for murder in the Supreme Court at Wanganui, was found guilty and sentenced to death. A month later, the sentence was commuted to life imprisonment and, in the following week, Phoebe wrote a confession admitting her guilt in Flossie's death.[15] Phoebe remained in prison in Wellington, to which she had been transferred in June 1883, until her death in 1891 of constitutional syphilis.[16]

In Christchurch in 1891, young Beatrice and Annie Coombs were gathering fruit in an empty garden when they found a baby's severed head among the bushes.[17] Nearby they discovered some rope and a shawl, both covered in blood. They told their mother of their grisly find and, after assuring herself of the veracity of her children's tale, she informed the police. A police search by lantern light revealed only the shawl; a hoax had been played upon the 'unsuspecting females', the police suggested.[18] Next day, however, they found the head under a gooseberry bush, where it had been dragged by a dog or a cat. Reporting such as this guaranteed high excitement in Christchurch, which escalated even further with the arrest for murder of police constable Daniel Flanagan and his wife, Anna. Their 32-year-old single daughter Sarah, the mother of the dead child, was arrested in Wellington, where she had travelled under an assumed name on a hurried passage to Sydney.

The family was well known around Christchurch and Lyttelton, and Sarah's second unwed pregnancy in two years caused family members considerable consternation. Sarah had been causing him 'some trouble', and doing some 'bad things', Daniel Flanagan told fellow officers as they arrested him.[19] Nonetheless he, and particularly his wife, had taken pains to conceal from neighbours and family the birth of Sarah's second child. Anna Flanagan arranged for a nurse to remove the child from his mother on the evening of the birth. Nurse Jane Freeman swore not to reveal the identity of the child's mother; Sarah was introduced to her as a Mrs Stevens whose husband was away on the West Coast. Sarah and Anna Flanagan claimed that, after collecting the baby a few days later from Nurse Freeman's house in preparation for joining Mr Stevens in Wellington, they were attacked by unknown assailants. The men snatched the baby from Sarah and severed its head, tied a rope around her waist and wrists and dragged her through the streets until she fell down, exhausted. The assailants made off when another unknown man came to Sarah's rescue and assisted her to get home.[20]

Daniel was charged with being an accessory after the fact, but the bill against him was thrown out at the Supreme Court; Anna and Sarah Flanagan stood trial for murder, were pronounced guilty and sentenced to death. Their sentences, too, were later commuted to life imprisonment. Anna's health and mental state deteriorated badly in prison. She was transferred to the asylum at Sunnyside in late 1892, where she remained until her release in 1895; Sarah was transferred to the Terrace Prison in Wellington in 1897 until her release in 1906, after serving 15 years of her sentence. Daniel Flanagan did not regain his position in the police force.[21]

⋆   ⋆   ⋆

Both cases were sensations for the eager crowds that filled the courtrooms. Women were a minority of the accused in Supreme Court trials, just as they formed a minority throughout the criminal justice system. Violent, deliberate actions that struck at the core of contemporary conceptions of womanhood were bound to garner attention. Of the few women who stood trial for murder in nineteenth-century New Zealand, even fewer were sentenced to death. Mythic stories of Minnie Dean, the only woman executed in New Zealand, overshadow those of other women, such as Veitch and the Flanagans, who were also condemned to death, but reprieved.

Despite a recent assertion that New Zealand women killed their babies 'all the time',[22] few women were brought to court on charges relating to the death of their children, either as murder – commonly called infanticide – or as concealment of birth. In the years bracketed by the Veitch and Flanagan cases, fewer than 20 women appeared in court charged with such offences.[23] The history of infanticide, as several scholars have noted, is difficult to trace, and the number of charges does not necessarily reflect the actual number of babies murdered or left to die by their mothers.[24] In New Zealand, as elsewhere, charges could be reduced to manslaughter, or women dismissed without conviction, as courts, the police and the public struggled to grasp the notion of women harming their offspring. Sometimes only desultory searches were made for the mothers of dead babies fished out of privies or found rolled in a mattress.[25]

But the sensationalism of and interest in the Veitch and Flanagan cases derived not just from their subject matter or their rarity. These trials were theatrical, spectacular events, which played out recognisable dramas of private life on a public stage. Each carefully crafted and sensationalised instalment of the murder sagas in the local and national press progressively heightened public interest: the discovery of a body or body parts, the arrest of the accused, the coroner's inquests and their appearance in the Magistrate's Court. The Supreme Court trials marked the final formal episodes in these dramas, and the expectant crowds were not disappointed. The question of justice was perhaps the last thing on their minds; they had come to share in the 'voyeuristic, transgressive pleasures of the criminal story', to explore that interplay between truth and sex in the confessional sphere of the courtroom, and to be part of a morality play, a ritual catharsis of judgment on unnatural actions, an affirmation of shared values about gender roles and motherhood.[26] As vicarious entrances into the domestic affairs of neighbours, the cases were performances as entertaining as anything to be found in the local theatres, and just as melodramatic.

In common with criminal narratives elsewhere in the nineteenth century, the stories of Phoebe Veitch, and of Sarah and Anna Flanagan, drew upon the language of melodrama to cast their experiences of economic vulnerability, sexual liaison and relations with men. With its characteristic hyperbole – its extreme representations of virtue and vice, guilt and innocence, romance and betrayal, good and bad – melodrama was a popular theatrical and literary form that had 'tremendous currency' in the nineteenth century.[27] Colonial New Zealand audiences particularly enjoyed tales of 'virtue triumphant', and hankered after the 'gentility and moral standards' of melodrama on stage and later in film.[28]

Melodramatic narratives depicted women and men as stereotypical characters. Plots – on the stage and in court – revolved around virtuous and wronged heroines seduced or driven to desperate acts by the duplicity and villainy of men. Perhaps not surprisingly, then, melodrama was a form of storytelling most available to women, as many recent studies of female crime and scandal have attested.[29] But the 'simple, stark moral claims' of the stock characters of melodrama also gave them an appeal across various social constituencies.[30] In courts, the public, the judges, jurors and counsel could understand, and perhaps even sympathise with, the narratives of the accused that told, in spectacular form, of the everyday challenges of their lives. As Angus McLaren has suggested, violence and conflict were intrinsic aspects of society, and murder provided a very distorted reflection of acceptable behaviour.[31] This was especially so in cases of infanticide or concealment of birth, where the motives prompting women's actions were understood, but the deeds condemned.

Criminal narratives and events in trials were intensely mediated proceedings. Many voices related different versions of a single event, as witnesses, police, lawyers, judges and newspaper reporters created and recreated explanations for the actions of the accused. The accused themselves rarely told their own stories in court; New Zealand legislation did not permit them to give evidence in murder cases until 1889.[32] Even after that, few defence counsel allowed the accused to take the stand, for doing so forfeited the defence right of having the last word – and hence opportunity to influence the jury – before the judicial summing up. Phoebe Veitch made a long statement about her life at the inquest but, apart from that, the accused in these two cases were denied a formal speaking part in their trials.

Police and court records, as well as newspaper accounts of trials, pose significant interpretive challenges over the use of historical evidence.[33] Many representations – 'truths' and 'lies' – make up such records, reminding us of the constructed nature of historical events and 'facts'.[34] Statements to the police or evidence in court could be given under abnormal conditions or in states of high excitement. Elisions, evasions, repetitions and silences appear in the record as the accused and witnesses told their stories. These verbal accounts were reworked again in the written record, although, as Natalie Zemon Davis reminds us, the transition from the spoken to the written was more a mediation than an alteration.[35] Moreover, the criminal narratives were rarely coherent stories. The accused and witnesses provided answers to questions posed by police, lawyers or judges, rather than offering their own narration of events. The narratives were, instead, criminal conversations, the results of the 'enforced collaboration' and 'social transactions' between the various individuals involved.[36] Examining these myriad 'conversations' enables us to explore both the contested nature of the narratives in the court and in wider circulation through newspapers, and to understand why some stories were seen to be more truthful and more acceptable than others.

Criminal stories and courts were mediated through gender as well. Courts were highly gendered environments that influenced the form and reception of criminal narratives. As Carolyn Strange has argued in the context of Canadian trials, women were bit players in the male domain of the court.[37] In New Zealand, too, men assumed the major roles in courtrooms until well into the twentieth century, dominating the bench, the counsel, the jury and usually the dock as well. Women such as Phoebe Veitch and Sarah and Anna Flanagan were often isolated figures in the court. Women may have sat in the public gallery, but female accused faced males fulfilling the most powerful roles in the justice system. Invariably, their accounts of gender relations, domestic affairs and moral choices received different emphases when rendered, advocated or judged by men.

The only man arrested in these two cases also had an anomalous position in the police and court process. Even though the case against him was thrown out at the Supreme Court hearing, Daniel Flanagan gave a statement to the police and appeared at the inquest and the hearing in the Magistrate's Court. The fact that he was a policeman complicated his position: arrested by colleagues in his house, which doubled as the local police station, questioned by his peers and with junior officers giving evidence against him, Daniel Flanagan was left with his professional standing in jeopardy. But it was his implication in a crime normally seen as women's business that made his position in the gendered trial process most equivocal; it was resolved, in the end, by the Flanagans emphasising Daniel's role as supportive father and husband acting in the best interests of his family.

Court trials were visual and oral spectacles, but they were also textual events. If attendance were impossible, the next best thing was to read about the trials in the local and national newspapers, or vicariously imagine the experience of witnessing them. Of course, newspaper accounts could not capture the emotional essence of the occasions: a bald description of Sarah Flanagan fainting as the details of the extensive injuries to her baby's head were read out conveyed the flavour of the courtroom drama, not its substance. Nevertheless, the reports of these trials were discursively structured for dramatic effect. Court reporting was part of the 'new journalism' of the last quarter of the nineteenth century, a literary style that relied on personal stories and anecdotes to map out social unrest and scandal. Such journalism foregrounded the significance of the criminal story, focused on the participants involved and invited readers to enter into judgment themselves.[38] Vivid language, evocative detail, accounts of crowded courtrooms and sensational subjects all underscored the drama of the events, suggesting their uniqueness and repeating the moral lessons to be learnt from them. As literary critic Ed Cohen has argued with respect to the Oscar Wilde case, trials involving sexual practices – and, by extension, sexuality more generally – constituted social dramas in which contests over social behaviour were played out; such scandals opened up a liminal space in which activities and attitudes were renegotiated.[39] These scandals and contests were inevitably gendered: in the Veitch and Flanagan trials, the social dramas regarding the roles and responsibilities of single mothers and elusive fathers, and of the moral dangers for women in urban areas, were all litigated in public.

The Supreme Court visited Wanganui only twice yearly. During its session, court reports filled half of the local newspapers and, one could surmise, most of the conversation around dinner tables and in the numerous public houses. The composition of juries, the details of cases and discussions of police, magistrates and counsel were mulled over for days afterwards as Phoebe Veitch remained newsworthy and her fate held up as just punishment for her actions. She was a minor celebrity during her brief sojourn in the town and by far the exceptional female offender in the dreary procession of petty thieves, prostitutes and drunkards who normally appeared before the court. Benevolent society ladies came to gaze on her in prison, and offered ministrations that Phoebe gratefully accepted.

She cut a dramatic figure in her court appearances by donning a black veil or wearing a thick bandage to hide her disfigured face.[40] Such garb prevented those in court from deciphering her demeanour, which was an important element in any murder trial, especially of women being tried for the murder of their children. The lack of emotional outbursts in court was more than made up for in the local newspapers, however, which repeated and fostered rumours circulating about the case: that police had found the child's father, pronounced to be a Chinese man working in a hotel in Nelson; that Phoebe had confessed to the crime and spoken of the terrible task of disentangling her child's fingers from her own as she pushed Flossie into the flooded river; or that her predicament was due to drink and poor upbringing.[41]

More cosmopolitan Christchurch put on an elaborate show of interest in the Flanagan case, and the fact that Daniel Flanagan was a police officer added further spice to the saga; the entire case was a voyeur's paradise. The proceedings at the inquest, the preliminary hearings in the Magistrate's Court and the trial at the Supreme Court were constantly full to overflowing. A scuffle broke out on the first appearance of the three accused in the Magistrate's Court, when a large group gathered to watch the prisoners' arrival. The crowd rushed the front door, and poured into the body of the court before they could be stopped. Newspapers reported a 'severe struggle in which there was some rough shoving and mauling'. The gallery too was 'crammed with spectators, and for a short time there was considerable noise, which only subsided after loud warnings by the police'. The arrival of Sarah Flanagan on the steamer from Wellington was a sensation in itself. An estimated 800 or 900 people crowded the wharf and the main street of town to see her disembark. Women going about their lawful business were mistaken for the accused: according to the *Press*, 'the lady passengers, as they came along the wharf, were subjected by strangers to a running fire of remarks as "Is that her?" &c, which must have been particularly annoying to them'.[42]

In both cases, the presence of women in court as spectators or as prison visitors was remarked upon in the press. 'Several females' were among the eager crowd jostling together in the Supreme Court to hear the Flanagan case, a local newspaper commented, evidently surprised that women would want to listen to grim details about a decapitated baby.[43] Like the women they watched in the dock, these female spectators occupied an ambiguous place in the gendered domain of the courtroom; no remarks were made on the presence of men in the public galleries of the courts. Observation of the sordid domestic dramas and personal affairs of criminal trials transgressed women's social and sexual roles, and exposed them to the 'unsavoury' details of life. As Deborah Nord has argued, once women became observers of events, rather than the objects of others' observations, their respectability, chastity and femininity were brought into question.[44]

★   ★   ★

The tale Phoebe Veitch told to police, and which she elaborated in her statement at the inquest, was a story of seduction, poverty, self-sacrifice and torment, of a woman wronged by men, who nevertheless tried to be a good mother.[45] Her husband, Robert, was a respectable man, with whom she lived happily for two years. Then Robert became bankrupt and Phoebe had to support the family. One day Robert arose at 3.45 a.m., telling Phoebe that he would be back in time for breakfast. He never returned. Deserted, and with three growing children, Phoebe worked hard to maintain her family. All the while, Flossie's father – Frank or Sam Timaru, alias 'Darky Sam' – tormented her: demanding that she return with him to Nelson or give him Flossie, and urging that things be 'settled' once and for all. He hid in the flax bushes behind her house at Feilding and threatened her with a pistol when she called him a 'two-faced villain' for annoying an unprotected woman.

According to Phoebe, Sam was adept at changing his appearance. Sometimes he sported short, cropped hair and a black moustache; at others he wore a black curly wig and full whiskers. He dressed well, and adorned himself with flamboyant jewellery and weaponry: a florid gold ring, a glass pin through which could be seen pictures of three naked women and a man, a sheath knife and a double-barrelled pistol about a foot in length which he kept 'hidden' in his breast pocket. Whatever 'Darky Sam's' nationality and race, he was neither white nor British. In all, he was a slippery, menacing figure who had no business with white women, even those of loose character such as Phoebe Veitch. In the end, Phoebe said, she moved to Wanganui to get away from him, but it was to no avail: he lurked outside hotels waiting for her, he hovered outside her house, he sent her letters and he threatened her in the street. Phoebe finally agreed to meet with him one evening by the river to discuss their future. In Phoebe's own words: 'He said, "Well, it must be settled one way or the other. Will you give up the child?" I said, "No, I'll not part with her, I've kept her till now and I love her as I love my life". . . . He said, "If you won't part with her, you shall have her corpse."' He threw the child into the water, and threatened Phoebe once again with the pistol: '"If you speak one word I'll blow your brains out. There shall be two corpses instead of one."' He kept watch on her house that night and the next day, stopping her from going to the police with more threats of violence.

Beneath the dramatic flourishes, Phoebe's story spoke of female economic and sexual vulnerability, and the potentially disastrous consequences for women of sexual relationships outside marriage. A series of liaisons with men – coerced, or in exchange for money and support – placed women like Phoebe in difficult social and economic situations. Pregnancy was often a severe blow for nineteenth-century women without male providers. Single women and deserted mothers experienced public disapproval of their status, and support from charitable organisations could be hedged around with censorious restrictions; economic prospects were poor, and employment opportunities limited for single women with children in tow.[46] Phoebe's elaborate stories about the fathers of her children become more explicable when read in these contexts.

Child care was a constant dilemma for sole mothers, who relied on the goodwill of friends and relatives, or who paid other women to look after their children. Phoebe knew of the informal and underground female networks for minding children. She had sent her eldest daughter to live with relatives in Feilding, and had discussed with neighbours the prospect of sending Flossie away to a paid child minder. Once in Wanganui, she repeated the notion to her son, to her neighbours and to prospective employers: she claimed she was about to send the child, via an aunt, to an unnamed 'dark lady' in Christchurch, who would bring up the child as her own. On the day of Flossie's death, Phoebe sent a letter to her brother and to a friend in Feilding, repeating the story of handing Flossie over to a dark lady at the railway station. The day after Flossie's death, she told the story again, embellishing it further with details of jealousy and revenge: the unnamed woman had once vowed to exact vengeance from Phoebe, she told her neighbour, Eliza Blight, in relating a dream where she imagined her daughter drowned and washed up on the beach. Phoebe's scenario grew more fanciful with each rendition, but she knew the basic ingredients in the plot of sending burdensome children away through a network of child minders.[47]

Sarah Flanagan's story conveyed other problems facing unwed mothers. For families like the Flanagans, concerned about community acceptance and status, an illegitimate child could be a traumatic stigma.[48] Sarah Flanagan came of a respectable Irish Catholic family. Daniel had been a police officer in New Zealand for 25 years, serving on the West Coast and then at the Addington station in Christchurch. Anna worked as a female searcher for the police when not raising her children. Sarah's brother, Michael, was landlord of the Mitre Hotel in Lyttelton. Sarah had kept house for him, but her regular employment was as a music teacher. Respectability was important for the Flanagans. In a 1901 petition for the remission of the remainder of her sentence, Sarah stated that she had brothers in 'very prominent positions' in Melbourne and Sydney who were seeking to restore her to her former position of a music teacher with 'very good connections'.[49]

The Flanagans' tale was equally as melodramatic as Phoebe Veitch's but, unlike Phoebe, they could take advantage of their respectability and standing in the community. Downplaying Sarah's little-known first pregnancy, the Flanagans positioned Sarah as a virtuous woman suddenly set upon by wicked men. The shame and social stigma of single parenthood alarmed the economically secure Sarah and her family. Presenting her as a married woman whose husband was away on the West Coast – a common enough scenario – was an attempt to salvage some respectability from her situation; illegitimacy and unmarried sexual relations were not things the Flanagan household could speak about as easily as Phoebe Veitch. Acutely aware of their position in the local community, the Flanagans tried everything they could to hush up Sarah's second pregnancy. The physician who attended Sarah's confinement had to enter and leave the Flanagan premises by the back gate, so that people would not 'make remarks', and the nurse who took the child also had to leave by the back gate, and under cover of darkness.[50]

Discreet child minding, with no questions asked, was the order of the day for the Flanagans. As Lynley Hood notes in her biography of Minnie Dean, there was a considerable demand for such services in colonial New Zealand, and women who took in babies for money revealed, rather than concealed, the 'ugly secrets' of the age.[51] Nurse Jane Freeman clearly knew what was expected of her in minding the unwanted children of the respectable classes. Two years earlier, she had nursed Sarah's other child, who died within a fortnight. Freeman did not ask questions about removing an hours-old child from his mother late at night, and she scarcely blinked when, as following the first delivery, the woman she knew as Sarah Flanagan was introduced as Mrs Stevens. Nor was she above accepting a bribe to keep quiet about the baby. Anna Flanagan visited Freeman the day following the newspaper accounts of the discovery of a child's head, and gave her £1 – from Daniel, she said – for her 'kindness' to Sarah. Anna Flanagan then informed the nurse of the 'most unfortunate affair' that had befallen herself and her daughter after they had removed the baby from her care. Freeman may have been sceptical of the tale, but she agreed that she would not speak of the matter unless obliged; she knew the unwritten rules about taking in illegitimate babies.[52] Throughout the trial, this and other attempts to cover the family's shame over Sarah's pregnancies, were presented as the natural reaction of caring parents doing their utmost to protect their family's name and daughter's reputation.

The care of children of single or deserted mothers, and of neglected children, was a topical issue in New Zealand from the late 1860s, partly as a result of an increase in child abandonment during the goldrushes. By the 1880s, government institutions and privately run homes in the major population centres took in indigent, illegitimate and destitute children. Ironically, Phoebe Veitch's young son, Herbert, was committed to one such government institution just two weeks after her sentence, on the grounds of having no visible means of subsistence – a bald, legalistic assertion that gave little clue to the boy's tragic family situation.[53] Phoebe Veitch and the Flanagans explored the less formal and unstructured world of non-institutional, paid child care. Such arrangements had come under official scrutiny by the 1880s as New Zealanders followed dramatic accounts of British and Australian 'baby-farmers' who neglected or wilfully murdered the children in their care. Coroners and newspapers reported instances of baby-farming throughout New Zealand, although an 1889 police survey into paid child care noted more honest child carers than questionable baby-farmers.[54]

Women who took in children were aware of the growing police and public interest in their work from the later 1880s. In response to Anna Flanagan's request to keep silent, Jane Freeman agreed so long as she did not lay herself 'open to get into trouble'.[55] An 1893 police report commented on the 'large extent' of baby-farming, which officers believed had expanded over the previous two years, perhaps in the wake of the depressed economic conditions in the 1880s. By the time that Minnie Dean, 'the Winton baby-farmer', was convicted of the murder of a child in her care in 1895, public feeling was running high. As Hood asserts, Dean's actions 'inflamed the nation', as if every family that had ever lost a child was 'convulsed' by guilt and recognition: 'angrily they tore at their own gnawing secrets and flung them in a frenzy of rage and relief at the monstrous babyfarmer. Then, intoxicated by their new-found purity, they howled for revenge.'[56] Occurring before such publicity into baby-farming, the Veitch and Flanagan cases did not tap such a rich vein of indignation, which may explain the repeal of their death sentences and the execution of Minnie Dean.

But if child-care services broke down, if women could not afford them or could not face the shame of entering into negotiations over the care of their children, then getting rid of unwanted or burdensome children through either concealment of birth or infanticide was the extreme end of the options for desperate and isolated women. As a kind of 'delayed abortion', disposal or wilful neglect of children was a final strategy for women struggling to survive within a limited frame of options.[57]

There was one avenue, however, which Veitch and the Flanagans did not explore. None of the women took steps to compel the fathers of the children (or her husband in the Veitch case) to pay maintenance towards the child, as they could legally do, and as did other sole women with children.[58] Perhaps the women did not want the fuss or the embarrassment of compelling the husband or the father to pay maintenance; they may have been afraid of these men, if indeed they knew who they were; or perhaps they were unaware of the legal avenues available to them. In both cases, the male figures remained as ciphers, with no responsibility, or expectation of responsibility, for their children and the mothers of their children. Single motherhood was female business, something to concern women and their families, rather than men. Physically absent fathers nevertheless facilitated an imaginary space that could be filled with stock male characters. 'Darky Sam' and 'Mr Stevens' may well have been living persons – and there is sufficient police and other evidence to testify to Sam's existence – but their participation in the events of the cases appears imagined, rather than real. Phoebe Veitch, and Sarah and Anna Flanagan, used the very elusiveness of the fathers of these dead infants to hint at seduced and abandoned motherhood, as they fashioned tales of virtuous women and villainous men who were implicated in the deaths of children.

The Veitch and Flanagan stories also spoke of other moral dangers facing women in urban centres: that of the stock figure of the evil male stranger lying in wait on city streets to accost women who journeyed alone and unprotected, or through parts of the town into which respectable women would not venture. Such a figure was a common aspect in nineteenth-century discourses of gendered sexual danger, as a number of historians have shown for other countries.[59] In New Zealand the idea was picked up, or perhaps inherited, as local moral reformers referred to the perils – and implicit excitements – of the country's burgeoning urban centres, where danger came in many guises, bringing Old World ills to the new land.[60]

The Flanagans enunciated a story of chaotic urban male danger striking from nowhere and at random. The women were not in the most salubrious part of central Christchurch, and witnesses who saw them expressed surprise at such respectable figures being out late in an area of town frequented mainly by 'bad women'. After leaving Nurse Freeman's home, Sarah said, she left her mother to farewell a friend who lived nearby. Walking down the dark street, however, she was stopped by two men who asked her where she was going. In her statement to the police, Sarah recorded her responses to the strangers: 'I said "For God's sake, let me pass." One of the men took the baby out of my arms, and the other tied a rope round my wrists and pulled me along until I fell exhausted. Another man came up and both the others ran away. . . . The man who took the baby was a short, stout, fair man, just like the father of the baby. The other man who tied my hands was a tall, dark man.' No one was ready to believe this tale – the absence of rope burns on Sarah's wrists suggested fabrication – but still the story captured the sense of popular fears about the potential dangers for respectable women on urban streets.[61]

Racial undercurrents simmered beneath the surface of Veitch's story. The image Phoebe evoked of a white woman and mother violated by a lascivious dark man was a powerfully sexualised one, which suggested unprotected white women and impotent white men. It was an image that resonated in a town that had experienced its share of conflict with Maori in the surrounding district. Wanganui locals quickly identified the dead child as Maori, they were ready to believe in the existence of a menacing dark man who lurked on street corners and outside public houses, and they were prepared to entertain the idea that he had some hand in Phoebe's predicament. The police found Phoebe's statement about the child's death unbelievable, but they searched thoroughly for the man she said was Flossie's father. Their enquiries revealed about a dozen Chinese, Indian and mixed-race men working in hotels, in shearing gangs and on steamers in the port towns and hinterlands of Napier, Nelson and Wanganui. The men constituted a loose network of acquaintances, drawn together by their non-white status and common occupation as cooks or hotel staff.[62]

One newspaper could scarcely contain its glee in the face of Phoebe's extravagant descriptions of the alleged murderer, whom it referred to as 'a half-caste from India, with a black wig and thick curly whiskers, a Scotchman with his hair cut close, and a half-caste Chinaman, three rolled into one'.[63] But Phoebe's portrayal of Flossie's father had created a mystery, and those who attended the court proceedings waited expectantly for the results of the police search. They were not disappointed. The police may not have located 'Darky Sam', but their self-professed 'anxiety' to give Phoebe every chance to prove her allegations led them to add their own theatrical flourish during the coroner's inquest. They arranged for one of the longer-haired men they had found to enter the room as Phoebe gave her statement, to enable them to check for mutual 'signs of recognition'. 'One could not of course swear to the wig,' the *Evening Post* reporter chortled, 'but it was perfectly evident that Mrs Veitch, during her description of a real or imaginary person, had in her mind's eye just such a man.' The 'great sensation' had the crowd and jurors abuzz with 'hurried whispers' suggesting that the man was indeed Sam, but the event left both Phoebe and the unknown man bewildered. 'As a matter of fact,' confided the *Post* to its readers, 'the visitor, who to most people present seemed to have "dropped in promiscu-ous-like" was a total stranger to Mrs Veitch, and had no more to do with her affairs and history than has the man in the moon.'[64]

Whether depicting themselves as wronged mothers or respectable women, Veitch and the Flanagans crafted a storyline that positioned themselves as victims – whether or not they were in their own lives – and allowed the men in court to play the valiant hero. For Daniel Flanagan in particular, it was a role that worked to his advantage and enabled him to overcome the anomalous part he played in the proceedings as both caring father and husband, and police officer upholding the law. In marked contrast to his wife and daughter, Daniel was depicted as a steady character. He was a 'quiet and inoffensive man', fully aware of the 'gravity of his position', who remained calm while his wife and daughter fainted or shrieked around him. His statements to fellow officers and witnesses suggested that he knew few details of the arrangements Sarah and her mother had made for the child. Caring for a baby may have been women's business, in Daniel's view, but he was completely aware of the circumstances surrounding the birth, and had striven to keep it a secret. Daniel had been the one to call the doctor to attend the confinement – which he apparently described as 'a bit of bad luck' – and, mindful of prying neighbours, had requested him to leave by the back of the property. He also knew that the child would not remain in his house, informing the doctor that the family 'must do the best they could' for the baby. Although Daniel had made the arrangements to send Sarah north, he maintained that he knew no more than what his wife and daugh-ter had told him of the baby's disappearance.

The Flanagans portrayed Daniel as the loyal father and husband who supported family and reputation, and who trusted his wife and daughter and acted accordingly. His counsel, Mr Stringer, reiterated this position in court, and stressed that Daniel reacted to the story of the abduction as any father would, by trying to help his daughter hide 'her shame' and acting to 'prevent disgrace falling upon himself'. Stringer argued that charges against Daniel should be dropped to allow him to continue his role as family pro-tector; charging him would 'deprive the females of the means of assistance' in gathering evidence to support their story, for he was the only one who could do this.[65] In the end, Daniel emerged from the case as a loyal father and husband, although not a suitable police officer; he may have had some involvement in a women's crime, but throughout, he had acted as the true family man.

Male counsel and jurors seized upon the apparent feminine frailty of the women to bolster their own positions in a system of 'chivalric justice' which assigned men as women's protectors.[66] The defence counsel in both of these cases eagerly accepted the position of gentlemanly defenders of the weak. They carefully avoided alluding to the difficult issues of their clients' single motherhood and illicit sexual relations, but this silence did not mean that illegitimacy was not important. Condemnation of unconventional female sexuality was expressed instead through assumptions about women's biology. Images of biologically driven, lying, manipulative women formed a strong part of nineteenth-century discourses on female criminality.[67] Both defence and prosecution employed this discourse in the Veitch and Flanagan cases, the one to condemn the women's actions, and the other to explain and to justify.

Veitch's counsel presented her as a valiant and victimised mother so traumatised by Flossie's father that she was powerless to prevent him throwing the child into the river. She was, her lawyer ventured, an emotional wreck, totally overwrought by the circumstances of her life and experiences on the river bank. 'No one present could put themselves in the position of a mother whose child had been murdered, or do more than imagine what her feelings would be,' he reminded the jury. She had become confused in her mind, and any discrepancies in her police statements and her inability to remember much about the child's father, were consequences of that state. Her lies and half-truths were linked with her emotionalism and a desire to screen the father of her child, whoever he may have been.[68]

Robert Stout, Sarah Flanagan's counsel, used the public shame of illegitimacy to justify her actions and those of Daniel and Anna in trying to protect her and their family name. In reference to Sarah's flight north under an assumed name, he suggested that it was utterly 'probable that she would to cover her shame use a false name'. Stout pressed witnesses on Sarah's secret drinking problem, trying to suggest that this may have accounted for her actions. He tried to link this with theories of puerperal and lactational insanity to suggest that Sarah, shamed and bereft of her child, took its life in a fit of sudden homicidal mania. 'Could they not tell what was the state of that girl, who they could see was hysterical, with the child taken away from her and her not nursing it?' he urged, deploying Sarah's frequent hysterical outbursts in court to advantage.[69] Stout quizzed doctors on temporary insanity following childbirth – something of which they had had little experience – in the attempt to build up an image of a biologically driven woman who had no control over her actions. Her fabrications and fanciful scenarios of an absent husband and unknown assailants were linked to her biology, to her emotions and to her sexuality.

If Sarah Flanagan was the 'disabled, reproductive female',[70] then the middle-aged Anna Flanagan was presented in court as the 'natural mother' who acted only to help her daughter. Anna's lawyer, Mr Stringer, emphasised her compassion for her daughter and her desire to help her screen the shame of the pregnancy. Sarah may have been 'insane' after the birth of the child, but Anna, he claimed, most definitely was not. In his view, Anna's story and her attempt to bribe Nurse Freeman were simply 'the natural effort on the part of a mother to shield her daughter'.[71] A defence of natural and loyal fatherhood may have worked for Daniel, but that of natural and loyal motherhood did not work in Anna's favour. Motherhood was an elastic and unstable ideal that could arouse compassion for women, but could also condemn them if they were seen to be acting 'unnaturally'.[72]

The clearest expression of criminal women defined by their sexuality and biological state occurred at the end of Phoebe Veitch's trial. As the judge prepared to deliver the sentence of death, Veitch's counsel declared her to be pregnant. For the only time in New Zealand legal history, a jury of matrons was empanelled to ascertain whether the prisoner was quick with child, a finding that would delay the sentence of death until the child had been born. Quickening was popularly believed to designate the point at which a foetus became a human being and at which life commenced: a pregnant woman could be executed before quickening without fear of murdering the unborn child.[73]

The announcement of Phoebe Veitch's pregnancy initiated a new drama in the courtroom, and one in which the prisoner's sexuality played a key part. With an all-female cast, the normal gendered dimensions of judicial proceedings were overturned. The jury of matrons gave women an important official voice in the court in a period when they were neither regular jurors, counsel, police nor magistrates. As 'expert witnesses' in the area of female sexuality and pregnancy at a time when most births still occurred at home, the women were called upon to ponder the mysterious secrets of another woman's body in the belief, perhaps, that it took a woman to know a woman.[74] In the end, the expertise of Phoebe's jury of matrons was not sufficient, and they had to call on the assistance of a medical doctor. Even with such professional input, the jury prevaricated for a considerable time before it declared that quickening had occurred; the arcane knowledge of a woman's body, it seems, could be beyond women as well as men.

* * *

The stories in these child murder trials expounded large issues on a small, personal scale and in a form with which listeners and readers could identify: problems of poverty and social isolation, of illicit sexual relationships and single motherhood, of marital strain and desertion, of potential or imagined dangers for women in urban centres. But there were conceptual limits to a believable story, and juries chose not to credit the Veitch and Flanagan tales of wronged women and wicked men, no matter how familiar that storyline, those gender roles or life situations may have been. At the conclusion of the trials, the accused were seen to get what they deserved. Daniel Flanagan, the loyal father, walked free, while his wife and daughter, like Phoebe Veitch, were depicted simply as lying, manipulative, loose women. Anna Flanagan had acted as an 'unnatural' mother, while Phoebe Veitch and Sarah Flanagan were not even credited with vestigial maternal feelings to redeem them. Such roles, of course, were part of other narratives of female sexuality – and sexual danger – in nineteenth-century culture. Individualised stories of good and bad characters, male and female, dispelled any need for contemporaries to enquire more deeply into the underlying reasons for the actions of the accused.[75] Poverty, single motherhood, irresponsible fathers and the paucity of economic options for women could all be ignored. Awkward implications about women of 'easy virtue' and the role that men's actions played in their situation could pass unnoticed. Clichéd tales of struggling women wronged at the hands of faceless, nameless blackguards, or of immoral, sexualised and heartless mothers fitted easily into perceptions of morally dangerous times and places and the cautionary tales that circulated around them.

1   Michel Foucault, *The History of Sexuality. Volume 1: An Introduction*, London, 1990, p. 3.
2   Jeffrey Weeks, *Sex, Politics and Society: The Regulation of Sexuality since 1800*, 2nd edn, London, 1989, p. 12.
3   James Kincaid explores sexual silences in his provocative *Child-Loving: The Erotic Child and Victorian Culture*, New York, 1992.
4   Peter Bailey, 'Parasexuality and Glamour: The Victorian Barmaid as Cultural Prototype', *Gender & History*, 2, 2, 1990, p. 148.
5   Kali Israel, 'French Vices and British Liberties: Gender, Class and Narrative Competition in a Late Victorian Sex Scandal', *Social History*, 22, 1, 1997, p. 1.
6   For good examples of the microhistorical approach to crime, see Edward Berenson, *The Trial of Madame Caillaux*, Berkeley, 1992; Karen Dubinsky and Franca Iacovetta, 'Murder, Womanly Virtue and Motherhood: The Case of Angelina Napolitano, 1911–1922', *Canadian Historical Review*, 72, 4, 1991, pp. 505–31; Michel Foucault, ed., *I, Pierre Rivière, Having Slaughtered My Mother, My Sister, and My Brother.... A Case of Parricide in the 19th Century*, Lincoln, 1972; Patrizia Guarnieri, *A Case of Child Murder: Law and Science in Nineteenth-century Tuscany*, Cambridge, 1993; Joëlle Guillais, *Crimes of Passion: Dramas of Private Life in Nineteenth-century France*, Cambridge, 1990; Angus McLaren, *A Prescription for Murder: The Victorian Serial Killings*

of Dr Thomas Neill Cream, Chicago, 1993 and *The Trials of Masculinity: Policing Sexual Boundaries 1880–1930*, Chicago, 1997; Amy Gilman Srebnick, *The Mysterious Death of Mary Rogers: Sex and Culture in Nineteenth-century New York*, New York, 1995; Carolyn Strange, 'Wounded Womanhood and Dead Men: Chivalry and the Trials of Clara Ford and Carrie Davis', in Franca Iacovetta and Mariana Valverde, eds, *Gender Conflicts: New Essays in Women's History*, Toronto, 1992, pp. 149–88. In the New Zealand context see Lynley Hood, *Minnie Dean: Her Life and Crimes*, Auckland, 1994.

7   For an excellent recent account of the close relationship between the court and the criminal story, see Ann-Louise Shapiro, *Breaking the Codes: Female Criminality in Fin-de-siècle Paris*, Stanford, 1996. See also Joan Sangster, '"Pardon Tales" from Magistrate's Court: Women, Crime, and the Court in Peterborough County, 1920–50', *Canadian Historical Review*, 74, 2, 1993, pp. 161–97.

8   Berenson, *The Trial of Madame Caillaux*, pp. 6–10; Thomas Boyle, *Black Swine in the Sewers of Hampstead: Beneath the Surface of Victorian Sensationalism*, London, 1989, p. 13; Ed Cohen, *Talk on the Wilde Side: Toward a Genealogy of a Discourse on Male Sexualities*, New York, 1993, pp. 120–38; Dubinsky and Iacovetta, 'Murder, Womanly Virtue and Motherhood', pp. 512–15; Karen Dubinsky, *Improper Advances: Rape and Heterosexual Conflict in Ontario, 1880–1929*, Chicago, 1993, p. 90; Guillais, *Crimes of Passion*, pp. 218–30; Ruth Harris, 'Melodrama, Hysteria and Feminine Crimes of Passion in the Fin-de-siècle', *History Workshop*, 25, 1988, pp. 31–63; McLaren, *The Trials of Masculinity*, passim; Shapiro, *Breaking the Codes*, passim.

9   The material in this and the following paragraph is drawn from *Wanganui Herald* (*WH*), 28 February and 1 March 1883; *Wanganui Chronicle* (*WC*), 2 March and 1 May 1883; Phoebe Veitch, Confession, 7 June 1883, Notes of evidence, J40, 83/604, Justice Department files, National Archives, Wellington (NA); Report of inquest, 2 March 1883, Notes of police questioning, 1 March 1883, P1, 1883/1079, Police files, NA; Pardon, 5 June 1883, J21/2, NA.

10   *WC*, 2 March 1883.

11   *WH*, 1 and 7 May 1883.

12   *The Yeoman*, 2 March 1883.

13   *WC*, 1 May 1883.

14   *WC*, 2 March 1883, 1 May 1883.

15   Phoebe Veitch, Confession, 7 June 1883, J40, 83/604, NA.

16   Report of surgeon on death of Phoebe Veitch, J40, 91/531, NA.

17   The material in this and the next paragraph is drawn from Christchurch *Press*, 8, 12, 14, 17 January and 24, 26 February 1891; *Auckland Weekly News*, 28 February 1891; Judge's notes of evidence, Notes on Anna Flanagan, J40, 95/720, NA.

18   *Press*, 8 January 1891.

19   *Press*, 17 January 1891.

20   *Press*, 12 January 1891.

21   Arthur Hume, Commissioner of Police, to Minister of Justice, 8 May 1905, J40, 906/99, NA; Richard Hill, *The Iron Hand in the Velvet Glove: The Modernisation of Policing in New Zealand, 1886-1917*, Palmerston North, 1995, p. 24.

22   Hood, *Minnie Dean*, p. 165.

23   Annual Reports of the Police Force, *Appendices to the Journals of the House of Representatives*, 1883–93.

24   For Australia see Judith Allen, *Sex and Secrets: Crimes Involving Australian Women since 1880*, Melbourne, 1990. For Britain see George Behlmer, 'Deadly Motherhood: Infanticide and Medical Opinion in Mid-Victorian England', *Journal of the History of Medicine and Allied Sciences*, 34, 1979, pp. 303–27; Carolyn Conley, *The Unwritten Law: Criminal Justice in Victorian Kent*, New York, 1991; Ann R. Higginbotham, '"Sin of the Age": Infanticide and Illegitimacy in Victorian London', *Victorian Studies*, 33, 2, 1989, pp. 319–38; Lionel Rose, *Massacre of the Innocents: Infanticide in Great Britain, 1800–1939*, London, 1986. For France see James M. Donovan, 'Infanticide and the Juries in France, 1825–1913', *Journal of Family History*, 16, 2, 1991, pp. 157–76; Rachel Fuchs, *Poor and Pregnant in Paris: Strategies for Survival in the Nineteenth Century*, New Brunswick, 1992. For the United States see Kenneth Wheeler, 'Infanticide in Nineteenth-century Ohio', *Journal of Social History*, 31, 2, 1997, pp. 408–18.

25   For other cases of the discovery of dead babies see Frances Porter and Charlotte Macdonald,

eds, *'My Hand Will Write What My Heart Dictates': The unsettled lives of women in nineteenth-century New Zealand as revealed to sisters, family and friends*, Auckland, 1996, pp. 342–4, 373–6.

26 Foucault, *The History of Sexuality*, pp. 55–63; Shapiro, *Breaking the Codes*, p. 11.

27 Harris, 'Melodrama', *passim*; Judith Walkowitz, *City of Dreadful Delight: Narratives of Sexual Danger in Late-Victorian London*, Chicago, 1992, pp. 86–91.

28 Peter Downes, *Shadows on the Stage: Theatre in New Zealand – The First 70 Years*, Dunedin, 1975, p. 92.

29 See Shapiro, *Breaking the Codes*, *passim*; Strange, 'Wounded Womanhood', *passim*; Walkowitz, *City of Dreadful Delight*, pp. 171–89. Angus McLaren has teased out the places in melodramatic narratives available to men on trial in *The Trials of Masculinity*, *passim*.

30 McLaren, *The Trials of Masculinity*, p. 38.

31 McLaren, *A Prescription for Murder*, p. 140.

32 For a discussion on nineteenth-century criminal court practice and procedure in murder trials see Francis Boyd Adams, ed., *Criminal Law and Practice in New Zealand*, 2nd edn, Wellington, 1971.

33 There is a large literature on the use of court records. For a good recent summary of this, with particular regard to the history of sexuality, see Steven Maynard, '"Horrible Temptations": Sex, Men, and Working-class Male Youth in Urban Ontario, 1890–1935', *Canadian Historical Review*, 78, 2, 1997, pp. 197–205.

34 Frank Mort, *Dangerous Sexualities: Medico-moral Politics in England since 1830*, London, 1987, p. 9.

35 Natalie Zemon Davis, *Fiction in the Archives: Pardon Tales and their Tellers in Sixteenth-century France*, London, 1988, p. 20.

36 Shapiro, *Breaking the Codes*, pp. 51–61.

37 Strange, 'Wounded Womanhood', p. 153.

38 Discussions of the new journalism and crime reporting can be found in Boyle, *Black Swine*, *passim*; Cohen, *Talk on the Wilde Side*, pp. 120ff; Karl Beckson, *London in the 1890s: A Cultural History*, New York and London, 1992, pp. 307ff.

39 Cohen, *Talk on the Wilde Side*, p. 120. Berenson, *The Trial of Madame Caillaux*, pp. 9–10 discusses the textuality of trial transcripts.

40 *WH*, 1 March 1883; *WC*, 1 May 1883.

41 *The Yeoman*, 9 March 1883; *WC*, 2 May 1883; *WH*, 7 May 1883.

42 *Press*, 14, 15 January and 26 February 1891.

43 *Press*, 26 February 1891.

44 Deborah Epstein Nord, *Walking the Victorian Streets: Women, Representation, and the City*, Ithaca, 1995, pp. 117–21.

45 The material in this and the next paragraph is drawn from *WC*, 2 March 1883; Notes of evidence, J40, 83/604.

46 See Margaret Tennant, '"Magdalens and Moral Imbeciles": Women's Homes in Nineteenth-century New Zealand', in Barbara Brookes, Charlotte Macdonald and Margaret Tennant, eds, *Women in History 2*, Wellington, 1992, pp. 49–75 and 'Maternity and Morality: Homes for Single Mothers 1890–1930', *Women's Studies Journal*, 2, 1, 1985, pp. 28–49.

47 *WC*, 2 March and 1 May 1883; Notes of evidence, J40, 83/604; Notes of police questioning, P1, 1883/1079.

48 Conley, *The Unwritten Law*, p. 112.

49 *Press*, 8, 12, 14, 17 January and 26 February 1891; Judge's notes of evidence, Daniel Flanagan to Arthur Hume, 3 November 1891, J40, 95/720; Petition of Sarah Flanagan, 10 August 1901, J40, 1906/99.

50 *Press*, 26 February 1891.

51 Hood, *Minnie Dean*, pp. 91, 116.

52 Minnie Dean also refused to divulge to police the names and addresses of the women who came to her with their children, Hood, *Minnie Dean*, pp. 101–14, 126–8.

53 *WC*, 9 May 1883.

54 Hood, *Minnie Dean*, pp. 91–3; Hume to Minister of Justice, 31 August 1893, J40, 93/598, NA. For more on baby-farming in the nineteenth century see Rose, *Massacre of the Innocents*, *passim*.

55 *Press*, 26 February 1891.

56 Hood, *Minnie Dean*, p. 130.

57 Fuchs, *Poor and Pregnant*, pp. 201–17.

58 Reports of women's applications for maintenance orders from 'fugitive fathers' can be found in Porter and Macdonald, eds, *'My Hand Will Write What My Heart Dictates'*, pp. 414–17.

59 Dubinsky, *Improper Advances*, pp. 35ff; Walkowitz, *City of Dreadful Delight, passim*.

60 The temperance movement provides one example of this; see also debate around the introduction of the Contagious Diseases Act 1869 in Charlotte Macdonald, "'The Social Evil": Prostitution and the Passage of the Contagious Diseases Act (1869)', in Barbara Brookes, Charlotte Macdonald and Margaret Tennant, eds, *Women in History: Essays on European Women in New Zealand*, Wellington, 1986, pp. 13–33.

61 *Press*, 17 January 1891.

62 See the descriptions of the various men in P1, 1883/1079.

63 *WC*, 3 May 1883.

64 *Evening Post*, 6 March 1883.

65 *Press*, 12, 15 and 19 January 1891.

66 There is an extensive literature on the operation of 'chivalric justice' which accorded women lenient penalties for violent crime, including infanticide, in the nineteenth century. See particularly Strange, 'Wounded Womanhood', *passim*.

67 See Shapiro, *Breaking the Codes*, passim, for a recent elaboration of this.

68 *WC*, 1 May 1883.

69 *Press*, 26 February 1891.

70 Shapiro, *Breaking the Codes*, p. 105.

71 *Press*, 26 February 1891.

72 Sangster, '"Pardon Tales"', p. 192.

73 Problems in its use, and medical challenges which dispelled the notion of quickening and questioned the expertise of 'untrained' women to settle matters of life and death, led to the demise of the jury of matrons during the nineteenth century. The English court system empanelled its last jury of matrons in 1879, and even that had been the first use for 30 years. Unlike other juries, no regulations or instructions surrounded its use. Given that women were unable to serve as regular jurors, no jury rolls existed from which juries of matrons could be drawn. In practice, older and married women were simply taken from the public gallery during the trial and ushered into side rooms to conduct the examinations. On the jury of matrons, see James C. Oldham, 'On Pleading the Belly: A History of the Jury of Matrons', *Criminal Justice History*, 6, 1985, pp. 1–64; Thomas R. Forbes, 'A Jury of Matrons', *Medical History*, 32, 1988, pp. 23–33. For a mid-nineteenth-century discussion of both the concept of quickening, and the means for ascertaining pregnancy, see 'Reviews', *Australian Medical Journal*, January 1857, pp. 47–51. I am grateful to Philippa Martyr for drawing my attention to this item.

74 Mary Beth Norton, on H-WOMEN@h-net.msu.edu, 22 September 1995. I am also indebted to Charlotte Macdonald for this suggestion.

75 Other historians have commented upon how such a focus on the criminal allowed contemporaries to overlook the crime itself, and the social conditions that gave rise to it. See Higginbotham, '"Sin of the Age"', p. 337; McLaren, *A Prescription for Murder*, pp. 139–40. A full exposition on nineteenth-century attention on criminals rather than crimes is Michel Foucault, 'About the Concept of the "Dangerous Individual" in 19th-century Legal Psychiatry', *International Journal of Law and Psychiatry*, 1, 1978, pp. 1–18.

This bronze sculpture of a naked male athlete, erected on the gateway to the Auckland Domain in 1936, caused a major controversy in the city.
Photograph by P. Brennan, Auckland Museum, C8700.

A Gendered Domain:
Leisure in Auckland, 1890–1940

Caroline Daley

When William Elliot bequeathed £10,000 to the Auckland City Council to fund a new entrance way into Auckland's Domain he could not have anticipated the furore his generosity would create.[1] There had long been a call for a more impressive entry to the city's premier recreation ground.[2] The 200-acre Domain, preserved as a central-city parkland since 1845, still lacked an appropriate entrance way in 1934, when Elliot's gift was made.[3] While Fletcher Construction built the gateway, artist Richard Gross was commissioned to provide the adornment. The resulting bronze sculpture, depicting a naked male athlete 'posed on one leg, with one arm reaching towards the playing fields to urge youth on to greater effort and prowess', was erected in 1936 and caused a major controversy.[4]

Among the first to complain to the council were the 1200 women of the Auckland District Women's Christian Temperance Union: 'the display of such statues in public streets are [sic] not for the moral uplift of the young people of our city'.[5] L. Carradine also objected to the statue, reporting that 'boys and youths are purposely taking girls [to the Domain gate] so that a forbidden topic may be raised, that illegitimate children will walk their lonely way through life'. Carradine did not think city councillors should 'bully' people into looking at 'the silly lump jutting into space'.[6] The 'silly lump' caused another 'decent man' some embarrassment too. He wrote to the council complaining that when he took his wife for a Sunday drive in the Domain, he could not drive through the gates, because a crowd of boys 'of all ages' was blocking the way: '[T]hey were screaming and laughing watching the statue. I got out of my car to see what was the cause. I can't express my disgust when I saw what they were laughing at[:] the rain was dripping from different points of the figure but the steady fall of water from a part that should not be exposed was the reason of the crowd and the laughter. I was so disgusted I told them I would call the police if they did not move away.'[7]

In the following months the council received many other letters and petitions condemning the public display of the figure of a naked male. Church leaders called for the statue to be altered to cover the athlete's genitalia,[8] as did a petition signed by 1152 people. The petitioners pointed out that 'public displays of nakedness and a low morality go together'. This was fine in 'Continental cities' with their morality 'far below that of Auckland', but it would not do for the city of sails.[9] Some were even moved to 'poetry'. Jean Batten's recent aviation feats were regarded as a more suitable subject for a bronze memorial than a naked male:

> For she'd sooner wear an aviator's suit,
> Than be seen in silks and satins,
> So Take down the Statue at the Domain,
> And put up one of Jean Batten, and her airoplane.[10]

The cartoonists in both of the city's newspapers drew comic strips about the statue and one radio company incorporated a picture of it in an advertisement.[11]

In the middle of 1936 the council took a vote and decided not to modify the statue.[12] Instead, they continued to receive communications from the public 'without comment'.[13] It seems that, having agreed to the original design, the councillors felt they must uphold their initial decision.[14] If they hoped the issue would go away they were to be disappointed. The debate flared again during the Second World War, and continued into the 1950s.[15] Not everyone opposed the work. Some wrote in support of the statue, praising it as a beautiful piece of art, but the critics were more vocal than the supporters.[16] Few could now walk through the Domain gates without being aware that a naked male was poised above them.

The fuss raised many issues for Aucklanders. Apart from concerns over whether or not it was art, the statue caused many heated discussions about sexuality, morality and how public donations were spent. Some of those debates speak to the ongoing, fraught relationship between women and men's use of leisure space and resources between 1890 and 1940, the focus of this chapter. The statue on the gates had sexual overtones, yet inside the Domain the citizens of Auckland were being encouraged to participate in 'wholesome' physical activities, team sports and games designed to sublimate rather than encourage sexual activity. This emphasis on physicality was directed far more at boys and men than girls and women. Here the statue raised another problem. The physicality of the male body had long been displayed and celebrated on the Domain's playing fields, but Gross's statue took that a step further by displaying the athlete's genitalia. Decades of organised sports had not created a stable situation regarding male sexuality. The male body could be publicly lauded but silence had to be maintained about certain parts of it. The statue and the ensuing outcry shattered that silence.

This tension between physicality and sexuality is an important aspect of my discussion about gender and leisure in the Domain. I begin by examining the joint use of the Domain by men and women, arguing that although mixed groups were frequent users of the ground, once through the gates they usually performed to a gendered script: males taking centre-stage, females very much in the wings. Not surprisingly, then, the second section of this chapter explores the ways in which boys and men commandeered the ground for their organised sports and military parades, how week after week they demonstrated their masculine power through a celebration of their physicality. In the final section, I turn to women's and girls' attempts to use the park for their own recreation. Two major obstacles stood between them and using the Domain: first, a culture of fear and danger deterred women and girls from using the park without a male protector; second, the council usually denied requests from women's groups for sportsgrounds and recreation sites. I argue, however, that women stood their ground and eventually achieved some successes. It was hardly surprising that a male athlete was chosen to model for the entrance gate, given how few women got to show their athletic prowess on Auckland's Domain, but the younger women of the city, especially, were increasingly dissatisfied with their relegation to a spectator's role.

It is also important to remember, though, that the Domain was more than just a recreation ground where tens of thousands of people went every year to relax.[17] For some, it was a place of work. Gardeners and caretakers were joined by prostitutes and soft-drink sellers, all trying to earn their keep. During the 1930s Depression, part of the Domain became a garden where the unemployed grew tons of vegetables to help feed the city's hungry. At times of war or civil unrest, the Domain was turned into a camping ground for troops and special constables, as it was during the 1913 waterfront strike. And for many throughout this period the Domain was home, a refuge for the city's vagrants.[18] This particular use of the park, though, raised fears among the general public. The Domain needed to be kept safe for recreation.

We know very little about leisure in New Zealand between 1890 and

1940. Although the period has long been regarded as critical in terms of the development of modern Pakeha society, what these people did in their growing spare time has received relatively scant attention from historians.[19] The emergence of rugby as a national passion is a notable exception to this neglect.[20] In recent years, more historians have regarded organised sports as a legitimate area of inquiry, but few have broadened this out to include other forms of leisure, or taken a specifically gendered approach to their work.[21] This chapter, therefore, is a first step, an initial attempt to make some sense of the gendered meaning of leisure for Pakeha.

Although the Domain was not a planned leisure ground like New York's Central Park, it was hoped that, as with other parks of the era, this piece of the country in the city would offer urban dwellers a sanctuary from urban evils.[22] Throughout the period, this meant men and women, boys and girls, joining together in informal and organised recreation. The Domain has always provided open spaces for games and displays, public space for active leisure. It also provided personal space, rustic seats under trees, secluded walkways through the bush, and allowed for passive leisure: sitting in a carriage or car, driving around the grounds, lolling in the pavilion, sipping tea in the kiosk.[23]

The growth of leisure and an increasing contemporary emphasis on this area of life epitomises modern New Zealand. In a more organised, urban society, with greater regulation of work and school hours, smaller families and better roads and forms of transportation, the scene was ripe for leisure to take on a new importance. Local and national bodies were formed to control existing sports and activities, and new entertainments sprang up.[24] Modern citizens talked on the telephone, went to the movies, listened to the radio, drove to the beach, shopped in the department stores and wore the latest fashions. Their leisure world was public and commercial.[25] They had time and money for leisure; collectively they bought public spaces for their enjoyment. But, these 'modern' citizens also continued to enjoy informal, unorganised, non-commercial leisure.[26]

The Domain offers a perfect site to explore the co-existence of old and new leisure. For the most part, entry into the park was free; couples, families and groups could spread the picnic rug, lie in the sunshine and read, stroll through the native bush. Occasionally, though, the city council let the ground to commercial enterprises. Citizens of Auckland who paid the admission price could embrace flash, new entertainments. The first exhibition flight in New Zealand, for example, saw tens of thousands of people cram into the

Domain in 1913. They were disappointed when 'Wizard' Stone and his monoplane only managed a 35-second flight. The angry crowd mobbed the pilot and damaged his plane.[27] A few years later they were stunned when a parachuting Father Christmas, sponsored by a department store, crashed through the glass roof of the Winter Garden, the Domain's hot-house. Santa managed to hand out gifts to children, as planned, after he had rearranged his beard.[28] Parachuting Santas competed with New Zealand's first budgerigar lawn parade in terms of novelty events held in the Domain.[29] Such occasions sat alongside cricket matches, athletic meetings, cadet parades and military pageants, new sports like baseball and sports new to the Domain like rugby union.[30] Few developments in leisure were not represented. Even the movies tried to come to the Domain, although the council would not allow film-makers to use the Winter Garden as a set.[31] In the summer of 1913–14 the Domain hosted the Auckland Exhibition, with its Wonderland funfair and numerous trade displays. In 1929 the Auckland War Memorial Museum, housed in the Domain, opened its doors to the public. But whatever people did in the Domain, and how their behaviour was regarded, had a decidedly gendered dimension.

The Domain was the community's playground and celebration site. It drew together families and couples, young and old. It was a means 'of "civilising" and cementing' Auckland society.[32] Each year, for example, thousands of children enjoyed their annual Sunday school picnic there. With friends and family they played cricket, enjoyed the merry-go-round, delighted in games of 'kiss-in-the-ring' and ate their fill.[33] Parents and others turned out every year to watch their children compete in school sports, and on summery Sunday afternoons hundreds gathered to hear the First Auckland Mounted Rifles or the Garrison Artillery brass band play in the rotunda.[34] Couples played tennis together.[35] At the 'Citizens' Tea Kiosk' men and women, girls and boys enjoyed strawberries and ice cream, tea and scones. Tea was taken very seriously in the Domain. Council rules stated that the kiosk's lessee must use fresh, not condensed, milk and ensure that their teapots did not let excess tea-leaves into the cups.[36]

The kiosk was part of the new, modern Domain. Apart from providing refreshments, at a price, it offered its customers a public, safe space in which to enjoy their leisure. Courting couples had a legitimate site for conducting their romances. The Domain had long been a place for young lovers, and it retained this function throughout these years.[37] The kiosk may have been safe but, for many, the attractions of Lovers' Walk and other secluded paths and areas were too great. There is a curious silence in the public records about homosexual sex in the park, but in the late nineteenth century 're-spectable' heterosexual couples were reputed to be the target of blackmailers:

> it is a well known fact that the place is infested by two or three gangs of blackmailers and larrikins, who will hesitate at nothing in their nefarious pursuits. One of their plans is to watch for an apparently respectable couple, and, immediately the pair pause in their walk or rest for a moment on one of the dilapidated benches, to rush out and demand hush money or threaten exposure for alleged immoral intentions. This ruse is very often successful, and the miscreants almost invariably get off scot free, as a policeman seldom, if ever, goes inside the park after dusk.[38]

The demand for 'hush money' brought romance and courtship into the commercial realm. It was more likely, though, that couples spent their money on the increasing number of legitimate, commercial events held in the Domain. 'Wizard' Stone's flight drew a large, mixed crowd, as did Albert Eastwood of the Beebe Balloon Company in September 1910. The assembled crowd first watched a game of rugby league, then listened to the City Band, before Eastwood began his act. As the photograph shows, a group of men held down his hot-air balloon until it was time for the ascent. High above the ground, on a trapeze suspended below the balloon, Eastwood performed a series of acrobatic feats. While the awestruck crowd strained

A group of men holding Albert Eastwood's hot-air balloon down before his performance in the Domain in September 1910.
Auckland Weekly News, 22 September 1910, p. 4. Auckland Museum, C10, 750.

their necks, he released himself and inflated his first parachute. He then cut himself loose, went into free fall and opened his second parachute. As the crowd gasped, he again cut himself free and, close to the ground, opened his final parachute, before landing safely.[39] It may have cost a shilling, but the crowd loved every minute of this most modern spectacle.

Every year there were numerous events to entertain the public, but nothing brought the populace together in a healthy but reverent way like a traditional, patriotic occasion. When the jubilee of the colony was commemorated, the Domain was filled with more people than had ever attended a fête in New Zealand.[40] Auckland's peace celebrations, at the end of the Great War, were held in the Domain.[41] Royal birthdays always drew large crowds, but if anything could bring loyal Aucklanders out of their homes for a mass celebration it was a royal visit. The Prince of Wales's 1920 visit saw a 'throng of restless humanity' descend on the Domain.[42] 'Never before,' said the press, 'had there been in Auckland such a vast family gathering.' Proud parents looked on as 1400 girls grouped themselves into the living word 'Welcome', then 2400 primary school boys marched to the tune of the 'British Grenadiers', and finally 3500 girls, wearing either red, white or blue caps, formed a living Union Jack. Parental pride was somewhat shaken when '[w]ith a sudden movement, like the onrush of a tide, almost every child on the course raced towards the Prince, and in a moment, he was literally mobbed'.[43] This 'charming incident' was repeated seven years later when the Duke and Duchess of York visited the Domain. This time a crowd of 80,000 gathered to watch the children welcome the royals. Twelve hundred little girls spelled out 'Haeremai', 1600 boys drilled and 3600 girls, wearing red or white bonnets, formed a living St George's Cross. When the royal car drove through the avenues made in the living flag, however, the girls broke loose. As the photograph shows, these 'loyal and patriotic' children could not contain their enthusiasm.[44]

On such occasions, mothers and grandmothers shepherded children to the Domain, and even fathers were seen 'smoking pipes and helping to pilot the youngsters through the crush'.[45] Although men and women looked on together, the boys and girls gave separate and different performances. Girls were decorative; boys were sombre and military. It was the same at the floral carnivals and military pageants. On a fine Saturday afternoon in 1914, 14,000 people gathered at the cricket ground to witness a floral carnival and sweet pea pageant. They watched as Miss Isabel Reeve, in her white satin dress, was crowned queen of the carnival. They saw other women parade in the 'decorative' section and the 'living posters' event. They applauded as 150

'Loyal and patriotic' girls mobbing the Duke and Duchess of York as they drove through the Auckland Domain.
Auckland Museum.

young girls, representing various varieties of sweet peas, processed around the ground. In the evening it was the men's turn. Now the crowd marvelled as 500 territorials and senior cadets gave a combined physical drill display, 300 senior cadets fired off rifle exercises, teams of engineers built a field observatory, relay races were run, a tug-of-war took place and military flares were set off as part of an attack practice display.[46] The events were part of the same programme, but they were as different as night and day.

It was not just on rare or one-off occasions that gender roles dictated performances. At the annual Labour Day parades and sports, the same pattern was repeated, year after year. Labour Day was the perfect holiday to celebrate with sports in the Domain. As a commemoration of the eight-hour working day, it reminded everyone that eight hours were also to be set aside for rest, and eight hours for leisure. A typical Labour Day in Auckland saw a parade wind through the city up to the Domain, where lolly scrambles and games were organised for the children, and sporting events were put on for the male apprentices and the men. Girls and women were not forgotten in all of this. They processed through the city, dressed as Britannia or Hibernia.[47] They ran in special 100-yard races for married and single

94

ladies. The girls danced around the maypole and played games of basketball in front of large crowds.[48] A new event was introduced in 1910, a baby show.[49] By 1921, with over 80 infants entered, 'some mothers and their infants had to wait for several hours before going before the judges. Here and there a man could be seen assisting his wife in a rather uncomprehending way, but for the most part this section of the day's programme was in the hands of the ladies.'[50] The expectations were clear. So was the importance placed on these female events: whenever the programme ran late, female events were jettisoned. In 1910, for example, the dancing competitions were abandoned since the sports ran over time.[51] And although the women in their bright gowns added 'the required touch of gladness' to the day, their dress was also the subject of ridicule.[52] In 1902 Mr F. Whitehead won first prize in the fancy dress competition by impersonating a 'New Woman', dressed in a '"rational" costume of the most-up-to-date style'.[53] The cross-dressing continued in 1910, when the driver of the Zealandia Laundry delivery cart 'dressed as a woman in well-laundered white clothing'.[54] Such ritualistic inversions allowed everyday life and gender roles to be parodied, safe within the confines of the picnic. Before darkness fell, Mr Whitehead would be back in masculine attire.[55]

Girls and women had a role to play in these joint events, but it was a gendered role. They could dance, play certain games and show off their babies. When they ran a race, it was restricted to 100 yards. Boys and men were also performing to a set script. They had to display their physical strength. Each year there was a tug-of-war competition, as well as endurance events to test masculine mettle. They were expected to be centre-stage for most of the day.

It was no accident that men and boys' activities dominated the Domain; park controllers had long prioritised male needs. By 1890 the need for organised, regular, masculine leisure was obvious to many Aucklanders. In particular, there were special concerns about the leisure requirements of boys and young men. Attempts to establish golf links in the Domain were thwarted by the presence of 'that social pest, the small boy larrikin', who destroyed the preparations for this 'coming' sport.[56] Boys had too much spare time on their hands. Rates of juvenile delinquency were causing alarm;[57] their energy had to be harnessed. There were also concerns about the feminisation of boyhood. Boys were raised by their mothers and taught by women teachers;[58] it was time for men to step in and take control. So the Domain took on some of the characteristics of a 'reform park', a place where the problems of industrial, urban life, such as juvenile delinquency, could be addressed by adult-organised physical activity.[59] In Auckland, as in American parks, reformers focused on the problems of boys and young men;[60] and organised team sports and military training were their favoured responses.

In a city full of vices, it was important that young males had legitimate, healthy outlets. Team sports were seen as a way for males to prove their manliness. The physicality required by games was a visible demonstration of masculine power. The ability to command space to play games, and audiences to watch them, reiterated both manliness and masculine power. This was the world the boys entered as they left the pavilion and took to the playing field.

The call for young males to have playing space was made again and again. When the council suggested exchanging some land in the Domain with the hospital, a group of boys wrote to oppose the plan: 'The land proposed to be taken is part of the playground for the boys in the district. . . . As this will be a great city by-and-by, we beg that the rights and privileges of the children not be taken away. You were boys once yourselves. Think of that, and please grant our prayer.'[61] By this time the boys were aware of the benefits of sports. Mercutio, a regular columnist in the *New Zealand Herald*, had told them that athletics saved them from '"mooning" in front of an hotel bar, talking soft nonsense to the Hebe who dispenses refreshments there, or leaning over the billiard table till three o'clock in the morning'.[62] The mayor had told them that the Domain was 'for the health and benefit of the citizens'. By citizens he meant young men. The mayor wanted more money spent on the Domain cricket ground since it 'employed hundreds of young fellows during their spare hours in an innocent and healthy way'.[63] His choice of words is instructive. Sport was the new labour; it replaced work as a way to reiterate masculinity.[64] The message did not wane. In the 1920s, the boys' work director of the YMCA pointed out that there was an 'outstanding' need for young males to have 'healthy outdoor recreation under expert supervision'.[65] The mayor saw the flattening of 13 acres of land in the outer Domain as an excellent development since the land had been 'rendered available as a playing area for the boys of the city'.[66] And the Auckland Labour Party pointed out that the 100-plus members of their Boys' Club needed access to free playing areas so that they could play sports and thus train to be 'good citizens'.[67]

At times boys and youths learnt how to be 'good citizens' by mimicking adult men. From 1893, the Auckland Amateur Athletic Club organised races for boys from the public schools, as part of their annual athletic meets.[68] Maori as well as Pakeha boys were meant to emulate their elders. The 'plucky' if 'swarthy' boys from St Stephen's, a school for Maori boys, 'elicited the most applause from the spectators'.[69] Sport was a way to bring Maori boys and men into the fold.[70] Cheap tickets also encouraged boys to be spectators at men's sports.[71] But, for the most part, men organised separate sporting events for boys and youths. Groups like the YMCA held athletic meetings and organised cricket teams.[72] Masters at schools like Auckland Grammar watched boys train and play team sports after school.[73] Organisations like the Auckland Primary Schools' Rugby Union made sure boys got to play at the ground on wintry Saturday mornings, while cricketers saw that 400-500 young boys took to the wicket on summery Saturdays.[74]

If sports were meant to make boys fighting fit, cadets and the Boy Scouts would make them disciplined and loyal. In the post-Boer War world, especially, military training was seen as essential.[75] Boys, youths, veterans and other men became involved in an ongoing display of New Zealand's military preparedness and loyalty to the empire. When they donned their uniforms they put on the clothes of masculinity: as they precision marched in front of adoring crowds they reiterated their manly control. The Domain was the perfect site for such displays. In front of 'the great captain of the Empire', Lord Kitchener, over 4000 'growing lads' marched, 'with patriotism a part of their character, with loyalty bred in their bones'.[76] On the hillsides around the sportsground 'feminine dress predominated': women were at the margins, spectators, while the boys and the returned contingents performed centre-stage.[77] The scene was repeated many times. Ten thousand spectators watched 4000 men and youths parade at the coronation celebration in 1911; by the King's Birthday of 1933 the only thing that had changed was the introduction of a fly-past.[78] Prominent among the marchers were boy scouts, the quintessential organisation for training future soldier-citizens.[79] Boy Scouts and cadets did more than march. They held military gymkhanas and sports meetings, where they competed for challenge cups.[80] Like their adult male counterparts, they knew the importance of physical fitness.

The physicality of men was never in question at the Domain. Every week, the ground witnessed men playing team sports. In summer cricket dominated, while in winter association football, rugby league, Australian rules, lacrosse and hockey struggled for supremacy. Athletic and cycling meetings were often held, and although these did not have the benefit of encouraging team loyalty, like the team games they, too, asserted the importance of the male body. The modern world no longer allowed many city-dwellers the opportunity to prove their physicality through work. The pen pusher, who might even be sharing his workplace with women, needed a venue to display his masculine prowess. For some men, the hotel, race-course and billiard saloon fulfilled this role, but for those who endorsed the eugenic call for fit, pure and fertile citizens, the playing field and running track held more appeal.[81]

Women, though peripheral to the action, were nonetheless important. Part of the appeal of sports was the attention a muscular body received from admiring females. As one journalist put it, reporting on a recent athletic meeting watched by 5000 in the Domain: 'It amazes us to see the abnormal amount of interest taken in cases of ultra-development in calves by the fair sex. The average "fashionable" girl, it seemed to us, after a stroll through the field on Saturday, would walk miles to gaze on the legs of athletic heroes.'[82] Without an audience, spectacular masculinity lost its resonance. Women were being encouraged to provide an adoring public: at athletic meetings the pavilion was set aside for them, and free tea was provided in a marquee on the grounds.[83] The La Crosse Association also made sure there were free seats in the pavilion for women spectators.[84] The athletes even introduced a 'Ladies' Bracelet Race', where all the men who ran had to be nominated by a young woman.[85] Cricketers and boys from Auckland Grammar involved females in a more prosaic way: women and girls made the tea.[86]

For men, as for boys, sports became an important way to prove man-liness. Men's ability to secure time, week after week, for their games was a visible sign of their power. Their unquestioned right to use the grounds at the Domain, and their access to money to pay for their kit and the use of the pitch, showed that even if they worked in an office they were still real men. In the Great War, men were urged to keep playing, to retain their readiness for war. The rugby league president reminded them that 'by con-tinuing to play football players were doing their duty to their country'.[87] During the Depression, when the breadwinning capacity of some men was undermined, the council allowed mid-week league teams to use the grounds free of charge.[88] By this time the council was quantifying the number of matches played each year. In 1933 men played 583 games of football of various codes and 428 cricket matches in the Domain.[89] Their dominating presence was immortalised on the Domain gates.

Although some Aucklanders may have suggested a clothed Jean Batten as a worthy replacement for the naked male athlete on the gates, the city's fathers never entertained such an idea. After all, women were generally passive users of the Domain. They watched men play sports, they supervised children at Sunday school picnics, and if they promenaded around the grounds they were meant to be on the arm of a man. In the 1930s the councillors saw women's use of the park as passive, largely because, over the previous 40 years, they had denied women a more active role.

The Domain was the people's park but the people were often assumed to be male. In theory, the citizens of Auckland had unrestricted access to the grounds, but throughout the period women and children were reminded constantly that danger lurked behind every tree.[90] If they were part of the crowd at an organised event, like the Labour Day sports, they were generally considered safe. They might fall foul of pickpockets, as during the 1927 royal visit when a group of professional pickpockets crossed the Tasman to try their luck, but their personal safety was not in question.[91] If, however, women or girls wanted to use their park for their own leisure, promenade without a male escort, explore the native bush, or sit on the rustic benches and enjoy the vista, they were warned that evil was just around the corner.

Sometimes that evil was morally offensive, rather than personally dangerous. It was assumed that women and girls would want nothing to do with the gambling going on in the Domain. Bookmakers were frequent visitors to sports meetings, and even went so far as to print up betting cards, giving the names of competitors in various races, noting their physical merits and their past histories. As the press reported, they called out the odds 'with as much boldness as if [the competitors] were horses engaged in a metropolitan race meeting'.[92] The council responded by passing a by-law to prohibit betting in the Domain, but gambling continued.[93]

Some women may have enjoyed a flutter, but the fear of physical assault restricted many women's use of the park. It was hard not to be afraid when the press carried so many stories warning that the Domain was 'not safe for women and children by day, much less by night'. Given that these were the words of the town clerk, they demanded to be taken seriously.[94] The Domain was said to be 'infested' with 'undesirable characters' who placed women and children at risk.[95] Even the mayor admitted that only 'able-bodied men' could safely use the park.[96] The official response was to cut back the undergrowth, 'in the interests of our womenfolk', so that there was less cover for undesirables, and to request a more visible police presence in the area.[97] After years of effort, the council declared in 1933 that 'The removal of the undergrowth and the constant patrolling by a police officer' had made the park safe.[98] Yet later that same year they were informed that the boundary hedge by George Street was 'popular as a place of refuge for inebriated persons and lends itself very frequently to most unseemly behaviour on the part of irresponsible people'.[99] A few years later 'Pro Bono Publico' reminded Aucklanders that 'even up till today women do not care to enter unprotected into [Lovers' Walk's] solitudes. There is too much cover for vagrants.'[100]

Some women certainly faced danger when they used the Domain. In 1908 there was a much-discussed assault on a woman in the park by two men.[101] In 1926 'A Disgusted Londoner' wrote to the *Herald* to complain about the behaviour she encountered during half a dozen walks in the Domain:

> on two occasions, I have been accosted by most objectionable types of men who have used indecent language to me, and on a third occasion in the afternoon a man of, presumably, the clerk class, called out to me good afternoon, miss! and, although I hurried on and sat on a seat near some people and occupied myself with reading a newspaper, as soon as they had gone the same man reappeared, and took their seat, so that I was obliged to move.

Although the clerk's intentions may have been honourable, the woman felt threatened. Whether women were in fact more likely than males to be the target of male violence was immaterial to many. As the Londoner noted, when she was out strolling alone she did 'not see any other ladies either walking or driving and not even nursemaids with their charges as is the case in our London parks'. She concluded that 'it is not customary in New Zealand for ladies to go out alone'.[102]

Presenting the Domain as a place of danger for women and children, with 'undesirables' lurking in the undergrowth, effectively inhibited women's use of the park. Although I would not like to suggest that this was a deliberate policy, designed to limit female leisure in the park, the net effect was that many females did not feel able to enjoy unorganised, female-only recreation in the Domain. And when they did want to participate in organised, female-only leisure, they faced other obstacles.

By the 1890s, people throughout New Zealand were already debating the merits and costs of girls and women engaging in physical exercise.[103] Middle-class women and girls had taken to the croquet green, the golf links, the hockey field and were even starting to cycle around the countryside. They were also playing tennis. Such activities could not pass without derisive comments from some males. Mercutio suggested that a proposed tennis court in the hospital grounds, on the edge of the Domain, had been 'hung up' after 'ladies' at some of the nearby clubs complained, fearing that their male tennis partners would find playing with the 'mob caps' too enticing.[104] Matchmaking, rather than match point, was the aim of their game, if Mercutio were to be believed.

Tennis, unlike many other sports, could be portrayed as a genteel game. Given that women often played paired with men, and men ran the national organisation, it was a game that could accommodate contemporary notions of 'proper' gender relations. Within a few years there were tennis courts within the Domain and each week, although never on a Sunday, mixed doubles were played.[105] But when it came to other sporting endeavours, Auckland's women and girls more often than not found themselves sidelined.

Very few women's organisations even requested sportsgrounds in the Domain before or during the Great War. It was not that Auckland women did not play sports – there were, for example, local hockey teams from 1899[106] – but when women asked to use this public park for their games, generally they were stonewalled. The honorary secretary of the Auckland Ladies Hockey Association Cricket Contingent waited in vain for a reply from the council to her 1909 request for a practice ground on Saturdays.[107] Four years later, the city engineer failed to respond to the YWCA's request for basketball grounds in the Domain, and his inaction never troubled the works committee.[108] Such silences were not common when men's organisations made requests. The only success women's clubs could claim was the permission granted to the Tui Hockey Club to use one pitch on Wednesday afternoons for women's hockey.[109]

While, in general, the interwar period might have seen a more relaxed, indeed encouraging attitude, towards women's sports, the Domain continued to be a male bastion.[110] In 1925 the superintendent of parks did agree that the YWCA could reserve space for girls' sports in the Domain 'except on Saturdays, when all space is taken up', but the parks committee ignored his suggestion. Even on weekdays, girls were not to play on the Domain's fields.[111] The parks committee was happy to defer indefinitely responses to requests from women's sports clubs for practice and playing grounds, or tell them that all grounds had been allocated.[112] Little wonder that when the first athletic carnival of the Auckland Girls' Sports Clubs was held in 1926, the 400 competitors from offices, factories, shops, warehouses and church and girls' associations, held their hockey and basketball matches, relay and novelty races at neighbouring Carlaw Park.[113]

But girls and women did not give up on the Domain. In spite of, or perhaps because of, the hostility they faced when they requested grounds, the 1920s saw more and more deputations to the council demanding space for female sports. In 1926, Councillor Ellen Melville introduced a group of women to the parks committee. The women, representing the Inter-House Girls' Sports Association, the Auckland Ladies Hockey Association, the Basket-Ball Association and the YWCA, wanted 20 acres of playing area set aside for female sports.[114] The following year, another deputation asking for girls' sportsgrounds waited on the committee.[115] Women's groups also began asking for special terms and conditions. As the Auckland Ladies Hockey Association pointed out when they asked for two grounds, the women needed dressing-rooms, since many of their players came straight from work and needed somewhere to change into their team uniform. They also thought that, since the majority of their players earned less than 'gentleman players', they should have the grounds at a cheaper rate. They were told no grounds were available.[116]

For the most part, the women's requests fell on deaf, or openly hostile, ears. But perseverance did pay off for some. In 1936, the general secretary of the YWCA asked for use of the area behind the War Memorial Museum 'for the purpose of organising recreation for girls'. The superintendent of parks was not sympathetic to the request. He did not think the museum and war memorial should be 'surrounded by sports grounds', especially since there was 'ample room' in other grounds for young women's sports.[117] Once again, the decision was deferred, but this time the committee actually returned to the issue, and when they were told that the only regular sports girls played in the Domain was tennis, they granted the YWCA free use of the area for girls' baseball for the next 12 months.[118] A new, regular sporting venture and venue had been secured. Girls and young women from training college and firms such as the Farmers' Trading Company turned up on Tuesday evenings and Saturday afternoons, paid their dues and played their game.[119]

Baseball was not the only success story. In 1938 the Ladies Sub-Committee of the Auckland Centre of the New Zealand Amateur Athletic Association was granted use of the outer Domain for athletic events.[120] The following year, the Girls' Life Brigade held games in the Domain on a Saturday afternoon.[121] But, like the baseball and women's athletics, the girls' games were held in the outer Domain, in their case around the statue of Robert Burns, far from the main sportsfields, and nowhere near the pavilion. Girls and women may have gained some ground, but they were not meant to have an audience.

Female sporting successes in the Domain were limited. Their sports were marginalised spatially, not just in terms of where they were sited, but also in terms of size. Men had 20 first-class cricket pitches; women had to be grateful for three baseball diamonds.[122] Nor is it surprising that their biggest triumph came with baseball. As others have noted, female sport tends to be better received if it is divorced from men's sport.[123] Few men had ever played baseball in the Domain. Since the game had not been masculinised, it was permissible to feminise it.

Women undoubtedly struggled for sporting space and resources in the Domain, but they did continue to fight, and they did not give up their sports. Nor were the battles and the successes limited to the sporting arena.

In 1926, the Domain hosted the largest rally of Girl Guides ever held in the country. In front of the pavilion, before the Governor-General, Sir Charles Fergusson and Lady Fergusson, almost 1000 young women and girls demonstrated that they were prepared.[124] At a time when female sports still found it hard to secure grounds in the Domain, the city council showed no hostility to the guides' rally. To many, the guide embodied the best features of the modern girl. She was feminine and decorative, while also loyal and selfless. Like the girls at Labour Day sports and royal visits, the guides did country dances, made living maps of the globe and demonstrated the core values of guiding: purity, friendship, courage.[125] The guides, however, were also challenging some contemporary notions of femininity. They were preparing for a changing world, a world where women and girls were the equal of men. Auckland's Girl Guides and Brownies were taught jiu-jitsu as an 'invaluable . . . weapon of the weak', but when the girls showed that they could now throw 'ruffians' twice their size over their shoulders, hold them on the ground and inflict pain on the men if they struggled, the crowd could see that these girls were not to be toyed with.[126] The following year, 1500 young women and girls demonstrated what to do if a bomb exploded in a public place. Not content with just tending to the injured, a group of guides chased the 'evil-doer', caught and bound him and brought him back in custody. Girls were fighting back, some taking on masculine attire. A group of guides, dressed as Robin Hood and his 'merrie men', held an archery contest in front of an admiring audience.[127]

When Mr Whitehead took off his 'New Woman' outfit after the Labour Day sports in 1902, his masculinity was intact. He had made fun of women who wore 'rational' dress and won a prize at their expense. When the guides took off their uniforms and Robin Hood outfits their femininity was a little less secure. The skills they had acquired while in their other garb were not unlearnt as the buttons of their uniforms were undone. In the same way, the young women in the Farmers' Trading Company baseball team were playing a new ball game, in more ways than one. Contemporaries may have been coming around to the idea of female sports for the sake of the children these women would one day bear, but there is little indication that this motivated the young women in question. The sports and leisure of girls and young women was unsettling notions of femininity.

Auckland's city fathers were not in the habit of making grand statements about the Domain's role in their city. The closest they got to such a pronouncement came in 1932, when the city engineer, in the course of a lecture to the councillors, said:

> Turning now to the question of statuary, the selection and placing of which demands most careful thought, the primary object of decorating parks with sculpture is to delight the imagination of the citizen, who, when desirous of escaping from the commonplace of a workday world, seeks quietude in the retreats of a park, and it has been said by a noted authority that the intellectual sanity of a City depends largely upon the wise provision of such places, and here in the Domain where we already have the Valkyrie and the Cain and Abel statues suitably situated, our sculpture should preferably be that of the idyllic or allegorical kind, but we may, also, with discretion, fittingly introduce historic personages.[128]

When the statue of the naked male athlete was erected on the Domain gates a couple of years later, many were less than delighted. No longer was the Domain characterised as the community's playground, a place of civilisation and good citizenship. Instead it became the site for a very public debate about morality, sexuality and the gender order. Gross's statue embodied many of the concerns of the modern age.

Beyond the gates, those tensions did not dissipate. From the 1890s through to the 1930s, the girls and boys, women and men who went to the Domain lacked an easy coexistence. They all participated in many transgender events, but these joint activities invariably required them to perform to a gendered script. At picnics and sports days, women were meant to provide the tea and be an adoring audience for male athletes. Their decorative and spectator status was reinforced at the new commercial events that developed over these years. Women went to watch Albert Eastwood and his amazing balloon act, but it was men who assisted him, holding down the balloon. The old and the new forms of leisure allocated men and women different roles. Arguably, the financial cost of modern leisure reinforced these roles, as men 'treated' women, demonstrating yet again their superior hold on the Domain.

To the women who tried to gain ground for their sports, men's hold on the Domain looked very secure. Yet throughout the period men and boys were constantly using the park to reiterate their masculinity. Week after week, through sports and military drill, the male body was monitored and reinscribed in an acceptable form. The statue on the gates was said to have been designed to 'stir Auckland youth to further conquests on fields afar': the men of Auckland were making sure those conquests were honourable.[129] Male sexuality remained ever problematic, as the many male critics of Gross's statue made clear.

The desire to harness male sexual energy through sports and drill can be seen as part of a larger campaign to clean up and modernise the Domain. The undergrowth of the native bush had to be cleared to 'civilise' and control nature.[130] Gambling and other illegal activities had to be stamped out. Vagrants had to be removed to make the park safe for leisure. Although boys and men would benefit from this, girls and women were seen as the main beneficiaries of a newly respectable Domain. Many saw the statue on the gates as a setback in achieving this goal. The modern recreation ground could hardly be civilised and safe, non-threatening and asexual, if visitors were greeted by the figure of a naked male.

Although fear limited many women's use of the park, others decided it was time to claim some ground for themselves. Beginning before the Great War, but intensifying after it, girls and young women's sports and recreation groups made repeated requests to the council for the right to play in the Domain. After many years of stonewalling, the council finally acquiesced. Like the girls who chased the Duke and Duchess of York in 1927, these young women understood and expressed their femininity in ways the city council, and others, found hard to comprehend, let alone accept. By the outbreak of the Second World War young women had won the 100-yard dash at the Domain. It was to be many years, though, before they were allowed to enter the marathon.

I would like to thank Deborah Montgomerie and Raewyn Dalziel for their insightful comments on an earlier draft of this essay.
1   Auckland City Council (ACC) 275, Town Clerk/Secretarial Department Classified Subject Files 1913-76, Box 199, Item 34/261: Donation of Sum to Allow for Erection of Arches and Gateways at Entrance of Auckland Domain, 1934-54, ACC Archives, Auckland.
2   In 1906 one city councillor complained that: 'There was no public park in Australasia that had an entrance in such a foul state. People entering the park there would think it only a grazing paddock.' *New Zealand Herald* (*NZH*), 14 April 1906, p. 6.

3 On the history of the Domain see *An Historical Guide to the Auckland Domain*, Auckland, 1979; G. W. A. Bush, *Decently and In Order: The Government of the City of Auckland 1840–1971*, Auckland, 1971, especially pp. 167-8, 274-5; lecture given by James Tyler, Engineer, to the Council, 25 February 1932, ACC 219, Works Department Subject Files, Box 57, Item 27/365 Part 1: Proposed New Drive from Stanley Street to Ponds Near Kiosk at the Domain, ACC Archives, Auckland.

4 *Auckland Star*, 29 June 1936, p. 9. The report noted that a 'well-known Auckland athlete posed for the sculptor'. According to an unsourced index card at the Auckland Institute and Museum Library, Allan Elliott modelled for the statue. Elliott was an Auckland sprinter, and represented New Zealand at the 1932 Los Angeles Olympics. Peter Heidenstrom, *Athletes of the Century: 100 Years of New Zealand Track and Field*, Wellington, 1992, p. 6.

5 ACC 275, Box 199, Item 34/261, 6 July 1936.

6 ACC 275, Box 199, Item 34/261, c. 20 July 1936.

7 ACC 275, Box 199, Item 34/261, c. 30 September 1936.

8 ACC 275, Box 199, Item 34/261, 5 April 1937. This petition was signed by leading members of the Anglican, Presbyterian, Methodist and Baptist churches, along with a Jewish rabbi and various other concerned citizens. The pastor of the West Street Church of Christ had also written to complain on 27 January 1937. When the statue was first unveiled there were similar calls for either a fig leaf, a pair of tights, or running shorts to be placed on the statue. See *Auckland Star*, 2 July 1936, p. 10; 3 July 1936, p. 8; 7 July 1936, p. 10; and *NZH*, 1 July 1936, p. 16; 2 July 1936, p. 15; 4 July 1936, p. 17; 7 July 1936, p. 13; 9 July 1936, p. 16.

9 ACC 275, Box 199, Item 34/261, 6 April 1937. See also the letter to the editor by W. Owen Garland, who was 'shocked' and 'ashamed' to look at the 'offensive' statue. *NZH*, 15 April 1937, p. 15.

10 ACC 275, Box 199, Item 34/261, c. 8 April 1937. The poem, 'A Protest Against the Domain Statue', was penned by E. C. Frost, K. R. Moore and M. Graham of Mount Eden. Emphasis in original. Electoral roll and street directory searches indicate that the three 'poets' were probably women.

11 The *Star*'s cartoonist, J. C. H., drew a 'The Diversions of Mickey Savage' strip about the statue forgetting to wear running shoes, *Auckland Star*, 4 July 1936, p. 10. That same day Mercutio noted the lack of running shoes on the athlete, *NZH*, 4 July 1936, Supplement, p. 4. Gordon Minhinnick in the *Herald* drew the statue dressed for all seasons, *NZH*, 2 July 1936, p. 13, and drew 'Sam' on a Sunday stroll walking past the Domain statue with a blindfold on, *NZH*, 11 July 1936, Supplement, p. 2. Sterling Stores advertised Cromwell radios alongside a photograph of the statue, claiming that their 'Magic Eye' radio, rather than the statue, was the talk of Auckland, *NZH*, 10 July 1936, p. 15.

12 *NZH*, 21 July 1936, p. 10.

13 *NZH*, 9 April 1937, p. 14.

14 The council had approved the plan of the gateway sometime before, having seen a miniature of the statue. *Auckland Star*, 2 July 1936, p.10.

15 See ACC 275, Box 199, Item 34/261, 2 July, 30 July and 13 October 1942 and 2 July 1946. There were letters in the *NZH* on 12 and 19 March 1954, and a report on 17 March 1954 that four youths were found at night with a 14-foot ladder at the Domain; they had tied a baby's nappy around the statue. These reports are contained in ACC 275, Box 199, Item 34/261.

16 See for example the letter from 'A Mother of Sons', praising the council for refusing to alter the statue, and the letter from 'Old lady lover of true Art not modern distortion', who thought that only people with 'dirty minds' could object to the statue. ACC 275, Box 199, Item 34/261, c. 20 July 1936 and 26 July 1947. D. Luckens, who was impressed with the 'striking and inspiring piece of work' and did not accept that a statue could corrupt the morals of the young, wrote a letter to the editor, *NZH*, 15 April 1937, p. 15.

17 Attendance figures for anything except paying events are very hard to ascertain. In the first week of February 1932 a survey revealed that during the week, over 7000 people visited the Domain; on the Sunday 950 men, 880 women and 300 children came in. Undated handwritten list of use of paths in the Domain, c. February 1932, ACC 219, Box 57, Item 27/365 Part 1.

18 As Tim Frank mentions in his chapter, people were living in the Domain during the Depression.

This was not a new development. See, for example, the case of recidivist vagrant Samuel Briggs, *NZH*, 24 June 1911, p. 5.

19 On the importance of the period see Erik Olssen, 'Towards a New Society', in Geoffrey W. Rice, ed., *The Oxford History of New Zealand*, 2nd edn, Auckland, 1992, pp. 254-84. Olssen mentions recreation facilities in passing on p. 259 and pays some attention to rugby, pp. 262, 284.

20 Analytical works on rugby for this period include Jock Phillips, *A Man's Country? The Image of the Pakeha Male – A History*, revised edn, Auckland, 1996, especially Ch. 3; Rex W. Thomson, 'Provincial Rugby in New Zealand: Otago's Academic Pioneers', *Journal of Sport History*, 23, 3, Fall 1996, pp. 211-27; Len Richardson, 'The Invention of a National Game: The Struggle for Control', *History Now*, 1, 1, 1995, pp. 1-8; Piet De Jong, *Saturday's Warrior: The Building of a Rugby Stronghold*, Palmerston North, 1991; Alan Manley, 'Antidote to Depression: Rugby and New Zealand Society 1919-1939', Post Graduate Diploma of Arts, University of Otago, 1991; John Nauright, 'Myth and Reality: Reflections on Rugby and New Zealand Historiography', *Sporting Traditions*, 6, 2, 1990, pp. 219-30; Keith Sinclair, *A Destiny Apart: New Zealand's Search for National Identity*, Wellington, 1986, Ch. 10; Len Richardson, 'Rugby, Race and Empire: The 1905 All Black Tour', *Historical News*, 47, 1983, pp. 1-6.

21 Apart from the New Zealand literature on rugby, women's sport has received some attention. In particular see Catherine Smith, 'Control of the Female Body: Physical Training at Three New Zealand Girls' High Schools, 1880s-1920s', *Sporting Traditions*, 13, 2, 1997, pp. 59-71; John Nauright and Jayne Broomhall, 'A Woman's Game: The Development of Netball and a Female Sporting Culture in New Zealand, 1906-70', *International Journal of the History of Sport*, 11, 3, 1994, pp. 387-407; Charlotte Macdonald, 'The Unbalanced Parallel', in Anne Else, ed., *Women Together: A History of Women's Organisations in New Zealand/Nga Ropu Wahine o te Motu*, Wellington, 1993, pp. 403-44; M. A. E. Hammer, '"Something Else in the World to Live For": Sport and the Physical Emancipation of Women and Girls in Auckland 1880-1920', MA thesis, University of Auckland, 1990; Ruth Fry, '"Don't Let Down the Side": Physical Education in the Curriculum for New Zealand Schoolgirls, 1900-1945', in Barbara Brookes, Charlotte Macdonald and Margaret Tennant, eds, *Women in History: Essays on European Women in New Zealand*, Wellington, 1986, pp. 101-17. On other aspects of leisure see Douglas Booth, 'Healthy, Economic, Disciplined Bodies: Surfbathing and Surf Lifesaving in Australia and New Zealand, 1890-1950', *New Zealand Journal of History*, 32, 1, 1998, pp. 43-58; Sue Upton, 'Women in the Club', *Women's Studies Journal*, 12, 1, 1996, pp. 43-60; Isabella Mitchell, 'Picnics in New Zealand During the Late Nineteenth and Early Twentieth Centuries: An Interpretive Study', MA thesis, Massey University, 1995; David Grant, *On a Roll: A History of Gambling and Lotteries in New Zealand*, Wellington, 1994. Claire Toynbee has written on gender and leisure for this period. Claire Toynbee, *Her Work and His: Family, Kin and Community in New Zealand 1900-1930*, Wellington, 1995, Ch. 9.

22 See Mark Billinge, 'A time and place for everything: an essay on recreation, re-Creation and the Victorians', *Journal of Historical Geography*, 22, 4, 1996, pp. 443-59, especially pp. 450-2; Andrew Davies, *Leisure, Gender and Poverty: Working-class culture in Salford and Manchester, 1900-1939*, Buckingham, 1992, p. 138; Hazel Conway, *People's Parks: The Design and Development of Victorian Parks in Britain*, Cambridge, 1991, *passim*; David Schuyler, *The New Urban Landscape: The Redefinition of City Form in Nineteenth-Century America*, Baltimore, 1986, especially pp. 4, 59. For similar sentiments being expressed about Auckland's Domain, see lecture given by James Tyler, Engineer, to the Council, 25 February 1932, in ACC 219, Box 57, Item 27/365 Part 1.

23 On the various purposes of nineteenth-century parks see Hilary A. Taylor, *Age and Order: The public park as a metaphor for a civilised society*, Gloucester, 1994, especially pp. 3-6.

24 For example, in the late 1880s the New Zealand Lawn Tennis Association, the New Zealand Amateur Athletic Association (which included cycling) and the New Zealand Bowling Association were formed. In the 1890s the New Zealand Rugby Football Union and the New Zealand Cricket Council came into being. In 1902, both the New Zealand Boxing Association and the New Zealand Hockey Association were instituted. From 1896, movies were shown in New Zealand.

25 For figures on movie attendances, telephone connections and radio licences see G.T. Bloomfield, *New Zealand: A Handbook of Historical Statistics*, Boston, 1984, pp. 125, 260-1. On the movies see also Nerida Elliott, 'Anzac, Hollywood and Home: Cinemas and Filmgoing in Auckland, 1909-1939', MA thesis, University of Auckland, 1989; Peter A. Harrison, 'The Motion Picture Industry in New Zealand, 1896-1930', MA thesis, University of Auckland, 1974. On the beach see Stephen Barnett and Richard Wolfe, *At the Beach: The Great New Zealand Holiday*, Auckland, 1993. Department stores and fashions are discussed in Danielle Sprecher, 'The Right Appearance: Representations of Fashion, Gender and Modernity in Inter-war New Zealand', MA thesis, University of Auckland, 1997.

26 As Claude S. Fischer has argued for America, this 'modern' period does not see a simple replacement of informal leisure with organised events, nor do commercial activities totally replace self-generated ones. Claude S. Fischer, 'Changes in Leisure Activities, 1890-1940', *Journal of Social History*, 27, 3, 1993, pp. 445-75. For a similar argument for England see Davies, *Leisure, Gender and Poverty, passim.*

27 *NZH*, 21 April 1913, p. 8. The crowd of 30,000 had to be controlled by mounted police.

28 *NZH*, 22 November 1937, p. 10. The jump was organised by the Farmers' Trading Company.

29 The budgerigar show had over 100 entries. Birds were shown in small cages. *NZH*, 22 February 1937, p. 5.

30 Union was played in various grounds around the city and only made it into the Domain on a regular basis after the First World War.

31 See ACC 275, Box 11, Item 16/60c: Winter Garden, Domain, 20 February and 8 March 1920; ACC, 275, Box 37, Item 21/201: Exhibition Glass House in Domain for Floral Display Purposes, 7 and 16 July 1921.

32 Taylor, *Age and Order*, p. 4.

33 See, for example, the *NZH*, 2 January 1890, p. 5 for a report of a picnic attended by 3000 children 'and fully as many more of their friends and relations'.

34 ACC 285, Town Clerk's Office Record Files, Box 41, Item 15: Record Files, Parks and Endowments, 1908-10, ACC Archives, Auckland, 9 October 1909. By this time the council had already been subsidising the bands in parks programme for 'some time'. The band rotunda was not erected until 1912. See *Auckland Star*, 20 March 1976, p. 16. Bands played in the Domain on a regular basis right through to the late 1930s. See ACC 107, Parks Committee Minutes, Item 5: Parks Committee Minutes, 13.11.36-5.12.39, ACC Archives, Auckland, 4 February 1938.

35 For example, in 1936 Noel Howard of Otahuhu wrote to the council requesting information about hiring a court on Saturday: 'My wife & I are rather anxious to play there'. ACC 275, Box 85, Item 24/753: Tennis Courts, Domain, 1924-39, 19 October 1936.

36 The kiosk was built during the exhibition and gifted to the city once the exhibition closed. See ACC 275, Box 7, Item 14/60B: Domain Kiosk, 1914-21; ACC 275, Box 55, Item 22/1050: Domain Tea Kiosk, 1922-24; and ACC 275, Box 84, Item 24/722: Domain Tea Kiosk, 1924-39.

37 See Clementine Fraser, '"Incorrigible Rogues" and Other Female Felons: Women and Crime in Auckland 1870-1885', MA thesis, University of Auckland, 1998, p. 74.

38 *New Zealand Observer and Free Lance*, 8 July 1899, p. 2.

39 *NZH*, 19 September 1910, p. 9.

40 *NZH*, 3 February 1890, p. 6.

41 *NZH*, 22 July 1919, p. 7. The celebrations were delayed due to the 1918 influenza pandemic.

42 *NZH*, 26 April 1920, p. 9.

43 *NZH*, 27 April 1920, p. 5.

44 *NZH*, 24 February 1927, p. 12.

45 *NZH*, 24 February 1927, p. 12.

46 *NZH*, 5 January 1914, p. 9.

47 *NZH*, 11 November 1890, p.5; 29 October 1918, p. 4.

48 See *NZH*, 11 November 1890, p. 5; 9 October 1902, p .6; 13 October 1910, p. 7; 28 October 1917, p. 6; 29 October 1918, pp. 4, 7; 28 October 1919, p. 9; 28 October 1924, p. 6.

49 *NZH*, 13 October 1910, p. 7.

50 *NZH*, 25 October 1921, p. 6.

51 *NZH*, 13 October 1910, p. 7.

52 *NZH*, 13 October 1910, p. 7.

53 *NZH*, 9 October 1902, p. 6.

54 *NZH*, 13 October 1910, p. 7.

55 On cross-dressing at picnics see Mitchell, 'Picnics in New Zealand', Ch. 2.

56 *New Zealand Graphic, Ladies' Journal and Youth's Companion* (hereafter *Graphic*), 1 December 1894, p. 512. The links were laid at Greenlane, and 'ladies' were allowed to play, except on Saturday afternoons.

57 On contemporary concerns with delinquency see Penelope Ann Gregory, 'Saving the Children in New Zealand: A Study of the Social Attitudes Towards Larrikinism in the Later Nineteenth Century', BA Hons Research Essay, Massey University, 1975.

58 On the 'mother-dominated, sentimental family' see Phillips, *A Man's Country*, p. 222. On the need for male schoolteachers, especially for boys, see Sandra Coney, *Standing in the Sunshine: A History of New Zealand Women Since they Won the Vote*, Auckland, 1993, pp. 208-9.

59 The term is Galen Cranz's. See Galen Cranz, *The Politics of Park Design: A History of Urban Parks in America*, Cambridge, Massachusetts, 1982, Ch. 2, and 'Women in Urban Parks', *Signs: Journal of Women in Culture and Society*, 5, 3, Supplement, 1980, pp. S79, S85-90.

60 Cranz, 'Women in Urban Parks', p. S79.

61 *Weekly News*, 24 September 1903, p. 22.

62 *NZH*, 22 March 1890, Supplement, p. 1.

63 *NZH*, 17 October 1890, p. 6.

64 On the language of sport and masculinity see Michael Kimmel, *Manhood in America: A Cultural History*, New York, 1996, p. 139.

65 ACC 275, Box 32, Item 19/742: Cricket Pitches, Domain and Victoria Park, 1919-20, 13 September 1920.

66 *NZH*, 13 October 1921, p. 9. Surplus money from the exhibition had allowed for the flattening of the land into a sports area.

67 ACC 275, Box 113, Item 26/334, Part 1: Parks, General, 1926-40, 2 September 1926.

68 *Graphic*, 25 March 1893, p.270.

69 *Graphic*, 25 March 1893, p.270.

70 In the New Zealand context this has been noted particularly for rugby. See Phillips, *A Man's Country?*, pp. 90, 95; Geoff Fougere, 'Sport, Culture and Identity: The Case of Rugby Football', in David Novitz and Bill Willmott, eds, *Culture and Identity in New Zealand*, Wellington, 1989, pp. 114, 119; Sinclair, *A Destiny Apart*, p. 152

71 For example, for a rugby league test, New Zealand v. Australia, schoolboys were admitted for 6d and everyone else for 1s. *NZH*, 6 September 1919, p. 13.

72 See *NZH*, 3 December 1917, p.7; ACC 275, Box 32, Item 19/742, 13 September 1920.

73 In the 1920s Grammar boys used the sportsgrounds in the Domain every afternoon after 4 p.m. Sometimes they were joined by youths and young men from the training college and technical school. ACC 107, Item 2: Parks Committee Minutes, 16.12.1924-18.12.1928, 20 June 1925; ACC 275, Box 119, Item 27/36: Domain, Lettings and General, 1927, 29 June 1927; ACC 107, Item 3: Parks Committee Minutes, 5.2.1929-6.12.1932, 11 February 1930.

74 On free rugby grounds see ACC 107, Item 2, 1 October 1926 and ACC 275, Box 119, Item 27/36, 29 June 1927. On cricket see ACC 107, Item 6: Parks Committee Minutes, 13.2.1940-12.12.1944, 13 February 1940. The Auckland Cricket Association had secured five wickets for schoolboys on Saturday mornings back in 1903. ACC 255, Streets Committee Minutes, Item 4: Streets Committee Minutes, 1901-1905, ACC Archives, Auckland, 4 November 1903.

75 From 1904, most senior primary school boys and boys in secondary education were required to do military drill. See Phillips, *A Man's Country*, Ch. 4, for a discussion of the growing military ethos in post-Boer War New Zealand.

76 *NZH*, 2 March 1910, p. 6.

77 *NZH*, 2 March 1910, p. 8.

78 *NZH*, 23 June 1911, p. 8; 5 June 1933, p. 11.

79 For example, see *NZH*, 15 December 1913, p. 9. The Boy Scout movement has attracted

much attention from historians of masculinity. See Kimmel, *Manhood in America*, pp. 168-70; Maurizia Boscagli, *Eye On The Flesh: Fashions of Masculinity in the Early Twentieth Century*, Colorado, 1996, *passim*; Allen Warren, 'Popular Manliness: Baden Powell, Scouting and the Development of Manly Character', in J.A. Mangan and J.Walvin, eds, *Manliness and Morality: Middle-Class Masculinity in Britain and America, 1800-1940*, New York, 1987.

80   For example, see *NZH*, 3 April 1922, p. 8.

81   The eugenic movement in pre-Second World War New Zealand is explored in Philip J. Fleming, 'Eugenics in New Zealand, 1900-1940', MA thesis, Massey University, 1981. On the importance of temperance to New Zealand men and ideas of masculinity see Phillips, *A Man's Country*, Ch. 2.

82   *Graphic*, 26 November 1892, p. 1163.

83   *NZH*, 15 March 1890, p. 3; 22 November 1890, p. 6.

84   ACC 258, Cricket Ground Minutes, 1899-1903, Item 1, ACC Archives, Auckland, 25 April 1900.

85   *NZH*, 17 March 1890, p. 6.

86   On 'ladies who supply tea at the Domain Cricket Ground' see ACC 104, Works Committee Minutes, Item 1: Works Committee Minutes, 1911-16, ACC Archives, Auckland, 18 January, 15 and 29 February 1912. On the girls providing Grammar boys with afternoon tea see *NZH*, 31 October 1919, p. 9.

87   *NZH*, 8 April 1915, p. 9. Many matches were fund-raisers for the war effort. For example, see *NZH*, 17 September 1917 p. 2; 15 October 1917, p. 3.

88   ACC 107, Item 3, 4 August 1931.

89   Schoolboy games were not included in this total; neither were games where the ground was not paid for, such as the mid-week league matches. ACC 107, Item 4, Parks Committee Minutes, 20.12.1932-23.10.1936, Annual Report, Parks and Reserves Department for year ending 31 March 1933.

90   See *NZH*, 24 June 1897, p. 4; *New Zealand Observer and Free Lance*, 8 July 1899, p. 2 and 15 July 1899, p. 2; *NZH*, 31 May 1905, p. 4; 1 June 1905, p. 6; 13 March 1906, p. 4; 14 April 1906, p. 4; 17 January 1908, p. 4; 23 February 1926, p. 7; 21 August 1937, p. 17.

91   *NZH*, 25 February 1927, p. 13; 26 February 1927, p. 14.

92   *NZH*, 15 March 1890, p. 6.

93   *NZH*, 24 May 1894, p. 4. In 1904 there were reports of card playing in the Domain. See ACC 255, Item 4, 10 August 1904.

94   *New Zealand Observer and Free Lance*, 15 July 1899, p. 2.

95   *NZH*, 31 May 1905, p. 4.

96   *NZH*, 1 June 1905, p. 6.

97   On the undergrowth see *NZH*, 17 January 1908, p. 4; ACC 285, Box 41, Item 18: Record Files, Parks and Endowments, 1908-10, OP, U, V, W, 7 January and 4 February 1908; ACC 285, Box 41, Item 17: Record Files, Parks and Endowments, 1908-10, H-N, 20 February 1908; *NZH*, 21 August 1937, p. 17. On improved police coverage see *NZH*, 30 May 1905, p. 6; 2 February 1906, p. 7; 14 April 1906, p. 4; ACC 285, Box 41, Item 18, 4 February 1908; ACC 255, Item 5: Streets Committee Minutes 1905-9, 23 January, 5 March and 2 April 1908; ACC 104, Item 1, 12 May 1913.

98   ACC 107, Item 4, Annual Report, Parks and Reserves Department, for year ending 31 March 1933.

99   ACC 107, Item 4, 19 December 1933.

100   *NZH*, 21 August 1937, p. 17.

101   See *NZH*, 17 January 1908, p. 4; ACC 285, Box 41, Item 18, 7 January and 4 February 1908; ACC 255, Item 5, 23 January, 5 March and 2 April 1908; ACC 285, Box 41, Item 17, 15 and 20 February 1908.

102   *NZH*, 23 February 1926, p. 7.

103   Charlotte Macdonald has referred to the period from the 1880s to 1920 as the 'foundation period' in the history of women's sport and organised recreation. Macdonald, 'Organisations in Sport, Recreation and Leisure', pp. 406-8. See also Scott A. G. M. Crawford, '"One's nerves and courage are in very different order out in New Zealand": recreational and sporting

opportunities for women in a remote colonial setting', in J. A. Mangan and R. A. Park, eds, *From 'Fair Sex' to Feminism: Sport and the Socialization of Women in the Industrial and Post-Industrial Eras*, London, 1987, pp. 161-81; Hammer, '"Something Else in the World to Live For"', *passim*.

104 *NZH*, 9 August 1890, Supplement, p. 1. The mob caps refer to the nursing staff.

105 On the establishment of the tennis courts see *NZH*, 14 April 1906, p. 6; ACC 285, Box 41, Item 18. Attempts to play tennis in the Domain on Sundays were thwarted throughout the period. See ACC 107, Item 4, 1 May 1934; ACC 107, Item 5, 29 August 1939; *NZH*, 11 May 1934, p. 8 and 26 October 1934, p. 8.

106 Macdonald, 'Organisations in Sport, Recreation and Leisure', p. 406.

107 ACC 285, Box 41, Item 15: Record Files, Parks and Endowments, 1908-10, 16 November 1909.

108 ACC 104, Item 1, 27 February 1913.

109 ACC 285, Box 41, Item 18, 11 May 1909.

110 Macdonald, 'Organisations in Sport, Recreation and Leisure', pp. 408-10.

111 ACC 107, Item 2, 21 April 1925.

112 For example, when Miss Stevenson of the YWCA asked for use of a hockey ground she was told that no grounds were available; ACC 107, Item 2, 20 June 1925. When a deputation waited on the committee asking for sports grounds for women and girls the decision was deferred for a fortnight and then nothing was done; ACC 107, Item 2, 3 April 1928. The Auckland Ladies Hockey Association was told that no grounds were available; ACC 107, Item 2, 3 April 1928. No decision was made when the Auckland Women's Cricket Association wrote to ask for 3-4 wickets in the Outer Domain; ACC 107, Item 4, 16 October 1934.

113 *NZH*, 22 November 1926, p. 13.

114 ACC 107, Item 2, 24 August 1926. The committee deferred their decision for the city engineer to report. No report was found in the minutes. In 1939 Ellen Melville Park, for women's sports, opened in Auckland.

115 ACC 107, Item 2, 14 June 1927. Again, a deferred decision resulted in no further action.

116 ACC 107, Item 2, 3 April 1928.

117 ACC 107, Item 4, 7 August 1936.

118 ACC 107, Item 4, 11 September 1936.

119 After the first year the diamonds cost 5s on Tuesday and 10s per Saturday. ACC 107, Item 5, 16 August 1938 and 10 October 1939. See press reports on the games in *NZH*, 17 February 1938, p. 20; 1 December 1938, p. 22; 5 December 1938, p. 18.

120 ACC 107, Item 5, 4 February 1938.

121 ACC 107, Item 5, 16 May 1939.

122 ACC 107, Item 6, 28 May 1940, Annual Report of Parks and Reserves Department for year ending 31 March 1940 and 29 October 1940.

123 For this argument applied to hockey see Coney, *Standing in the Sunshine*, p. 248; with regard to cricket see Hammer, '"Something Else in the World to Live For"', pp. 39-42.

124 *NZH*, 12 April 1926, p. 11.

125 On dances see *NZH*, 12 April 1926, p. 11; for the living map see *NZH*, 11 February 1935, p. 12; on the values of guiding see *NZH*, 26 November 1928, p. 11.

126 *NZH*, 12 April 1926, p. 11.

127 *NZH*, 21 November 1927, p. 6.

128 ACC 219, Box 57, Item 27/365 Part 1, 25 February 1932.

129 *Auckland Star*, 29 June 1936, p. 9.

130 On picnics as a form of colonisation and a way to tame the wilderness see Mitchell, 'Picnics in New Zealand', Ch. 3.

Males were seen as the energetic breadwinners of 1930s
New Zealand but several of the products this image
supported were made by women workers.
New Zealand Herald, 20 August 1938.

Bread Queues and Breadwinners: Gender in the 1930s

Tim Frank

Oh you had to *look* for work. Oh boy, I knew fellas out of work for three years without a job. . . . You had to fossick round. The saddest thing that I witnessed in the depression was one day I was out of work, I had a round of bread with me. I walked along the waterfront . . . and there was a couple of young fellas sitting on the waterfront . . . and they were hungry. And they were living in the Domain. . . . And I can remember sharing this round of bread with them, bread and jam. And the poor little lads they were hungry, and had no work. I had none, but I had a home to go to. . . . So I went up and I sat down at St Patrick's Church. . . . And on that side there must have been a hundred and fifty women, young women . . . elderly women, women with little babies crawling over their shoulders, poverty-stricken. Oh it was dreadful. . . . And there were all those women kneeling in front of that statue of a crucified Christ asking for bread. They weren't getting any though. The poor devils. . . . And I got outside that church – I don't know much about history or religion, but I thought, 'Well, Christ you're supposed to have taken your people out of the land of Egypt into a land of milk and honey. But', I said, 'by Christ, those kids in there have got none'. The poor devils, they were hungry. . . . That's how it was. . . . It was dreadful. Those poor kids. I can see their eyes now. They were *hungry*, you know? All those mothers, praying, you know, for jobs for their husbands. It was a hell of a state to be in you know.[1]

David Hill's vivid recollection highlights some of the realities of Depression-era New Zealand. Throughout the 1920s, the New Zealand dream of home, family and prosperity was predicated on male breadwinning. Recession threatened this idyll. The crisis also exposed raw nerves as various solutions to Depression woes were debated. Issues of gender were implicit in these differing opinions. The Depression focused public attention on male breadwinning priority and reputation. Yet it also forced many New Zealand families to consider alternatives and supplements to sole male breadwinning, especially with regard to women and youths seeking work. The Depression, therefore, highlighted two fundamental issues regarding work and gender in the 1930s: the place of women in the paid workforce, and the performance of men as breadwinners.

The male breadwinner ideology was the dominant paradigm relating to masculinity and work in New Zealand in the first half of this century.[2] By the 1930s, this ideology was a powerful public convention and the images it conjured up had developed tremendous appeal. Yet the breadwinner role is not a fixed characteristic of being masculine; it was constructed in response to a specific historical set of social and economic interactions.[3] Consequently, like all social conventions, the ideas about male breadwinning concept were neither static, nor immune to subsequent disruption, contravention and subversion. The 1930s New Zealand labour market was largely gendered, and prioritised male breadwinning. Even so, strict adherence to the traditional gender ideology governing paid work does not satisfactorily account for men's and women's workforce participation and attitudes during the recession and the post-1935 recovery.

Much recent work on gender in interwar New Zealand, particularly concerning employment, economic citizenship and dependency, has focused on women.[4] The primary intent has been to acknowledge women's struggles in the arenas of politics, economics, paid work, health and reproduction. Because there has been little close examination of men's lives and experience, the picture of unchallenged male breadwinning has been preserved relatively intact. This has been due partly to a failure to fully acknowledge the impact of labour market trends, and social, political, economic and legislative change, on breadwinning activity and attitudes, and partly because male work has been scrutinised chiefly in terms of labour relations and legislation.[5] This chapter argues that, although paid work and breadwinning ideology were gender-biased in the 1930s, both women and men adjusted their attitudes to gendered employment, and to their workforce participation. These changes occurred in deference to the pragmatics of shifting economic fortunes, and often in defiance of male breadwinner ideology conformity. Both the Depression and the Labour government's policies contributed to the adjustments. Adopting less rigid attitudes about gendered employment, and assuming more relaxed expectations of male workers, were just two of many individual and household responses to the calamitous circumstances.

But the lean years wrought other responses too. Out of the climate of recession, and the Coalition government's insistence that the country could afford little compromise on the issue of male breadwinning and the principle of 'no work, no pay', Labour secured the working man's 'right' to work, together with more favourable employment conditions. Yet while Labour's social and employment policies depended on the male breadwinner supporting women and children, they also contributed to an improving economy that, ironically, gave greater scope for households to make choices about employment. These choices did not always conform to Labour's gender-loaded expectations. In the late 1930s, Labour's outbursts upbraiding male workers for lack of effort and its policy statements reveal its continued commitment to male breadwinner ideology. They also hint at Labour's failure to comprehend the significance of employment trends in an improving economy. Throughout the 1930s, the necessity for households to find work – any work – quietly widened the distance between actual workforce participation and well-established gendered attitudes to work, breadwinning and dependency. By late 1939, workforce participation trends indicate a relaxation of the imperative for men to work and the insistence that breadwinning was a solely male domain. This implies that, by the end of the 1930s, a gendered work ideology was not necessarily the most important factor influencing private decisions about workforce participation.

David Morgan has suggested that 'unemployment might almost be seen as a paradigmatic example of masculinity under challenge'.[6] This certainly states the case in Depression-era New Zealand, where masculine identities constructed around employment, occupational status and breadwinning were undermined. Work was more than simply the inalienable right of men. It was also closely allied to the achievement of household goals of comfort and modest affluence.[7] One man articulated the relationship between work activity and the object of work: 'We demand the right to work and provide our wives and children with the comforts of life, gotten by our own efforts and toil'.[8] The value many men placed on work was likely to be closely allied to the value they placed on their families, and to the satisfaction of providing for them. Unemployment and recession sorely tested breadwinners' capacity to provide more than just bare necessities for their loved ones (bearing in mind that nearly two-thirds of men aged 16 and over were married).[9]

For many men living in the shadow of recession exigencies and spartan 'work for work's sake' government policies, work was reduced to a means of survival. One man expressed his situation in stark terms: 'It was simple. If you didn't work you didn't eat.'[10] Although some men were never in danger of losing their employment, for others the competition for jobs was fierce. David Hill recalled, 'You had to be a champion to hold [your job], believe you me.'[11] Francis Leabourn explained his motivation for enduring arduous employment: 'It was hard work because in those days you had to *work* too. If you didn't work there was someone breathing down your neck waiting to take your place.'[12] Rather than supporting strikes that would jeopardise workers' standards of living, many adopted a survival mode characterised by a reluctance to rock the boat.[13]

When the government-appointed Unemployment Inquiry Committee released its full report late in February 1930, it provoked much public comment on the causes of, blame for and solutions to unemployment.[14] The committee's brief, as it saw it, was not to concern itself with 'immediate provision of relief measures', but to propose a more long-term plan: 'first, to find methods of preventing unemployment as far as possible; and, second, to indicate methods of providing for the unemployed with the minimum of loss to the community'.[15] Chief among its wide-ranging recommendations for minimising and relieving unemployment was the immediate provision of an unemployment insurance scheme, followed by the more far-reaching goal of broadening the industrial base in order to fully absorb available labour. Furthermore, it was the committee's 'unanimous opinion' that unemployment was not simply an industrial problem, but primarily a social one. Its remedies required the full participation and co-operation of the whole society, and for attendant costs to be spread as equitably as possible.[16] Yet public response to these recommendations indicated that many people viewed causes and remedies in narrow economic and structural terms, although they differed widely on which particular aspects were considered pertinent. Putting men 'back on the land', the perennial panacea to employment and economic woes, was one solution revived and embraced with ardent vigour.[17] This was a significant nod in favour of the traditional masculine iconography of the hard-working, resilient, rural worker, even though, by 1926, industrialised, urban male workers outnumbered primary sector workers by two to one.[18] Some recognition of the part male urban workers had to play in the fight against recession was obliquely acknowledged in the 1930 'Buy New Zealand Made Goods' campaign (depicting consumer support for the stalwart urban labourer's efforts) and by ministerial statements encouraging secondary industries.[19] At the very least, such proposals indicated that people much preferred alternatives to taxpayer-funded relief work, and hoped that if the right economic structures were put in place, the 'honest toiler' would literally dig New Zealand out of trouble.[20]

The 1930 'Buy New Zealand Made Goods' campaign stressed consumer support for the efforts of the stalwart urban worker.
Dominion, 28 August 1930.

Clearly, though, some also believed that unemployment exposed a fault in the modern worker's integrity, a suspicious weakening of the traditional male resolve to find a job and work hard. Although the Unemployment Inquiry Committee had partly attributed 'industrial troubles, economic bad times, and unemployment' to the 'continuous demand by all workers' for higher wages and lower prices, it did not specifically target worker attitudes.[21] But some criticised the committee's decision to recommend 'dole' and relief payments, and for proposing a universal income tax to finance it.[22] One critic was disappointed that the committee's desire that 'Work, and not a dole, should be provided' was not reflected in its recommendations, while another offered the simplistic dictum that the 'solution of unemployment is work'.[23] Another man vehemently opposed any form of government assistance, indignantly pronouncing this to be 'unadulterated charity', and defiantly proclaiming that it was 'every man's duty to find his own opportunities in life'.[24] The concern that men had become 'soft', and did not work as hard as in days gone by, led to very unsympathetic comments about 'loafers', 'idlers', 'parasites' and the 'lazy'.[25] Behind this attitude lay the notion that 'worker' and 'breadwinner' were designations of (male) independence, and all unwaged people were 'dependants'. By the 1930s, this 'dependency' had developed 'good' and 'bad' connotations: the first, household dependency, applied to wives and children, and the second, 'bad' dependency, was associated with charity, including relief recipients.[26] Public reaction to unemployment measures emphasised the importance of appropriate attitudes to work in maintaining and perpetuating an ordered, stable, and functioning society.

Similar views were expressed in Parliament. When speaking on Reform party policy, Gordon Coates stated that: 'So far as this party is concerned, we wish to indicate quite clearly that we are opposed to any proposal which is in any sense a dole. The principle is wrong, and it should not be initiated in this country – indeed, Parliament might very well go further and declare that there be no pay if there is no work.'[27] In early 1931, Prime Minister Forbes reiterated the government's 'no work, no pay' principle.[28] The newly formed Coalition government sanctioned this principle in its refusal to authorise sustenance payments from the Unemployment Fund in its first year of operation.[29] Such views held men who did not work for work's sake in scant regard. Not to work threatened the very core of breadwinning masculinity: above all else, men worked, and not to do so was a failure of national significance. There was a genuine fear that provision of sustenance or dole payments would undermine men's character, independence and motivation to work.[30] Consequently, despite strong recommendations that all relief work should be productive, the government felt it was imperative that work, any work, be found to occupy men.[31] As Louis Wilson recalls of the men employed on local body unemployment relief schemes: 'They had to cut the edges of the grass, anything – like clean the beaches – anything that was given, so they could have ten shillings a week'.[32]

Attitudes to 'dole', relief and sustenance were not all negative, however.[33] Some commentators, mindful of the strain recession placed on households, sympathetically distinguished between the genuinely 'industrious' unemployed and the 'other kind', the 'imposters'.[34] Acceptance of the need for relief measures implicitly acknowledged that, in a capricious work environment both families and the nation required flexible employment solutions. Orthodox views of suitable male work were reinforced through the Coalition government's flat refusal to pay a dole, the introduction of the No. 4 and No. 5 Schemes employing men on public works and, later, the Small Farms Relief of Unemployment Act of 1933 placing men in rural occupations. But in regard to the type of work sought and the question of

Women's most valued role in Depression-era New Zealand was as consumers, especially when they bought local products. This 1938 advertisement echoed those used for the 1930 'Buy New Zealand Made Goods' campaign.
New Zealand Herald, 17 September 1938.

who should work, both men's and women's accounts of the Depression reveal the emergence of a more pragmatic spirit, 'just to live, just to exist, just to exist'.[35]

So, the Depression offered an opportunity for some to relax their views on women's paid work and to seriously contemplate some adjustments in women's economic position. Letters written at the 'kitchen table' in early March 1930 reveal widespread community ambivalence about the propriety of women's paid work and economic dependency.[36] For some, working women were a luxury, especially in recession. At best, they comprised the lowest tier of a breadwinner hierarchy favouring men, and family men most of all. At worst, women in paid work accentuated male unemployment by taking men's jobs, lowering the status and remuneration rates of some jobs and jeopardising the nation's health by fatiguing themselves in the workforce.[37]

Women's most valued and suitable economic role was as consumers, especially as purchasers of local products.[38] But, given the extent of household hardship, others believed working women were a necessity, and nothing should prevent them from working. Some even queried whether anyone had the 'right' to deny women paid work.[39] For those debating the merits of women's employment versus the propriety of men's work, the principle of sole male breadwinning often competed with a pragmatic recognition of the contribution women's paid work made to New Zealand households.[40] In this way, male work was problematised not only by the *fact* of male unemployment, but also by the *implications* of women's employment to supplement household incomes.

Not unexpectedly, the government gave scant acknowledgment to the extent or value of women's paid work, regarding the 'one-fifth' of women in employment (compared with 'over three-fifths' of men) as of little consequence.[41] This dismissal of women's employment was exemplified by government attitudes to female unemployment. When the Unemployment Bill first appeared in July 1930, Labour was concerned that it overlooked women.[42] The Coalition gave men first consideration, but issued assurances that later, perhaps in 1931, women might also be considered. Besides, including women immediately might 'jeopardise' the scheme for men[43] – 'we should learn to walk before we try to run'.[44] In fact, as far as women were concerned, the walk became a crawl, and it would take a change of government before women's economic status was given any significant recognition.[45] The Coalition government's assurances and preferences were based on an unquestioning commitment to an ideology of male breadwinning that inevitably made unemployed women and their suffering invisible, while attaching no importance to female employment. Early in the 1930s, one government minister betrayed such blindness when he refused to acknowledge homeless, jobless women. He preferred to believe that any claims of penniless women sleeping outdoors were simply a plot to discredit unemployment committee initiatives.[46]

The concept of hegemonic masculinity (denoting the power relations one group of men, often supported by women, have over other men and women) explains why issues of women's employment and workforce participation trends attracted little or no serious official attention.[47] Class and gender relations of alliance, dominance and subordination in interwar New Zealand society, accentuated by the male breadwinner ideology, ensured that women's employment was considered inexpedient, at best, and improper, at worst. The class and gender politics inherent within masculinity also explain why little or no change in male employment trends was acknowledged. Those institutions and structures embodying the male breadwinner ideology, such as the government, could not conceive that the role prescribed by their particular brand of exemplary masculinity could, or would, be compromised or adjusted by the present crisis, or by social reaction to events in general.

Some employers echoed government conviction against considering women's employment on a par with men's. In March 1930, for instance, a *School Committee Journal* article deprecated the practice of employing 'the married woman who has no necessity to teach'.[48] But even if some situations resulted in a victory for the male breadwinner, Depression conditions could mean that achievement was one of *principle* only. Jo Aitken's study of the effectiveness of a marriage bar imposed on women teachers in the Depression illustrates how women's (especially married women's) employment clashed with the ideology of domesticity. Although there was much support for the bar, the parameters of the measure, and the women's economic circumstances, meant that few were actually dismissed.[49] Commitment to gender ideology was not, in this case, necessarily sufficient to override economic pragmatism, even where it could be argued that working women contributed to male unemployment and threatened male breadwinning. In fact, Melanie Nolan has argued that examinations of paid labour in the interwar period 'have missed a slowly changing logic' in women's economic citizenship, one that served to undermine, or 'fracture', domesticity and the *concept* of the breadwinner's wage.[50] Women's Depression employment did not burst the dam of male breadwinner priority any more than later wartime women's workforce participation did. But, as with the wartime experience, the Depression intensified the conditions permitting a greater seepage of women into paid work.

In some occupational sectors, employers' qualms about women workers decreased. In 1931, the Canterbury Freezing Workers Union objected to a New Zealand Refrigerating Co. Ltd application to redefine an award clause regarding 'work suitable for females in the preserving department'.[51] The company wished to allow women to perform work previously done by men. In this case, the Arbitration Court supported the employer's request. The court had grown impatient with disputes over what it considered to be 'infernally stupid' and trivial definitions of women's work.[52] In another instance, involving the Coachworkers' Award, Judge F. V. Frazer commented that relaxing attitudes to women's employment was necessary for local trades and industries to be cost-effective against foreign competition.[53] Of course, while employers' acceptance, even encouragement, of women's paid work ostensibly denoted a liberal attitude, they employed women primarily for their own advantage. Employers always had the option of forgoing women's employment if lesser pay rates could not be secured. But the increasing use of women as clerical, retail and factory workers indicates that employers found women to be ready, convenient and acceptably priced employees.

Although women seldom competed with men for jobs, the economic crisis had engendered some willingness to promote expediency over propriety. That such cases were exaggerated entirely out of proportion to the small numbers of women involved, and provoked a high degree of outrage in some quarters, also hints at an uneasy acknowledgment that women's paid labour represented defiance, both in action and in attitude, of the sexual division of labour.[54]

But regardless of whether women took advantage of the jobs on offer at reduced rates, or whether they were simply taken advantage of (as some thought), their entry into the workforce was not necessarily at the behest of employers. In a study of New Zealand workforce composition in the interwar years, Keith Rankin argues that pressure on the household income from 1927 on resulted in a greater use of cheaper female and youth labour, especially in factories.[55] Rankin believes that workforce composition throughout the 1920s and 1930s was determined more by labour supply than demand: New Zealanders, particularly women and youths, entered or left the workforce more on the basis of whether or not individuals and households earned a minimum income, rather than as a response to labour demand or the wage mechanism.[56] During the Depression, single and, to a lesser degree, married women sought and secured work despite social discrimination against women's employment, low demand for labour, and low expectations of finding employment.[57] Rankin argues that women's propensity to pursue some form of paid work was probably higher during and immediately after the Depression than at any other time between 1920 and 1960.[58] Marriage and fertility trends in the 1930s provide some support for Rankin's picture of female workforce participation. Marriages were delayed, the marriage age rose and birth rates fell.[59] In general, 1930s New Zealand experienced 'a structural shift towards permanently higher rates of female participation', a trend Nolan has noted, arguing that '[paid] work was the typical female experience' in the interwar years, at least before marriage.[60]

This did not pass altogether unnoticed at the time. In 1930, for example, the *New Zealand Herald* reported that since 1896 increasing numbers of women had been working for pay, and that their occupational profile had changed, though the 1926 census revealed a 'slight retrogression' in female labour force participation.[61] In 1936, the *Dominion* detailed a rise in the number of women entering factories in the early 1930s.[62] Yet the significance of such trends was disguised by the overt discrimination against women in employment, and by the fact that official statistics and government reports recognised only the formally and fully employed and unemployed. It appears that many thousands of men, women and youths worked on a part-time, casual or intermittent basis during the Depression, but were not acknowledged as workforce participants. By early August 1933 57,313 male workers were officially jobless, a ten-fold increase from August 1930.[63] In September 1933, Elizabeth McCombs, the Member for Lyttelton, stated that 'official figures – the latest I have, at any rate – for unemployment register eighty thousand unemployed' but that the figures underestimated unemployment by two-thirds, since they did not include women or youths, and failed to count men working casually, half-time or part-time, or 'earning no more than relief rates of pay'.[64] McCombs suspected that many New Zealanders, male and female, participated in the workforce in ways that official figures did not acknowledge. Not only that, many who were classed as 'employed' did not have full-time jobs. The Coalition government admitted as much in 1931 when Gordon Coates called on employers to continue practising shared employment, a request entirely in keeping with its own policy of rationing relief work.[65] Consequently, it is highly probable that many more people 'worked' during the Depression than official figures admitted, including many more women than has been supposed.[66] Many breadwinners could not sustain their dependants on their own, and families were forced to supplement the household income in a variety of ways, including sending youths and women to work.[67]

Certainly, women's Depression workforce participation suggests some disregard for the social conservatism where '[g]ender and marriage became crude but convenient demarcation lines that determined who could be breadwinners and who could not'.[68] But pragmatic acceptance of women's employment did not overthrow the general social principle of male breadwinning. Nor did it incite general abandonment of the *notion* of men's prior claim to the jobs available in a time of economic downturn. Even so, growing public dissatisfaction over the government's handling of unemployment schemes throughout the Depression illustrates how, by the mid-1930s, there was more tolerance for men who failed to support their families. There was public outrage in September 1935 when the government attempted to downplay unemployment by excluding those on subsidised work from published unemployment figures.[69] The Coalition government's view that relief work ought to function to rebuke unemployed men's moral failures was increasingly unpalatable to the public the longer and harder unemployment bit into households' economic viability. People's growing sympathy for the unemployed, and their growing impatience with the 'go-nowhere' nature of relief work, contributed to the growing unpopularity of the government's work schemes.[70] Arguably, failure to appreciate this difference cost the Coalition government the 1935 election.[71] Displeasure over government performance created a mood favouring less stringent fiscal responses to social need, a mood tailor-made for the Labour Party to exploit with its promises of prosperous security.[72] The Depression did not topple the edifice of male breadwinning, but it shook the belief of many New Zealanders that the male breadwinner could always work, and that his work alone was sufficient to support his household.

As early as 1930, the Labour Party had articulated what it felt to be the fundamental desires of most New Zealanders. In the debate on the Unemployment Bill, Harry Holland had stated that: 'What the workers want, and what they demand, is the right to work. . . . If men are to live they must have the right to work.'[73] In the same debate, Michael J. Savage announced Labour's social vision: 'Boiled down, it comes to providing men, and women too, with an opportunity of making a home and a living. That is all there is in it.'[74] John A. Lee later endorsed that sentiment, pointing out that men wanted more from life than subsistence, and that their aspirations reached beyond working for work's sake. They 'want wives and they may have some desire to see themselves fashioning homes for themselves and bringing children into the world'.[75]

In early 1936, the new Labour government clearly signalled that its social vision required increased production and consumerism.[76] In announcing the findings of a preliminary report into unemployment relief, Hubert Armstrong, Minister of Labour and Employment, outlined immediate plans for 'progressive and productive employment' in the nation.[77] His blueprint relied on increasing land development, expansion of existing industry and developing secondary industries.[78] Quickly passing employment, labour and industry legislation, Labour immediately set in place the basic building blocks of its vision. It instituted a 40-hour working week, a basic wage and wider Arbitration Court powers.

But Labour maintained one important link with Coalition philosophy.

Its ideal society, where waged workers prospered from productive use of national resources, was based on the ideology of male breadwinning. Labour's male-oriented employment legislation was designed to strengthen the male breadwinner's position. Although both adult men and women were included, Armstrong's basic wage plans stipulated that a man should receive a wage 'such as to enable him to maintain a wife and two children at a standard of comfort to which it is considered they are entitled'.[79] William Anderton endorsed the relationship between employment and masculinity when outlining Labour's employment policy: 'It is the duty of the Government . . . to place . . . 35,600 men, together with the thousands of women unemployed, in useful occupations, so that they shall receive a standard of living that will give back to them that character of manliness and womanliness which they have lost in the past few years'.[80] However, his admission that 'I cannot find any statistical evidence as to whether we have any women unemployed', emphasised Labour's gender bias on employment. Although Labour included women in its unemployment relief legislation, honouring promises made earlier, its studied silence about initiatives to promote women's employment revealed how it prioritised men's access to paid work.[81] By 1937 Labour was convinced 'there was no unemployment as far as women were concerned', evincing a confidence in its gendered ideology and policies. Perhaps it also believed that negligible female unemployment meant women had found 'useful occupations' in the home.[82] There was little acknowledgment of the alternative possibility that some women, especially young women, had adopted the practice of 'do[ing] what she likes, and earn[ing] what she likes', and were engaging in paid work; Labour preferred instead to focus on how its policies had reduced women's need to work.[83]

In contrast to what it styled as the Coalition's spartan 'work for work's sake' stance, Labour presented its own approach to work as refreshingly new and liberating.[84] Labour did not regard work as an end in itself, but as a *means* to an end. That end was to supply people with 'all the necessaries and some of the luxuries of life'.[85] Its policies were worker-friendly, and for the good of the nation. In the previous 'years of desolation', males had not only been starved of bread but also of job opportunities, and reduced to queuing for both food and unemployment relief.[86] The policies of the previous government, and the years of Depression, had demoralised men, taught them how to loaf, 'drown[ed]' and 'submerged their manhood' and reduced them to 'mere automata'.[87] Labour's immediate job was to 'commence teaching [men] to work again', and to remove the propensity for apathy, laziness and idleness.[88] Labour would provide incentives to work, and its policies would restore men's work, their manliness and New Zealand's rightful position as 'God's Own Country' and 'a paradise for useful people to live in'.[89] Reduced work hours, higher wages and increased work efficiency would secure higher living standards and increased leisure for workers and families.[90] Charles Williams, one of Labour's newest members, encapsulated government philosophy and hopes most forthrightly. He was certain that eventually Labour would 'completely alter the attitude of people, both to life and to work'.[91] A society would emerge where it was not considered a shame to work, and where the male 'parasites', and those content 'to serve as consumers only', would develop into producers and 'useful people'. Robert Semple, the Minister of Works, quickly made it clear that a carrot-and-stick approach would characterise transactions between the State and the worker. Male workers could expect help from the government, but only if they relearned the 'masculine knack' of working hard. The slacker would get nothing.[92] Remarkably, while posing as the workers' friend, Labour appeared dissatisfied with employee performance, and its inferences and suspicions only fuelled a revival of Depression-style charges of worker laziness.[93]

Basing its social vision on hard work and a gendered society created tensions for Labour in its approach to workers. Annabel Cooper and Maureen Molloy's study of women's economic dependency in the 1930s provides evidence of Labour's commitment to a gendered view of society.[94] Examining the effects of Labour's social legislation on women, Cooper and Molloy demonstrated the 'tensions and counter-currents' with respect to 'the meanings of "women" and their relation to "men"' inherent in Labour's policies.[95] They noted that assigning restrictive roles to women also prescribed men's roles, and that Labour's policies embodied ambiguities and ironies for both sexes. Labour's gender-loaded employment legislation not only endorsed the priority of the male breadwinner and his right to secure sufficient provision for his family, but also implied an expectation that he would do so. Ironically, Labour's adoption of a 'surrogate husband and father' role through its social security legislation hinted at low confidence in men's capacity to provide for their families.[96]

Labour's policies reflected a determination to overcome prevailing economic structures and a desire to compensate for the poor performance of male breadwinners. Expectations that men could, should and would work hard were offset by the conviction that they needed to be taught to work again. Speeches heralding employment, industry and social security policies expressed hopes of significantly increased male productivity. Labour joined a hard-work ethic to its ideal of male breadwinning but it courted disappointment and difficulties, even disaster, if it could not engender worker appreciation and acceptance of this strategy. Labour's unwavering commitment to the efficacy of its gendered breadwinner ideology and its social policy programme left it vulnerable to the risk of failing to acknowledge changes in workforce participation and social attitudes brought on by an altered economic environment.

By the time Labour presented its Social Security Bill in 1938, male breadwinner ideology and increased worker productivity were firmly fixed in its social and economic vision. Successful realisation of Labour's plans required co-operation and productivity from all citizens. One man's charge to the government might have served as a Labour slogan: 'Build our prosperity ... on work, thrift, and perambulators'.[97] The principal burden of supplying the labour essential for generating long-term national prosperity fell to the male breadwinner. The overall strategy of boosting male work-rate and efficiency was quickly coupled to plans to expand the secondary sector. Women, as wives, mothers and consumers, were equally crucial to household and national prosperity; they were the designated 'professional' managers of consumption. Ironically, even though its plans for increased production might have benefited from encouraging women to enter factories, Labour's ideological and policy imperatives prevented endorsement of women's industrial employment. This near-sighted gender ideology also blinded Labour to the important strategic possibilities of reskilling women and relief workers for its planned industrial expansion.[98] Overall, then, the essential elements in Labour's plan for prosperity and progress were reassertion of women's traditional domestic role, high expectations of natural male breadwinner co-operation and expansive plans for industry.

Not everyone was reassured by Finance Minister Walter Nash's confidence that Labour could fund social security spending with industrial growth, population expansion and further land development.[99] At the very least, it was felt that much would depend on the government's ability to find new markets for its projected increases in local produce.[100] The 'New Zealand Made Goods' campaign, rejuvenated just before the 1938 election, was a fillip to the government's industry plans. Its representations of men as hard-working labourers in secondary industries, and women as consumers, were exactly what Labour had in mind.[101] These images coincided with Labour's election promotion depictions of men and women, and reinforced its notions of gendered citizen participation.[102] Promotional campaigns such as these reflected Labour's belief that a prosperous

PUT 'NEW ZEAL' *into New Zealand*

NEW ZEALAND

Bigger Factories
More Labour
Bigger Outputs
Greater Wealth
Greater Prosperity!

BUY THE PRODUCTS OF YOUR OWN LAND

The 'Buy New Zealand Made Goods' campaign was revived by the Labour government before the 1938 election. The men were depicted as hard-working labourers in secondary industries; women as consumers. New Zealand Herald, 26 November 1938.

New Zealand depended on progressive policies supporting and supplementing, but not supplanting, the traditional male breadwinner.

Labour secured an overwhelming election win in late 1938, but, before it could implement its promised development plans, a foreign exchange crisis and impending difficulties over British loan repayments forced the government into hasty measures to shore up the economy.[103] One of its initiatives exposed Labour's suspicions regarding unhealthy employee attitudes to hard work. Early in 1939 Michael Savage and other Labour politicians embarked on a whistle-stop tour of North Island industries to encourage both workers and local production.[104] This 'encouragement' included warnings and threats to 'loafers', slackers and those not pulling their weight.[105] The Minister of Labour also announced a departmental initiative to carefully scrutinise men engaged under the government's Employment Promotion Fund, a reaction to continuing beliefs that some men were deliberately 'not playing the game'.[106] These were not empty initiatives, as five men could testify when they were sacked from the New Brighton sand fixation scheme, allegedly for 'loafing on the job'.[107]

Of course, men employed on public works schemes were a soft target for criticism, since their pay and performance were politicised and open to public scrutiny. Government concerns regarding worker attitudes inevitably attracted some public support. Just as they had in 1936, many lamented some men's preference for the soft option of sustenance to actual work.[108] By 1939, the extent of male worker dishonesty, lack of integrity and poor work ethics seemed exemplified for some by revelations that, during 1937-38, 3257 men had defrauded the Employment Promotion Fund by making false statements regarding their work.[109] Some felt that fraudulent behaviour indicated a growing unwillingness to work hard and a lack of moral fibre.

But others argued, again just as in 1936, that the failure was the government's, since its policies curbed work and encouraged loafing.[110] Such arguments echoed earlier warnings, even from advocates of the government's work promotion initiatives, that Labour's policies might be counter-productive.[111] Its actions were construed as state interference in a private matter. Some even accused the government of usurping the breadwinner role.[112] Reactions to several complaints of slacking dealt with by the New Brighton Borough Council illustrate how tolerant many had become in their attitudes to male workers. Where officialdom often happily accepted loafing as a catch-all category with which to define and remedy workplace problems, others were not so dogmatic.[113] Although few dismissed slacking behaviour and attitudes lightly, many, as in the New Brighton case, were loath to insist that workforce problems simply required greater worker application. In another case, comments made by the Waimairi Council Chairman that workers were unable to use a difficult piece of roading machinery because they were 'too damned lazy to do the work', were strongly rebuffed by councillors and the public alike.[114] Such cases reveal strong reaction against officials and employers who too quickly dismissed workers' problems, failed to appreciate their efforts and failed to consider *all* the factors influencing male work habits.

In this vein, even some employers criticised the government for formulating policies based on unrealistic expectations of worker performance and industry capacity. Even when employers agreed with the government's aims of increased production, they did not always agree that low production levels were entirely due to worker laziness.[115] In early March 1939 Auckland manufacturers issued a statement on worker output, conceding that statistics showed a 'drop of hourly output a man of from 10 to 15 per cent in recent years'.[116] They felt, however, that the 'New Zealand worker is not lazy', and that the low output was not 'a result of any conscious policy' to slow production. It derived more from an inexperienced workforce struggling to cope with a developing manufacturing industry environment. True, 'strikes and stop-work meetings' indicated that 'some sections of workers' did not appreciate the benefits of high production for both employer and worker, and a 'speeding up by workers was essential'. But this would not come unless workers were educated to understand industry needs in the modern machine age. Manufacturers also recognised the benefits to greater productivity of employing women. Earlier, the secretary of the Auckland Manufacturers' Association had noted that many industries were indicating substantial capacity for expansion, most notably those employing women.[117] Few disputed government assessments of lower than expected worker output. But some employers looked beyond poor male worker attitude to explain it, and baulked at impugning workers' effort as a remedy for the situation. While the government was congratulated for its industry initiatives at the 1939 New Zealand Labour Party Conference, others felt that industries themselves had a better appreciation of factors influencing productivity and labour market trends, and should be supported rather than directed.[118]

The New Zealand labour force underwent many changes in the interwar years, although the lack of data makes it extremely difficult to accurately chart male and female workforce participation trends. As indicated earlier, Keith Rankin estimates that, by the end of the 1930s, the rate of adult women entering the workforce slowed after a sustained period of significantly increased involvement from the late 1920s.[119] The introduction of the government's social welfare policies early in 1939 only added to a trend away from workforce participation already apparent after 1936. Census data, viewed in the light of Rankin's estimates, does nothing to dispute such a 'trend', although it cannot confirm it. Between 1921 and 1945, the number of women classified as 'Breadwinners' rose from 109,880 to 163,561, an increase of 48.8 percent.[120] However, though women's workforce participation increased by 32 percent between 1921 and 1936, that net increase slowed to 12.7 percent between 1936 and 1945.[121] Miriam Gilson argues that, during this period, New Zealand women did not enter the paid workforce in the same proportions as in nations of comparable urban-industrial development. This, she believes, had less to do with economic factors than with 'our society's interpretation of the feminine role'.[122] Rankin argues that although social pressure inevitably biased women away from paid work, many adult women engaged in calculated reactions to 'cyclical developments in the economy' and supplemented the household income.[123]

An improving economy in the late 1930s reduced the need for women to hold jobs, and allowed them to marry, have children or pursue opportunities for leisure or voluntary community work.[124]

The trend of women leaving the workforce was, therefore, not necessarily a triumph for the male breadwinner ideology *per se*. Labour's gendered conception of social roles resonated favourably with many. Certainly, there was widespread agreement that men should work, but this did not mean that, by 1939, society had universally revived the traditional belief that women should *not* work. Many simply believed that it was better for a woman, and her family, if she had no *need* to work. But many also realised that exclusive male breadwinning was not an option for some households. Others felt working women were motivated only by greed, selfishness or the lust for luxury.[125]

Male employment trends provide some further evidence that attitudes to breadwinners and breadwinning were not blithely maintained quite as they had been, or as the government wished them to be. Overall male participation in the workforce had been steadily decreasing since the 1890s.[126] Although, numerically, male workforce participation was still increasing, the ratio of participation compared with the total number of working-age males (aged 15 to 64) was dropping.[127] Examination of age-specific male workforce participation rates reveals that, while workforce involvement of males aged 25–44 remained steady (at about 98 percent), fluctuations occurred, mainly in the under-25 and over-45 age groups.[128] By the late 1930s, paid work participation levels for older and younger men were lower than during the economic recovery of the mid-1930s.[129] The reasons for this are many and varied: employers spurned older workers in favour of employing women at cheaper wage rates and investing training costs in younger workers; more older men retired as social security and pension schemes became available; and an improving economy lowered expectations that young males should work, allowing them to remain at school, go on to tertiary training, support family businesses on an informal basis, or simply refrain from seeking work.[130] By the late 1930s, proportionately fewer male workers (most typically between their mid-twenties and mid-forties) were supporting a population with increasing rates of female, youth and aged non-participation in paid work.[131] Although Labour assisted the male breadwinner through policies delivering pensions, free education and health benefits, achieving its goals of increased production meant not only that men would have to work harder but, apparently, that *more* of them than ever would need to work.

While New Zealanders committed themselves to private prosperity, waiving gender orthodoxy as they did so, the government showed itself to be equally committed to national prosperity founded on a gendered view of New Zealand society. By mid-1939, the government was conceding that its plans had not produced the desired effects. Labour felt that its role as the worker's friend had not been returned in kind. The workers had not played ball: they took too many liberties, and too often exhibited a wasteful propensity for work stoppages and strikes.[132] It was time to rein them in. Trade unions were targeted as a major culprit, when on 18 July 1939, the government proposed an amendment to the Industrial Conciliation and Arbitration Act intended to nullify any action impeding production.[133] The 'workers' government' was understandably reticent about implementing such an unpopular employment directive. But, to its quiet relief, the outbreak of war saved the government from acute embarrassment, and certain criticism, over this issue. In September the government enacted Emergency War Regulations, substantially strengthening the intent of the earlier Industrial Conciliation and Arbitration Act amendment.[134] From this point on, Labour was more able to forthrightly adjust the composition of the industrial workforce.

David Hill described Depression-era New Zealand as a 'hell of a state to be in', but he may have been more positive by the end of the decade. Wages had risen, unemployment was down, social security was assured and prospects for prosperity seemed brighter. Under Labour, the milk and honey flowed more freely in the workers' Canaan. Most importantly, people seemed to have more choices. Certainly, women and children did not appear to be quite as dependent on male breadwinning as they once had been. It also seemed to be less imperative for males, especially the old and the very young, to work. Out of the grim years of recession, and in the years of recovery, there had been, for many, a 'quiet fracturing' of social attitudes regarding the value, place and conception of the breadwinner. This eventuated despite the efforts of two governments to maintain, then intensify, gendered roles featuring males as rightful, proper and primary breadwinners. Neither government entirely succeeded in securing workforce participation that corresponded with their ideology. Both the Coalition and Labour showed themselves to be inflexible in adjusting employment policies to public sentiment, worker expectations and employment trends. They underestimated the determination of men, women and households to tailor their work participation to their own economic needs, even in defiance of traditions of gendered work. Although male breadwinning priority characterised the public face of 1930s labour participation, New Zealand society loosened its grip on the belief that it was unnecessary for women to enter paid employment, even while it lamented this development.

I am grateful for the helpful comments made by Caroline Daley and Deborah Montgomerie in the writing of this essay. I also acknowledge the assistance of Simon Taylor in preparing the illustrations.

1 David Joseph Hill, 'Auckland in the 1930s' Oral History Project, 90-OH-067, Special Collections, Auckland City Libraries, Auckland.

2 See Margaret McClure, 'On Work: Perceptions of Work in Late Nineteenth Century New Zealand, 1870-1900', MLitt thesis, University of Auckland, 1993, pp. 18-19, 133; Bev James and Kay Saville-Smith, *Gender, Culture and Power*, 2nd edn, Auckland, 1994, pp. 32-49; Claire Toynbee, *Her Work and His: Family, Kin and Community in New Zealand 1900-1930*, Wellington, 1995, pp. 86-94. For the implications of this ideology for women see Erik Olssen, 'Women, Work and Family: 1880-1926', in Phillida Bunkle and Beryl Hughes, eds, *Women in New Zealand Society*, Auckland, 1980, pp. 159-83.

3 Wally Seccombe, 'Patriarchy Stabilized: The Construction of the Male Breadwinner Wage Norm in Nineteenth-Century Britain', *Social History*, 2, 1986, pp. 53-75.

4 Barbara Brookes, 'Aspects of Women's Health', in Linda Bryder, ed., *A Healthy Country: Essays on the Social History of Medicine in New Zealand*, Wellington, 1991, pp. 149-64; Julie Park, ed., *Ladies a Plate: Change and Continuity in the Lives of New Zealand Women*, Auckland, 1992; Maureen Molloy, 'Citizenship, Property and Bodies: Discourses on Gender and the Inter-War Labour Government in New Zealand', *Gender & History*, 4, 3, 1992, pp. 293-304; Melanie Nolan, '"Politics Swept Under a Domestic Carpet"? Fracturing Domesticity and the Male Breadwinner Wage: Women's Economic Citizenship, 1920s-1940s', *New Zealand Journal of History (NZJH)*, 27, 2, 1993, pp. 199-217; Charlotte Macdonald, *The Vote, the Pill, and the Demon Drink: A History of Feminist Writing in New Zealand 1869-1993*, Wellington, 1993, pp. 89-120; Jo Aitken, 'Wives and Mothers First: The New Zealand Teachers' Marriage Bar and the Ideology of Domesticity, 1920-1940', *Women's Studies Journal*, 12, 1, 1996, pp. 83-98; Annabel Cooper and Maureen Molloy, 'Poverty, Dependence and "Women": Reading, Autobiography and Social Policy from 1930s New Zealand', *Gender & History*, 9, 1, 1997, pp. 36-59; Louise Shaw, 'From Family Helpmeet to Lady Dispenser: Women Pharmacists 1881-1939', *NZJH*, 32, 1, 1998, pp. 23-42.

5 See for instance, John E. Martin, 'The Removal of Compulsory Arbitration and the Depression of the 1930s', *NZJH*, 28, 2, 1994, pp. 124-44.

6 David H. J. Morgan, *Discovering Men*, London, 1992, pp. 99-100. For representative discussions of this issue, see Eleanor Rathbone, *Family Allowances*, London, 1949; Joseph H. Pleck and Linda Lang, 'Men's Family Work: Three Perspectives and Some New Data', *The Family Coordinator*, 28, 4, 1979, pp. 481-8; Hilary Land, 'The Family Wage', *Feminist Review*, 6, 1980, pp. 55-77; Jessie Bernard, 'The Good-Provider Role: Its Rise and Fall', in Michael S. Kimmel and Michael A. Messner, eds, *Men's Lives*, New York, 1989, pp. 223-40; Margaret Marsh, 'Suburban Men and Masculine Domesticity, 1870-1915', in Mark C. Carnes and Clyde Griffen, eds, *Meanings for Manhood: Constructions of Masculinity in Victorian America*, Chicago, 1990, pp. 223-40; Morgan, *Discovering Men*, pp. 72-120; Colin Creighton, 'The Rise of the Male Breadwinner Family: A Reappraisal', *Comparative Studies in Society and History*, 38, 2, April 1996, pp. 322-5.

7 F. M. Fisher, 'Women in Industry', *New Zealand Herald (NZH)*, 24 February 1934, Supplement, p. 6; T. A. Hunter, 'Some Aspects of Depression Psychology in New Zealand', *Economic Record (ER)*, 10, June 1934, pp. 40-1.

8 *NZH*, 23 March 1932, p. 14.

9 *New Zealand Census*, 1936, Vol. IV, p. 32. In 1926 64.1 per cent of men were married, while 5.15 per cent were either legally separated or widowed (both categories quite possibly having

dependants). In 1936, 63.41 per cent of men were married, while 5.42 per cent were separated or widowed.

10 Robert Howard White, interview with Tim Frank, Auckland, 30 October 1996. Tape held by the author.

11 David Hill, 'Auckland in the 1930s' Oral History Project. Hill was farming on the Hauraki Plains in the 1920s but lost the farm when the Depression arrived. Subsequently, he moved to Auckland and found work in a variety of occupations, including roading, sewer building, tunnelling, grounds caretaking and mental hospital orderly duties. He was unemployed for a total period of nine months.

12 Francis Edward Leabourn, Glen Innes Oral History Project, 90-OH-006, Special Collections, Auckland City Libraries, Auckland. (Verbal emphasis on tape.) As a young man, Leabourn worked as a window-dresser until he lost his job in 1931. He was not able to find regular work until 1932 when he was employed at a flour mill.

13 Terry Colling, *Beyond Mateship: Understanding Australian Men*, Sydney, 1992, p. 16. An analysis of New Zealand statistics on the number of labour disputes and of workers involved in direct strike action between 1926 and 1932 confirms this reluctance, indicated by a reduced willingness to engage in militant worker action against employers during the Depression. While the numbers of workers involved increased, the number of disputes decreased. The numbers involved in sympathetic strikes supporting other workers also dropped dramatically. *New Zealand Official Year Book* (*NZOYB*), 1932, p. 742; *NZOYB*, 1937, p. 720.

14 The Unemployment Inquiry Committee had earlier released the first section of its report outlining what it believed to be the economic factors affecting unemployment in New Zealand. 'Unemployment in New Zealand', First Section of Report of Committee Appointed by the Government on 17th October, 1928, and 26th February, 1929, *Appendices to the Journals of the House of Representatives* (*AJHR*), 1929, H-11B.

15 *AJHR*, 1929, H-11B, p. 1. See also 'Unemployment in New Zealand', *AJHR*, 1930, H-11B.

16 *AJHR*, 1930, H-11B, pp. 2-4.

17 *NZH*, 14 March 1930, p. 17; 18 March 1930, p. 14; 'Unemployment Cure', 21 March 1930, p. 15; 24 July 1930, p. 14; 29 July 1930, p. 12; *Dominion*, 25 March 1930, p. 12. See also *Dominion*, 13 April 1931, p. 11; 21 April 1931, p. 11; *Otago Daily Times* (*ODT*), 29 July 1930, p. 8; *NZH*, 26 March 1932, p. 13; Gordon Coates, Public Works Statement, *AJHR*, 1931, D-1, pp. i-ii; Gordon Coates, Unemployment Statement, *AJHR*, 1931, H-35A, pp. 1-3; A. N. Field, *The Truth About the Slump*, Nelson, 1931, pp. 176-84; D. O. Williams, 'Small Holdings for the Unemployed in New Zealand', *ER*, 9, June 1933, pp. 76-81.

18 *New Zealand Census*, 1926, Vol. XVII, p. 67. Figures for industrial distribution in 1926 reveal that Pakeha male workers in primary industry of all types numbered 138,550, while Pakeha men in secondary and tertiary industry together numbered 276,499 (excluding 47,384 'not specified' workers).

19 For example, 'Won't you help to lay Another Brick?', *Dominion*, 28 August 1930, p. 6.

20 *NZH*, 4 March 1930, p. 12; 12 March 1930, p. 14; 14 March 1930, p. 17; 'Finding Employment', 15 March 1930, p. 12; 24 March 1930, p. 12; 16 June 1930, p. 12; 21 July 1930, p. 12; 22 July 1930, p. 12; 8 August 1930, p. 16; *Dominion*, 26 July 1930, p. 13.

21 *AJHR*, 1929, H-11B, pp. 1-2.

22 *Dominion*, 3 March 1930, p. 12; 4 March 1930, pp. 10, 12. At the 1931 Salvation Army Congress in Wellington, Commissioner John Cunningham invoked St Paul's injunction against men eating if they did not work, in support of the 'no dole' principle. *Dominion*, 20 April 1931, p. 8.

23 *NZH*, 8 March 1930, p. 10; 'Unemployed Relief', 11 March 1930, p. 11.

24 *NZH*, 22 March 1930, p. 14.

25 'Finding Employment', *NZH*, 15 March 1930, p. 12; 19 March 1930, p. 16; 11 March 1930, p. 12; 17 June 1930, p. 12; 7 August 1930, p. 12; *Dominion*, 7 March 1930, p. 13; 24 July 1930, p. 13; 30 July 1930, p. 13.

26 Nancy Fraser and Linda Gordon, 'A Genealogy of Dependency: Tracing a Keyword of the U.S. Welfare State', *Signs*, 19, 2, 1994, p. 320. See 'Unemployment', *ODT*, 9 August 1930, p. 19.

27 *New Zealand Parliamentary Debates* (*NZPD*), 1930, 224, p. 402; *Dominion*, 19 July 1930, p. 12. The 'No work, no pay' principle was later repeated by Robert A. Wright. *NZPD*, 1930, 224,

p. 521. Despite their opposition to some of the principles behind the government's Unemployment Bill, even Labour politicians agreed with such sentiments. For instance, in the same debate, Harry Holland stated that the 'only true solution [to unemployment] is to provide work'. *NZPD*, 1930, 224, p. 404.

28 *Dominion*, 22 January 1931, p. 8.

29 See the Unemployment Act 1930, *New Zealand Statutes*, 1930, Session III, pp. 56-7, and *NZOYB*, 1932, pp. 710-11. The Unemployment Board had announced plans to provide sustenance in January 1931 but was overruled by the government in February 1931.

30 *NZPD*, 1930, 224, p. 521; *NZH*, 2 April 1930, p. 16; 'Something For Nothing', *Dominion*, 23 January 1931, p. 8; Hunter, 'Depression Psychology in New Zealand', p. 40; R.T. Robertson, 'Government Responses to Unemployment in New Zealand, 1929-35', *NZJH*, 16, 1, 1982, pp. 22-3.

31 Both the Unemployment Committee's report and Michael Savage, in the debate on the Unemployment Bill, had made such recommendations. *AJHR*, 1929, H-11B, p. 3; *NZPD*, 1930, 224, p. 415; R. M. Burdon, *The New Dominion: A Social and Political History of New Zealand 1918-1939*, Wellington, 1965, p. 140.

32 Louis Wilson, Oral History (1978), DOHP 78-OH-025, North Shore Oral History Archive, North Shore Libraries.

33 'Dodging Work', *NZH*, 12 March 1930, p. 14; 13 March 1930, p. 12; 20 March 1930, p. 14; 25 March 1930, p. 14; 16 April 1930, p. 18; *Dominion*, 18 July 1930, p. 13; 28 July 1930, p. 14.

34 *NZH*, 11 March 1930, p. 12; *ODT*, 9 August 1930, p. 19.

35 Louis Wilson, Oral History (1978). See Tony Simpson, *The Sugarbag Years*, 2nd edn, Auckland, 1984, pp. 79-137, 186-96; Wellington Branch, Society for Research on Women in New Zealand (Inc), *In Those Days*, Wellington, 1982, pp. 78-85.

36 For example, see the extended 'discussion' in the *NZH* in response to Edna Macky, 'The Economic Position – Husband and Wife', *NZH*, 3 March 1930, p. 15. In all, 42 letters and four articles were published on the topic in the *NZH* from 10 March to 4 April 1930. Multiple submissions from some individuals notwithstanding, the *NZH* published correspondence from men and women in approximately equal numbers. The letters appeared under the headings of 'Married Life' and 'Husband and Wife'.

37 'Engineering Industry', *NZH*, 28 May 1930, p. 14; 26 May 1930, p. 12.

38 *AJHR*, 1931, H-35A, p. 4.

39 *NZH*, 15 April 1930, p. 14; 19 March 1932, p. 14; 21 March 1932, p. 12; 24 March 1932, p. 14; Christine Comber, 'Women in Industry', *NZH*, 3 March 1934, Supplement, p. 6. This was one of four articles on the issue of women wage-earners that appeared in the *NZH* on successive Saturdays from 10 February 1934.

40 'Women in Industry', *NZH*, 17 February 1934, Supplement, p. 6; Fisher, 'Women in Industry', p. 6.

41 *NZPD*, 1930, 225, p. 432.

42 *NZH*, 18 July 1930, p. 10; 19 July 1930, p. 13; 24 July 1930, p. 13; 25 July 1930, p. 8; *Dominion*, 30 July 1930, p. 13. See the comments by Henry E. Holland, Michael J. Savage, Walter Nash and William E. Barnard, *NZPD*, 1930, 224, pp. 406, 416, 430, 517-18; *NZPD*, 1930, 225, p. 427.

43 *NZPD*, 1930, 225, pp. 435, 432.

44 *NZPD*, 1930, 225, p. 431.

45 See Molloy, 'Citizenship, Property and Bodies', pp. 293-304; Nolan, '"Politics Swept Under a Domestic Carpet"?', pp. 199-217; Cooper and Molloy, 'Poverty, Dependence and "Women"', pp. 36-59.

46 The reference is to comments made by the Minister of Health, Arthur J. Stallworthy, in Auckland to a delegation from the Women's International League for Peace and Freedom, cited in Sandra Coney, *Every Girl: A Social History of Women and the YWCA in Auckland 1885-1985*, Auckland, 1986, p. 200. In early 1931, Stallworthy was reported as saying that there was 'no reason why any decent young woman, or any young woman at all, should sleep out of doors, or go hungry in the city of Auckland'. *Dominion*, 14 April 1931, p. 10. He was not alone in holding such views. In the debate on the Unemployment Bill in July 1930, an Independent/

Reform politician, William D. Lysnar, refused to believe there were either unemployed or destitute women on the basis that 'women are more resourceful than men' and 'will find [their] feet better than a man', and that 'a woman will take any kind of work, whatever the pay, so long as she can provide for herself'. *NZPD*, 1930, 224, pp. 406, 424.

47 R. W. Connell, *Masculinities*, St Leonards, 1995, p. 37.

48 Quoted in *NZH*, 13 March 1930, p. 10. For a contrasting view see *NZH*, 15 April 1930, p. 14. Significant support for married women teachers came from the Auckland Education Board chairman, Mr A. Burns, who was reluctant to pursue Education Department requests for details of married women teachers with employed husbands. *NZH*, 19 June 1930, p. 13; *ODT*, 19 June 1930, p. 7.

49 Aitken, 'Wives and Mothers First', pp. 83-98.

50 Nolan, '"Politics Swept Under a Domestic Carpet"?', p. 201.

51 See *New Zealand Awards*, 1931, 30, pp. 512-13.

52 'A Stupid Thing', *Dominion*, 25 July 1930, p. 10.

53 *ODT*, 16 August 1930, p. 10; *Evening Post* (*EP*), 16 August 1930, p. 7; *Dominion*, 16 August 1930, pp. 4, 10. The application to make provision for female machinists was rejected in this case, but only on a technicality. The Court did state, however, that the proposal had merit, recommending that it receive serious reconsideration.

54 An article in the *NZH* summarised statistics and trends of female work in the previous 34 years and highlighted the competition for jobs between men and women that had been created as a result. *NZH*, 14 June 1930, p. 13.

55 Keith Rankin, 'Labour Supply in New Zealand and Australia: 1919-1939', MA thesis, Victoria University of Wellington, 1990, pp. 123, 142.

56 Rankin, 'Labour Supply in New Zealand', pp. 142, 157, 182, 189-91. See F. M. Fisher, 'Women in Industry', *NZH*, 24 February 1934, Supplement, p. 6. E. P. Neale noted the increasing need for women to supplement family incomes as one of a number of factors influencing women's motivation for paid work participation. E. P. Neale, 'Economic Notes', *The Accountant's Journal*, 14, 11, 20 May 1936, pp. 286-7.

57 Rankin, 'Labour Supply in New Zealand', pp. 139, 161, 190-1.

58 Rankin, 'Labour Supply in New Zealand', pp. 91-2, 157, 181-3, 189-92.

59 Miriam Gilson Vosburgh, *The New Zealand Family and Social Change: A Trend Analysis*, Wellington, 1978, pp. 34, 37, 40-1, 62-3; Erik Olssen and Andrée Lévesque, 'Towards a History of the European Family in New Zealand', in Peggy Koopman-Boyden, ed., *Families in New Zealand Society*, Wellington, 1978, p. 14; Rankin, 'Labour Supply in New Zealand', pp. 48-53.

60 Rankin, 'Labour Supply in New Zealand', pp. 181-2; Nolan, '"Politics Swept Under a Domestic Carpet"?', p. 215.

61 'Women Who Work', *NZH*, 14 June, 1930, p. 13. Such 'retrogression' would be consistent with Rankin's argument that many women left employment as economic circumstances and marriage prospects improved. Rankin, 'Labour Supply in New Zealand', pp. 65, 91-2.

62 'Women Workers in Factories', *Dominion*, 23 April 1936, p. 11. Figures include the numbers of women employed in factories, and their per centage of total employees (presumably in factories).

63 *NZOYB*, 1935, p. 616. Just 5279 men were registered as 'Totally Unemployed' on 3 August 1930. *NZOYB*, 1933, p. 608. These figures represent only those men registered as 'Unemployed' (that is, for whom no work at all could be found) with the Unemployment Board. They do not include men working on relief jobs, either full-time or part-time, or simply unplaced or ineligible for relief work. For instance, therefore, the 1933 'Unemployed' figures do not include the 72,966 men registered but engaged on board relief schemes, or the 5125 registered but unplaced or ineligible for relief. *NZOYB*, 1935, p. 618.

64 *NZPD*, 1933, 236, p. 157. What McCombs bases this on is not indicated. It is perhaps a reference to the 79,435 men *registered* with the board but engaged, unplaced, or ineligible by 30 September 1933. (See *NZOYB*, 1935, p. 618.) It may also be an estimate of men underemployed and on low wages but not registered with the Unemployment Board. McCombs suggests that, combining all unemployed and underemployed categories, some 240,000 people were 'in such a position that they were unable to provide themselves and

their dependants with a sufficiency of even the bare necessities of life'. Keith Rankin estimates that, in 1933, a total of 224,100 working-age New Zealanders were 'fully or partially unemployed', lending some credibility to McCombs's claims. Rankin, 'Labour Supply in New Zealand', pp. 6-7, 105, 117-23.

65 *AJHR*, 1931, H-35A, p. 4. Coates's appeal was made in his capacity as the Coalition's Minister of Unemployment.

66 Efforts to compile a temporary register of unemployed women in Auckland in late 1935 can be directly attributed to a growing awareness that women's unemployment had been severely understimated. See *NZH*, 15 November 1935, p. 16.

67 Hunter, 'Depression Psychology in New Zealand', p. 40.

68 Rankin, 'Labour Supply in New Zealand', pp. 88-90. See, for instance, the series of articles on 'Women in Industry', *NZH*, 10 February 1934, Supplement, p. 6; 17 February 1934, Supplement, p. 6; 24 February 1934, Supplement, p. 6; 3 March 1934, Supplement, p. 6.

69 R. T. Robertson, 'The Tyranny of Circumstances: Responses to Unemployment in New Zealand, 1929-35, with Particular Reference to Dunedin', PhD thesis, University of Otago, 1978, p. 413.

70 Hunter, 'Depression Psychology in New Zealand', pp. 42-3.

71 Robertson, 'Government Responses to Unemployment', pp. 34-8. Both Alexander Moncur and Hubert Armstrong ascribed the Coalition's defeat to public unrest over its unemployment policies. *NZPD*, 1936, 244, pp. 472, 647. David Morgan has noted the relationship between unemployment and political dissatisfaction in Britain and the United States in the interwar years. Morgan, *Discovering Men*, p. 105.

72 Anthony Ashton-Peach, 'The Social Effects of the Depression in Auckland 1930-35', MA thesis, University of Auckland, 1971, pp. 126-7.

73 *NZPD*, 1930, 224, p. 404.

74 *NZPD*, 1930, 224, p. 415.

75 *NZPD*, 1933, 236, p. 730.

76 Note, for example, the comments of Walter Nash, Robert Semple, Michael J. Savage, William J. Lyon, Alexander F. Moncur, Arthur S. Richards and Leonard G. Lowry. *NZPD*, 1936, 244, pp. 370, 377, 404-5, 409, 422, 472, 584-5; *NZPD*, 1936, 245, p. 134.

77 *EP*, 5 February 1936, p. 10.

78 *NZPD*, 1936, 244, p. 450.

79 *EP*, 11 March 1936, p. 12. Armstrong later stated that the basic wage would provide for a 'man, his wife, and *three* children up to a reasonable standard of comfort'. *NZPD*, 1936, 244, p. 528 (emphasis added). Note also that the new basic wage rates revealed by Armstrong in the House on 21 April 1936 showed adjustments from old rates in the categories of 'Married, wife only', 'Married, wife and one child' and 'Married, wife and two children'. Rates for all other categories remained as they were. It was noted at the time that the move was designed to be a marriage and parenting incentive as much as anything else. *NZPD*, 1936, 244, p. 451. For discussion on the emergence of Australasian welfare states built on the family wage and female dependence on the male breadwinner, see Frances G. Castles, *The Working Class and Welfare: Reflections on the Political Development of the Welfare State in Australia and New Zealand, 1890-1980*, Wellington, 1985, especially Ch. 4.

80 *NZPD*, 1936, 244, p. 50.

81 Labour's commitment to include women in unemployment relief measures was expressed consistently from 1930 on. For example, note the comments of Henry E. Holland, Michael Savage, Walter Nash and William Barnard expressing dismay at women's exclusion from provisions of the Unemployment Act 1930. *NZPD*, 1930, 224, pp. 406, 416, 430, 517-18; *NZPD*, 1930, 225, p. 427. See also *NZPD*, 1932, 231, pp. 749-93, 808-53; 1932, 232, pp. 1-12, 240-4; *New Zealand Worker*, 15 March 1933, p. 2; 29 March 1933, p. 4; 11 April 1934, pp. 1, 7; Labour Party Manifesto, 1935, *Labour Has a Plan*, Propaganda Pamphlet 3, Wellington, 1935.

82 *NZPD*, 1937, 248, p. 1028.

83 *EP*, 18 February 1936, p. 8; Rankin, 'Labour Supply in New Zealand', p. 136.

84 *NZPD*, 1936, 244, p. 568.

85 *NZPD*, 1936, 244, pp. 367, 370-1, 375-6, 397, 477, 482, 527, 568.

86 *NZPD*, 1936, 244, pp. 472, 530, 632, 704.
87 *NZPD*, 1936, 244, pp. 367, 397, 420-1, 477, 704. See Hunter, 'Depression Psychology in New Zealand', p. 43.
88 *NZPD*, 1936, 244, pp. 367, 371, 375-6, 395, 397, 472-3, 477. See Editorial, *Dominion*, 6 February 1936, p. 8.
89 *NZPD*, 1936, 244, pp. 396-7, 530, 698, 706; *NZPD*, 1936, 245, p. 9.
90 *NZPD*, 1936, 244, pp. 370, 569, 723; *NZPD*, 1936, 245, pp. 116, 132, 255.
91 *NZPD*, 1936, 244, pp. 465-7.
92 *Dominion*, 4 January 1936, p. 10; 5 February 1936, p. 10; 6 February 1936, p. 8; *NZH*, 6 July 1936, p. 11; *NZPD*, 1936, 244, pp. 395, 397. Bob Semple often expressed such remarks in specific reference to men employed on public work schemes. But their being made in the context of debates on the Employment Promotion Bill and the Industrial Conciliation and Arbitration Amendment Bill clearly indicates they were also intended to cover all male workers.
93 For instance, 'Fifty Arrests', *NZH*, 29 August 1936, p. 14, referred to a public outcry over sustenance men gambling in cities when they could be working in the country. Two articles headed 'Work Refused' outlined reasons why men preferred sustenance to work. *NZH*, 6 November 1936, p. 11; 7 November 1936, p. 15. See also 'Work and Sustenance', *NZH*, 2 September 1936, p. 15; 7 September 1936, p. 12; 8 September 1936, p. 13; 10 September 1936, p. 15. For a more positive response to Labour's policies see 'Work and Wages', *NZH*, 26 September 1936, p. 17, and negative reaction to this response, *NZH*, 26 September 1936, p. 17.
94 Cooper and Molloy, 'Poverty, Dependence and "Women"', pp. 37-8, 45.
95 Cooper and Molloy, 'Poverty, Dependence and "Women"', pp. 36-8.
96 Cooper and Molloy, 'Poverty, Dependence and "Women"', p. 53. Labour ministers referred to the government's surrogate breadwinner role in speeches on various bills. For example, Walter Nash expressed the government's role in people's lives in 'provider' terms during the debate on the Social Security Bill. *NZPD*, 1938, 253, pp. 61-2; *Dominion*, 3 September 1938, p. 10. For statements indicating the parental and providing role of the state, see *NZPD*, 246, 1936, pp. 806, 809, 841.
97 *Dominion*, 14 November 1936, p. 13.
98 J. O. Shearer, 'The "New" Policy of the Labour Party', *ER*, 15, October 1939, p. 137.
99 *NZH*, 1 September 1938, pp. 12, 15; *Dominion*, 12 September 1938, p. 11.
100 See, for instance, the letter 'Increased Production', *NZH*, 5 September 1938, p. 12.
101 For instance, see the advertisements run by the Auckland Manufacturer's Association, 'Our Workers', *NZH*, 20 August 1938, Supplement, p. 11; 'Put "New Zeal" into New Zealand', *NZH*, 26 November 1938, p. 11; 'Certainly we must shop on the right side of the street – New Zealand Made Goods are always Best Value', *NZH*, 17 September 1938, Supplement, p. 11. The advertisements used in 1938 were similar to those used previously. For example, *NZH*, 24 July 1930, p. 19; *Dominion*, 14 August 1930, p. 8; 21 August 1930, p. 6; 28 August 1930, p. 6. A similar 'Buy New Zealand Made Goods' campaign had been advocated and instituted as an employment promotion measure in 1930. The National Council of Women had specifically highlighted the value of women's participation in it as a contribution to solving unemployment. See 'Women and Local Industries', *NZH*, 29 May 1930, p. 14, and 'Made in New Zealand', *NZH*, 30 May 1930, p. 13.
102 'I've got a job – help me to keep it!', *NZH*, 8 October 1938, p. 21; 'Here's MY reason for voting LABOUR', *NZH*, 19 September 1938, p. 17.
103 Sixteen of the 28 points in Labour's 1938 election manifesto were concerned with extensive plans for increased production, industrial expansion and land development.
104 See various statements to this effect made by Michael Savage from 24 February 1939 on. For example, *NZH*, 24 February 1939, p. 11; 2 March 1939, p. 12; 4 March 1939, p. 15.
105 *NZH*, 4 March 1939, p. 18; 10 March 1939, p. 10.
106 *NZH*, 23 February 1939, p. 13; *Press*, 24 February 1939, p. 12.
107 *Press*, 4 February 1939, p. 22. The work was controlled by the Public Works Department under the No. 13 Scheme.

108 *Press*, 17 February 1939, p. 12; *NZH*, 2 June 1939, p. 15; Editorial, *NZH*, 22 June 1939, p. 12.

109 *Press*, 29 March 1939, p. 8; *AJHR*, 1938, B-1, p. xix. This was an increase from 357 noted cases in 1936. *AJHR*, 1936, B-1, p. xiv.

110 Letter from J. M. Waddell, *Press*, 22 March 1939, p. 3; Editorial, 29 March 1939, p. 8; 'New Zealand Morality', *Dominion*, 11 April 1939, p. 10; 13 July 1939, p. 11; 24 July 1939, p. 13; *NZH*, 25 July 1939, p. 13. For examples of 1936 attitudes, see *Dominion*, 11 January 1936, p. 11; 'Work and Leisure', *NZH*, 26 August 1936, p. 15; 'Men and Work', *NZH*, 1 September 1936, p. 15; *NZH*, 21 September 1936, p. 9 and 29 September 1936, p. 13 for a rebuttal.

111 For instance, see the comments made by Sir Albert Atkey (a delegate to the Empire Chambers of Commerce congress) and Professor Winifred Cullis (a member of the National Institute of Industrial Psychology in Britain). *Dominion*, 29 October 1936, p. 12; 2 November 1936, p. 8.

112 *Dominion*, 24 August 1938, p. 13; 'Rights of the Family', *Dominion*, 3 September 1938, p. 13. See also 'Hard Work', *Dominion*, 12 August 1938, p. 13, which criticised government policy for depriving men of their right of control over their own circumstances.

113 *Press*, 14 February 1939, p. 9; 15 February 1939, p. 17.

114 *Press*, 16 February 1939, p. 12; 25 February 1939, p. 20; 27 February 1939, p. 7; 28 February 1939, p. 13.

115 For instance, see the comments of M. R. O'Shea, Secretary of the New Zealand Manufacturers' Federation. *NZH*, 31 August 1938, p. 15.

116 *NZH*, 1 March 1939, p. 13. It was generally agreed by commentators that reduced working hours had affected industrial production in the late 1930s, but there was some disagreement between commentators over the degree to which production had declined, or whether it had declined at all. See, for instance, E. P. Neale, 'Recent New Zealand Data Regarding the Incomes of Individuals', *ER*, 17, June 1941, pp. 79-80, and a reply by R. F. Wilson, 'New Zealand Production', *ER*, 17, December 1941, pp. 252-4.

117 *NZH*, 24 February 1939, p. 11.

118 *Dominion*, 15 April 1939, p. 13; *Press*, 6 February 1939, p. 5.

119 Rankin, 'Labour Supply in New Zealand', Table 6I, p. 183. Female youth (under 21 years) workforce participation had begun to decline earlier, from 1933 on, after both adult and youth female categories had experienced sharp increases between 1927 and 1932.

120 *NZ Census*, 1921, Section XIV, p. 134; 1936, Vol. X, p. i; 1945, Vol. X, p. ii. Note that figures used for these calculations have required some adjustment to standardize the results across the various censuses.

121 Possibly the 1945 figure was lower than previous years because, by 1945, some women who had taken up wartime employment were beginning to surrender their jobs to returning servicemen.

122 Miriam Gilson, 'Women in Employment', in John Forster, ed., *Social Process in New Zealand: Readings in Sociology*, Auckland, 1969, pp. 185, 189, 191. Rosemary Novitz argues that a woman's obligation to be a wife and mother was the greatest single factor mitigating against women's entry into the New Zealand workforce in the years between 1871 and 1936. Rosemary Novitz, 'The Priority of the Mother Role: An Investigation of the Importance Women Give to Their Employment Behaviour', MA thesis, Lincoln University, 1976, p. 52.

123 Rankin, 'Labour Supply in New Zealand', p. 189.

124 Rankin, 'Labour Supply in New Zealand', pp. 136, 142, 154-7, 190-1. See also *Dominion*, 28 April 1939, p. 10; *Dominion*, 6 November 1936, p. 10.

125 See the debate 'Married Women in Jobs' in the *NZH* in late 1938. *NZH*, 14 November 1938, p. 12; 16 November 1938, p. 19; 18 November 1938, p. 15; 21 November 1938, p. 14; 22 November 1938, p. 15; 23 November 1938, p. 17; 24 November 1938, p. 17; 26 November 1938, p. 19; 29 November 1938, p. 15.

126 P. M. Revell and Peter Brosnan, 'New Zealand Labour Force Participation: The Ninety Years to 1981', *New Zealand Journal of Industrial Relations*, 11, 1986, pp. 79-80.

127 Rankin, 'Labour Supply in New Zealand', pp. 179-80, 183.

128 Revell and Brosnan, 'New Zealand Labour Force Participation', pp. 80-1; Rankin, 'Labour Supply in New Zealand', pp. 179-81.

129 Rankin, 'Labour Supply in New Zealand', p. 95; Revell and Brosnan, 'New Zealand Labour

Force Participation', p. 81. See E. P. Neale, 'Population Prospects and Problems in New Zealand', *ER*, 15, October 1939, pp. 87-8 for an assessment of the economic and industrial impact of the rise in age at which males began work and a lowering retirement age, as well as a rising average age for workers caused by a lowering birth rate.

130 S. Leathem, 'Policies and Trends in New Zealand', *ER*, 15, June 1939, p. 50. Rankin, 'Labour Supply in New Zealand', pp. 64-79, 95, 182, 194-5; Revell and Brosnan, 'New Zealand Labour Force Participation', p. 81.

131 Rankin, 'Labour Supply in New Zealand', p. 195; Revell and Brosnan, 'New Zealand Labour Force Participation', p. 80.

132 *Standard*, 20 April 1939, p. 2.

133 *NZPD*, 1939, 254, pp. 454-5. See the Industrial Conciliation and Arbitration Act Amendment 1939, *New Zealand Statutes*, 1939, pp. 5-6, and earlier press announcements, *NZH*, 30 June 1939, p. 10; 1 July 1939, p. 12.

134 See War Measures, *NZPD*, 1939, 256, pp. 45-7; Emergency Regulations Bill, *NZPD*, 1939, 256, pp. 110-127; Emergency Regulations, *New Zealand Statutes*, 1939, pp. 41-7; Strike and Lockout Emergency Regulations 1939, *Statutory Regulations*, 1939, pp. 847-9; Labour Legislation Emergency Regulations 1939, *Statutory Regulations*, 1939, p. 735; Labour Legislation Suspension Order 1939, *Statutory Regulations*, 1939, p. 736.

Good Clothes are Good Business: Gender, Consumption and Appearance in the Office, 1918–39

Danielle Sprecher

For both women and men, the popular cliché of 'dressing for success' is a well-worn one in business. The ways in which people modify their outward appearance beyond the simple necessity of covering the body for protection and comfort are constrained by cultural, historical and social norms. By locating dress and appearance in a wider social and historical context, this study goes beyond the purely narrative, pictorial and élite tendencies of much fashion history. New Zealand writing about the history of fashion has consisted largely of either narrative histories of dress, outlining progressions of style, or accounts that treat fashion and appearance as an exclusively feminine affair.[1] Men's clothed appearance has largely been ignored. In 1945 Gordon Mirams denied that New Zealand men had any interest in clothing or fashion and for the most part his assertion has been uncontested, at least in the academic literature.[2] Histories of masculinity in New Zealand have concentrated instead on the physical male body, especially in sport and war.[3] In contrast, this chapter challenges the usual assumption linking fashion, concern with appearance and femininity, and considers the implications for definitions of masculinity as well. Rather than concentrating simply on clothing and dress, the ways appearances have been constructed and represented and the consumption of those appearances are also discussed.

The problems with New Zealand studies of dress are typical of much fashion history. Newer accounts, however, have introduced wider issues of culture and the relationships between the body, clothing, identity, appearance and consumption.[4] More complex approaches to gender have been employed, as has an increasing recognition of the importance of fashion and appearance to definitions of both masculinity and femininity. Material evidence over the years demonstrates that men, as well as women, have

In this 1928 photograph, the female secretary's jacket, blouse and necktie mimics the attire of her male boss.
Gordon Burt Collection, Alexander Turnbull Library, National Library of New Zealand, Te Puna Mātauranga o Aotearoa, G-1572-1/1.

constructed their appearance and have conformed to fashionable images.[5] Gender conventions and the oppositions by which they are defined are signalled through men's and women's appearance. Like other gendered conventions, the codes of appearance and dress are relational. Differences in clothing have reinforced physical and social differences between men and women and are inextricably tied to the cultural enactments of masculinity and femininity. The use of gender as an analytical tool, particularly its use as a relational concept, and the problematisation of masculinity and femininity, have changed the way in which appearance is viewed.[6]

The interwar period in New Zealand was a time of major change and upheaval. During these decades the cumulative effects of the social, economic, technological and demographic developments of the late nineteenth and early twentieth century became increasingly obvious and began to have a significant impact on New Zealand society. Erik Olssen, in his survey of the period between 1890 and 1940, argues that, by the 1920s, New Zealand society can be accurately described as modern.[7] The most common defining aspect of modernity is its fixation with change, and a constant concern with newness, the present and the future, rather than the past. The department store was one of the institutions that epitomised modernity. During the 1920s and 1930s, department stores were remodelled and extensively modernised. Large imposing buildings were erected, which became premier shopping venues and attractions in urban areas. These stores were marvels of modern technological innovation, containing escalators, lifts and huge window displays blazing with electric light. They were filled with numerous departments of consumer durables and expendables, such as the increasingly important area of beauty products and cosmetics. They also offered new services to customers including toilets, tearooms and restaurants, car parking, free buses, telephones, lounges, fashion shows and children's playgrounds. They emphasised and encouraged consumerism and spending through substantial investments in displays, advertising and promotion. Some stores made buying even easier by introducing time payment.[8] These changes and developments were not necessarily uniform. Consumerism and modernity were substantially represented as white: Maori participation was invisible and Maori were represented as traditional as opposed to modern. But the context of self-conscious modernity during this time is important in considering gendered appearance, and the ways that representations of gender were displayed for consumption.

Another area that became identified as modern was the office. According to some figures, by 1926 up to 45 per cent of the workforce were engaged in the tertiary sector of the economy.[9] Auckland in particular saw a boom in office building during the 1920s.[10] Office work and office workers were becoming a recognisable and important part of the modernising economy and what these workers wore helped to 'define and redefine' gender boundaries.[11] In the public sphere of work, clothing has not always been worn purely for reasons of practicality or efficiency; what is deemed to be appropriate attire is often culturally prescribed.[12] The white-collar sector of business and office work has been no exception. The appearance of the businessman or male office worker in New Zealand has been characterised by the modern tailored suit. Three- or two-piece, coupled with a plain shirt and tie, the man's suit is an emblem of white-collar work and masculinity. Conformity, regularity and conservatism have been the prescriptions for office menswear. New Zealand women working in the white-collar environment have also been subject to codes of appearance. Unlike men, women have not had a single marker such as the suit and changing definitions of femininity have been crucial to shifts in women's correct business attire.

Recently, greater historical attention has been paid to the importance of men's appearance in definitions of masculinity.[13] During the nineteenth century, the modern men's suit of a sack-type coat and trousers of the same material became the standard dress for office and business wear. Men dressed to confirm their involvement in the new industrial order; from the 1880s there was more concern with men's participation in the business/office workplace, 'which required a suitably serious and practical outlook and appearance'.[14] Part of this new appearance was the adoption of dark and sombre colours in direct contrast to the lighter and brighter tones worn by women.[15] It has been argued persuasively that one of the reasons this occurred was a fear of ridicule. Jo Paoletti's study of men's clothing change in late-nineteenth-century America found that the old models of men's clothing were challenged by a new model of masculinity represented by the adoption of the business suit.[16] The suit also became a sign of modernity. Anne Hollander makes the point that the tailored suit set a standard of sartorial modernity that women's clothing achieved only in the 1930s.[17] It was loose-fitting but streamlined, followed the form of the body and allowed ease of movement. Moreover, the business suit became a neutral form of dress and a comparatively desexualised one.[18] During this period women's bodies became more sexualised, while the uniform and exclusively masculine suit became the clothed norm against which women in the office were defined. By the early twentieth century, in New Zealand and elsewhere, the image of the suited businessman had become a familiar representation of authoritative masculinity.

In New Zealand throughout the interwar period, advertisements and clothing advice directed towards white-collar men emphasised the importance of having a correct appearance for business and career success. One writer considered that too many men 'regard clothes as merely a covering, instead of garments which can make or mar their appearance, and which often play a big part in hindering or developing their career'.[19] Earlier, Geo. Fowlds Ltd, a men's outfitters in Auckland, had launched a campaign to educate men to dress better. One of the brochures they published to further their aims was reprinted in 1926 in the *New Zealand Draper, Clothier and Boot Retailer*, a trade journal for retailers. 'The Best Dressed Man in the World' contained photographs of the then Prince of Wales correctly dressed for various occasions, with quotes about the importance of being well dressed: 'Business success of any kind requires that a man should be well dressed'; 'Clothes beget confidence. Clothes overcome obstacles. The business world makes way for the well dressed man. He carries the hall mark of prosperity. He invites and receives consideration. He advertises success. Clothes do not make the man – they advertise him. Ill-fitting clothes advertise carelessness; shabby clothes, poverty; freakish clothes, shallowness.'[20] Men could be transformed through their clothing, just as advertising persuaded women they could be transformed through beauty products. 'The Same Man – But What a Difference a Smart Suit Makes!' declared the Farmers' Trading Company, illustrating the advertisement with a man dressed in an impeccable suit.[21]

The idea that a man's good appearance was essential to achievement remained consistent through to the 1930s. And men had to buy that appearance. The business suit clearly represented an authoritative white-collar masculinity that had been strengthened and intensified because of its conservative, and largely unchanged, nature. Dorothy Dix in the *New Zealand Woman's Weekly* felt no compunction in declaring that: 'it is because we all instinctively dress our part that makes it a pretty safe bet to judge people by their clothes'. She continued by arguing that if a man 'is slovenly, if he is unshaven and unshorn, if there are spots on his waistcoat, and his linen is soiled, he is almost invariably lazy, unwilling to work or take trouble about anything, and generally no-account'. On the other hand, 'if a man is always immaculately dressed, if his clothes are well chosen, though cheap, if his shoes are polished and his clothes pressed, if he has made the very best he can of his circumstances, then he is a good man to hire, go into business with, or marry. He will succeed.'[22] The *Ladies Mirror* men's fashion pages were adamant that good dressing enhanced confidence which, in turn, 'naturally increases ability' and 'will open the way to a more complete life, both within and outside of business circles'.[23]

This theme was echoed in advertisements and in business literature, particularly during the 1930s. 'Good clothes are good business' declared an advertisement for Gifford tailors in a 1932 edition of the *Auckland Chamber of Commerce Journal*. 'No one knows the value of clothes more than the successful business-man', it continued.[24] The shoe company Hannahs named their line of men's business shoes 'Conquest', ensuring that the authority and manliness of the businessman was affirmed.[25] Hallensteins argued that their suits were a good investment: 'Invest in better appearance for yourself – it's a proved business asset!'[26] The illustration accompanying the advertisement for Klipper ties was more explicit. A businessman sitting at an imposingly large desk intently scrutinises the tie of the hopeful applicant opposite, the direction of his vision indicated by a dotted line.[27]

It was not just advertising that played up the importance of appearance to the success of the businessman. The September 1933 issue of the *Commerce Journal* was subtitled the 'Business men's apparel number' and contained numerous articles considering the importance of correct attire to the modern businessman and giving advice on how to achieve this. J. R. Rendell argued that, although the older businessman might consider that he had achieved success without worrying about clothes, the younger generation was 'fast qualifying as exponents of good style and dress'.[28] Anxiety about the deteriorating economic situation and the increasing availability of cheaper, stylish clothing encouraged retailers to stress the importance of dress and appearance. In 1935 Hugh Wright, Jnr. continued the theme in 'Personal Appearance – An Aid to Business'. He addressed the 'executives of to-morrow', commenting that 'it will probably be through personal appearance that they will have their first opportunity of showing their ability'. Having a good appearance was essential to the modern business world. It showed that these young executives had 'personality and ambition, and confidence in their ability to rise to yet greater heights if given the chance'. He finished the article with an appeal to the men of the Chamber of Commerce to become more 'clothes conscious', to 'show your fellow citizens how important such pride is, and how greatly it contributes to success in the business world of to-day'.[29]

Buying a suit was a ritualistic affair. It confirmed a particular type of male status and masculinity. During the immediate aftermath of the First World

War, New Zealand men were explicitly targeted as consumers by men's outfitters and tailors. They were encouraged to exchange their military uniform for the 'uniform' lounge and business suit. In 1919, Fowlds reassured men: 'Back to Civil Life. It sounds good, and it IS good. It gives a man a comfortable feeling to know that he can throw aside the shackles of Military Discipline – that he has done his duty as a BRITISHER – and that he is "a free man." The Clothing Question is now to be considered – and it is here that Fowlds can help you.'[30] Later in the year an advertisement for Hugh Wright Ltd stated: 'The Government Clothes the Soldier and Hugh Wright the Civilian'. This was illustrated by a man in military uniform looking into a full-length mirror and his civilian-suited reflection: 'You may wish to keep your Service togs as an heirloom, but you'll welcome the change into "civvies" and the resumption of civilian attire'.[31] The change into 'civvies' would not undermine masculinity if the 'civilian attire' was a suit.

Looking at the British tailor Montague Burton, Frank Mort and Peter Thompson found that, during the 1950s, the 'initiation into the culture of the suit was part of a broader initiation rite into manhood . . . purchase of "the suit" was a public sign of male status'.[32] This event was also important in the lives of young men before the Second World War. As a 1924 advertisement for the men's outfitters Falkner & Co. showed: 'His first Suit with Long Trousers. How proud he feels when he dons his first Suit with long trousers, particularly when he knows that they fit perfectly, and make him look smart and manly.'[33] By the 1930s the shift made from school to work, and the donning of the suit, was more dramatic. 'He's starting out in LIFE!' declared the headline of an advertisement for department store George Court's:

It's an immensely big step, that first step from schoolroom to job. Your boy will need more than just luck to help him make it firmly and confidently. His whole future is bound up with it . . . success or failure. You can't do much to help him once he's stepped out into life, but you can see that he starts off with fair chances. You can see that he's well dressed – good clothes give him self-confidence and command respect.[34]

The accompanying photograph showed a suited father proudly shaking hands with his newly suited son in front of the looming shadow of a schoolmaster. The youth's suit exactly resembled that of the older man.

The uniformity and sobriety of men's clothing contrasted with the ever-changing fashions associated with femininity. 'The Man About Town', writing the men's fashion column in the *Ladies Mirror*, complained in 1929 that the 'subject of men's fashions is always one likely to provoke discussion, and very frequently adverse criticism, by those who think it effeminate for a man to take an interest in his clothes, except from a purely practical stand-point of neatness and tidiness. . . . The trouble is that a select few so-called "well-dressed men" are so perfectly immaculate in a feminine way that they arouse the ire of more masculine types.'[35] This threat of effeminacy meant men's clothes tended to be conservative whereas some level of fashionability was considered important for female office workers. Female contemporar-ies often lamented the dullness of men's clothing. In 1928 Joan Kennedy declared in the *Ladies Mirror* that man 'condemns himself to drabness and heavy materials . . . Sartorial tyranny holds him to-day – a conservative clinging to drabness.'[36] That same year it was argued that whereas modern woman had 'thrown off the mid-Victorian vogue to stiff-necked collars, whalebone-ribbed corsets, pink flannel petticoats, and long skirts', modern man 'still continues to wear what his grandfather wore – style only has changed . . . Thus every business man's suit nowadays must be in three pieces, neither more nor less, unless he openly scorns convention or is an exceptionally bold young man.'[37] Men's business suits were subject to some fashionable variation, but the conservative nature of their dress, and the lack of change, was important in upholding the power and strength of the suited businessman's masculine image.

Stability was represented as one of the keynotes of male participation in modern consumer culture. In a survey of advertisements appearing in vari-ous American media during the 1920s and 1930s, Roland Marchand found that the businessman attired in a suit consistently appeared as generic man, or 'Mr. Everyman'.[38] The association of the business suit with masculinity, status and power meant that it was an effective buffer against any perceived threat of effeminacy. This was especially the case when men were being targeted and represented as consumers. Contemporaries associated con-sumerism with femininity. Like Australia, the United States and Britain, New Zealand saw an increase in advertising, the growth of a mass market, modernisation of retailing and the rise of the department store in this pe-riod. Advertisers and retailers constructed both male and female consumers in distinctly gendered ways. Representations of femininity emphasised the naturalness of shopping and its pleasurable nature. This was especially the case with fashion and beauty products, which were deemed to be the pri-mary object of desire for women. Despite the usual construction of New Zealand masculinity as rough, practical and uncaring of appearance, during the interwar period retailers and advertisers experimented with images of the stylish and fashionable man who cared about how he looked. This image was not dominant, but it was used to sell men all forms of attire. Care did have to be taken that these representations did not cross the line into effeminacy and that the manliness of the correctly attired man was established. This was particularly the case for men buying a business suit, where the modernity of the office required an up-to-date appearance, not a 'slovenly' one. The emphasis was placed firmly on the power and success a good suit could ensure.

Department stores and men's clothing stores catered for male shopping habits and concerns. In general, despite the increasing scholarly interest in early-twentieth-century consumption, men have been ignored as consumers in the interwar period. In contrast, contemporary literature concerned with the selling of men's clothing recognised the male shopper as well as his female counterpart. One article classified three types of male customer: the careful dresser, the slovenly dresser and the 'sheik type'. The salesman was advised to use these classifications to decide on the sales technique: 'Give the careful dresser enough time to make decisions. Work fast with the slovenly dresser, because he is anxious to get it over. And with the "sheik", give him all the rope he wants.'[39] These three categorisations of the male consumer give a valuable insight into the different ideals of masculinity between the wars. The most common masculine stereotype was that of the slovenly dresser, the man who did not dress well or care about his appearance. To target this man, retailers used women. The careful dresser could be advertised to directly, and appealed to with copy that employed 'dress for success' sales methods. The 'sheik' was the exception: interested in clothing to a dangerously feminine degree, he required little guidance. The fact that retailers in the 1920s and 1930s were aware of these three types and used them in their advertising throws doubt upon the ubiquity of the usual stereotype of the rugby-playing, hard-drinking bloke who did not care a toss about what he wore or what he bought. The stereotype we are familiar with is only the 'slovenly' construction of masculinity: the man who proved his masculinity 'through work, sport, drinking and war, through a robust physique and fatherhood'.[40]

The masculine consumer existed in the so-called 'Adamless Eden' of the department store.[41] In her history of women and department stores in the United States, Susan Porter Benson found that, by the 1910s, there was a consensus as to the layout of department stores: 'Street floors offered cosmetics, notions, gloves, hosiery, jewelry, and other small wares – glamour and impulse items to waylay women on their way to the upper floors – and

Good clothes are *good business*

No one knows the value of clothes more than the successful business - man. Gifford - tailored suits are the type styled in accordance with the expressed wish of keen business - men. Cut in alert, yet conservative lines, these suits show the way to success in dress, and at the same time with welcome economy. Our tailoring charges have recently been reduced to conform with conditions. Come in and see the new materials.

Business Suits

Tailored To Order from 6 guineas

GIFFORD
LIMITED
The Tailors of Vulcan Lane

This Milne & Choyce advertisement stresses the masculinity of its men's department ('The Man's Floor'), disassociating it from feminine overtones.
New Zealand Herald, 27 September 1934.

clothing and furnishings for men who were presumed too timid to venture farther into the store'.[42] Gail Reekie has argued that, by the 1930s in Australia, it was an accepted 'psychological fact' that men had an aversion to walking through women's departments.[43] Merchants in New Zealand followed these conventions.

Retailers believed that they had to adapt their stores to enable men to shop. A 1923 advertisement for the House of Flackson, an Auckland department store, demonstrated the lengths to which retailers went to ensure that men felt comfortable shopping. Announcing the opening of its 'handsome new building', the store asked: 'Did You Know? ... THAT in our new premises we have a Men's Suit and Overcoat Department that is absolutely separate from the remainder of the establishment, and that has a street entrance all of its own'.[44] While the office environment increasingly mixed men and women, stores constructed separate masculine spaces. Many department stores developed what they called 'men's shops' within the store designed to cater to male consumers. For example, the Auckland department store Milne & Choyce advertised their men's department as 'The Man's Floor'.[45] Display managers were warned to '[a]void the use of flowers with men's wear merchandise. It gives the merchandise a too effeminate appearance.'[46] Menswear shops also had to ensure they preserved their 'manly atmosphere'. The interior of the establishment was to 'conform rather to the reception room than the shop' and contain '[g]ood furniture, a carpet, a table bearing copies of current clothing and general publications, and, perhaps, an easy chair or two . . .', while, a 'box of cigarettes from which the customer may help himself is a surprisingly effective method of putting the customer at his ease and convincing him that here is the atmosphere in which he can buy his clothes with pleasure'.[47] The masculine atmosphere of the men's outfitters was regarded as an environment that allowed men to consume items otherwise tainted by associations of effeminacy. It was suggested that a menswear store was the best place for a man to buy men's toilet preparations. The 'masculine security of his favourite man's shop' would assure a man that the products 'are absolutely safe for him to use'.[48] The effete male had no place in retailing or in advertising images.

The 1920s and 1930s saw the recognition and intensification of the masculine symbolism of the businessmen's suit. The conservative nature of the suit and the lack of significant change in tailoring during the period, apart from a few minor style details, made it easier to entrench as a symbol of white-collar masculinity and power. Advertisers spoke to male white-collar consumers in ways that identified them as a legitimate market and reinforced the cultural importance of the business suit. Buying a suit was a special event, particularly for a young man, and was conducted in very carefully created masculine surroundings. Masculine consumers were constructed in ways that defined them against the impulsive and frivolous image of the feminine consumer. The idea of 'dress for success' and its embodiment in the three-piece suit confirmed masculinity in opposition to threats of effeminacy from the 'feminine' consumption of clothing.

Just as the business suit became vital to the definition of a white-collar masculinity in New Zealand, the clothes and appearance of women who worked in offices aimed to reinforce certain ideas of femininity. While men in the office were required to conform in quite rigid ways to certain standards of dress, women often found themselves in ambiguous situations. Women, and especially young single women, were taking a wider role in public life and had greater access to public space. An increasing proportion of the thousands of predominantly young and single women who entered New

Zealand's paid workforce in the early twentieth century were employed in offices.[49] In 1921 the occupational category of 'clerk' was second only to 'domestic servant' in the list of principal occupations for women.[50] A young woman sitting behind a typewriter became the emblem of this changing femininity; she was represented as being young, 'modern', earning her own living, freer and more independent than her mother. Women entering the paid workforce, especially in the white-collar sector, were forced to develop a style of clothing that could be worn in the new office setting. Women's clothing, which was commonly viewed as frivolous, decorative and subject to the whims of fashion, had to adapt to the practical and professional constraints of the office environment. Women's dress could not, however, mimic male attire exactly because of the symbolic importance of the business suit to white-collar masculinity and because of women's subordinate position in the office.

These social and economic changes were marked by changes in the representations and definitions of femininity. There was a close relationship between women's increasingly public role and the seductive new consumer culture of the period. Fashion and the new female accessories of cosmetics and beauty products epitomised this new consumerism. The modern office-working woman was subject to these changing modes of femininity as, by the 1930s, youth, attractiveness and sexual allure all became increasingly important in idealised representations of women.[51]

By the 1920s, the modernity of women as public beings was widely noted. This was especially the case for women office workers. They were considered to be 'modern' in their clothing, their actions, their consumption and their paid work. The *Ladies Mirror* during the 1920s constantly referred to 'the modern girl'. There were articles attempting to define who and what she was and what made her different from other girls, both present and past. Paid work and less cumbersome, confining clothing were two of the commonly cited attributes of the modern girl. An article titled 'The Modern Girl' argued that, in the past, it was the 'artificial thwarting of the masculine in women that not only made girls wish they were boys, but also bred the feminist; it gave us the "advanced" woman and the modern girl – the wage-earning, sports-loving girl – as well as the professional woman, the woman in public affairs'.[52] J. Jefferson Farjeon, in 'The Ultra-Modern Girl', considered that the modern girl 'has during the past dozen years, either acquired or increased her regard for: – Drinking and smoking; Paint and powder; Slang; Pastimes demanding physical vigour; Work, apart from the household variety; Individual independence and freedom of action; Speed;

Late hours'.[53] Another sign of modernity was the dramatic break by young women with the style of their mothers and the traditional notion of adult women putting their hair up. The 'bob' and 'shingle' fashions for short hair were avidly followed during the 1920s and were significantly different from the long hair and cumbersome styling of the pre-First World War period. These modern women were not necessarily viewed with approval, however. One writer deplored the changes that were occurring in fashionable femininity, especially the use of cosmetics in the new consumerist beauty culture: 'Years ago, while women may have been vain, as they went out to show off their clothes; they are now merely depraved, as they go out to show off themselves'.[54]

The modernisation of the office involved the use of specialised machinery and tasks with which women came to be associated. Advertisements for typewriters and other business machines were usually accompanied by illustrations of attractive young women manipulating the keys. The Imperial typewriter was photographed with a smiling young woman demonstrating its efficiency, as was the Sundstrand Accounting Machine.[55] Women were almost inseparable from business machines. The *Ladies Mirror* was enthusiastic about the entry of women into the business world and the importance of the typewriter in their success. A 1931 editorial argued that it was the typewriter that put women on the direct road to independence and emancipation.[56] 'The modern girl never has a moment's anxiety these days', declared an advertisement for Southalls sanitary pads illustrated by the image of a young girl sitting at a typewriter.[57] The image of a girl in front of a typewriter became one of the recognised representations of feminine modernity.

These young working women had disposable income to spend on their appearance and significantly more freedom to choose what they wore than many women in other occupations. The working dress of nurses, shop girls and factory girls was rigidly defined by uniforms and overalls. Office girls were generally believed to dress well, and to actively participate in modern consumption. A report from London published in the *Draper* in 1928 made the point that the English working girl at least 'has an excellent sense for the right thing in dress. She is out for simplicity and simple good effects, not ostentation, and if she likes to spend five guineas on a coat which is a replica of the costly simplicity of the 50 guineas model worn by her favourite actress, why shouldn't she?' Moreover, '[t]o all intents and purposes there is very little difference in appearance – whatever the difference in dress bills – between the working girl and the society debutante, which is really a score for the former'.[58] The *New Zealand Woman's Weekly* was also positive about improvements in the working girl's appearance. In a 1933 article titled 'Girls Who Earn Their Livings. A Change for the Better Since the War', Mrs James Rodney argued that the working girl was a 'picture of neatness, with well-cared for complexion. Smart silk hose and well-cut clothes. There is no more attractive collection of healthy, good-looking girls anywhere than those who step off their buses to-day in the early hours of the morning.'[59] In the late 1930s, the Farmers' Trading Company even organised a 'Business Girls' Fashion Show' at which 'all the new advance spring and summer fashion goods suitable both in style and price for the business girl will be shown'.[60]

These new, modern, working women were frequently advised about behaviour and dress in the office. Advice to working women about the appropriate attire for the office during the interwar period remained largely the same: articles and comments in women's magazines and fashion pages emphasised the need for women to fit in with the businessman's suited seriousness and yet not exactly reproduce the masculine emblem of the suit. Women earned less than men, were usually young and were often in positions of lower status. They had to ensure they did not upset the gender order too dramatically by what was termed 'the invasion of women' into men's so-called 'paths of industry and business'.[61] Women had to 'strike the balance between business-like conservatism and feminine sexual attractiveness' when deciding how to present themselves.[62] In 1919 the women's page of the *New Zealand Herald* carried some advice for 'the business girl' in terms of her special clothing needs. Those necessities, the coat and skirt, should be 'made very simply of material of a dark colour, or, more economical still, of a gentleman's suiting'. She also required two or three blouses and a 'simple frock of a dark material'. These sober and masculine styles of clothing were important because of the requirement for women not to be excessively feminine in the office. It was suggested that they have a few good clothes and that they should not try to follow fashion too closely. Individuality, however, was also important, and young women were advised to ensure they looked their best by wearing 'what is becoming to you'.[63]

Images of office workers also demonstrated the middle path that women had to take. A 1928 photograph by Gordon Burt showed a man in a dark suit and tie while his female secretary wore a softer version of his business suit: a jacket, blouse and necktie.[64] Neatness, quietness of colour and practicality were the requirements for the clothing of the office girl; fashionability was of less importance. The *New Zealand Woman's Weekly* gave an illustrated example of appropriate attire with captions such as: 'A small cheeky hat on clusters of curls is wrong'; 'The office is not a ballroom! High heeled slippers are out of place'; 'Glaring necklaces and ruffled collars – No!'; and 'Do not use the office to wear out old evening or afternoon frocks. Plain, becoming styles are essential.'[65] In a later beauty column, the ideal appearance and manner of the businesswoman was outlined: 'Dress well but simply . . . clothes do not need to be expensive, but they must be in good taste, with simple lines and becoming colour'. Other suggestions included not wearing too much make-up or high French heels, keeping seams in stockings straight and thinking of 'perfume as a social-hour exigency, not a business day one'.[66]

While men had to ensure they were not effeminate, women in offices ran the risk of being considered frivolous, silly and too feminine. They were encouraged to compartmentalise their lives in ways that men were not. Men were never urged to be excessively interested in their appearance. In contrast, women in the office were expected to moderate and tone down what they wore, while out of the office acceptable expressions of femininity included avidly following and consuming fashion. 'Girl Clerks', a 1921 article in the Farmers' Trading Company staff magazine the *Optimist*, contained numerous complaints about female office workers. The author argued that while a male clerk started work swiftly, his female counterpart did not: 'First there's the hair to arrange and fluff up, the blouse to pull straight, the complexion to examine and restore with a surreptitious dab of powder'. Moreover, the writer was anxious that his staff 'should know that plain shirt blouses are much more to their employer's mind than fancy affairs of lace and open-work with more or less pink and blue ribbony things below. I would like to stick up a notice, "no powder or lip salve to be used during office hours".'[67] The danger was being identified with the 'butterfly brigade', as a 1928 article put it: 'Feminine vanity is all very well in its place, but it should be sternly repressed in the neighbourhood of filing cabinets and typewriters'.[68] By the late 1930s, similar complaints were still appearing. An article in the *Ladies Mirror* argued that women office workers were wearing, 'sleeveless, low-cut dresses, quantities of barbaric jewellery, and other frivolities' which were out of place in the office. Moreover, it was not just their clothes that caused problems; other associated elements of female office workers' femininity were also annoying: 'Boy friends, cinemas, permanent waves, dances and what not – yes I am all for them – BUT NOT IN OFFICE HOURS'.[69]

The new consumer culture of beauty products and accessible fashion associated with femininity was problematic for female office workers. While

representations of femininity in advertising, films, and magazines all idealised the fashionable and 'made-up' woman, cosmetics in the office were a
subject of tension. The question of the appropriateness of make-up at work
made an appearance in the *New Zealand Woman's Weekly*. 'Indignant', a correspondent to the regular beauty page, wrote that she had been asked to
forgo the bright nail polish she wore during the business day, and another
girl had been told to do her powdering and rouging in the dressing room.
In reply Antoinette Donnelly wrote:

> Powdering and making-up is part of a ritual that should be performed be-
> hind closed doors. Whatever may be said for the privileges extended to the
> coquettish type, who pulls out her vanity-case at a supper table, this has noth-
> ing to do with office managers and office behaviour. . . . There is a time and
> place for everything. Paint the nails like a fire alarm after hours if you choose,
> but use your head about conservative decoration when you are on the seri-
> ous job of earning your money. No one is asking you not to use powder,
> rouge, and lipstick, nor to tint the nails [*sic*]. But remember that good form
> for occasions is also part of the smart girl's programme of smartness.[70]

Although women office workers could be overly obsessed with how
they looked, they still had to demonstrate their femininity through some
concern for their appearance. Increasingly they also had to be sexually attractive. During the interwar period the ideal of femininity underwent a
shift. Marilyn Lake has argued that, in Australia in the 1920s and 1930s,
advertisements demonstrated this change. The importance of having a youthful appearance was stressed in representations of femininity, as was the new
emphasis on heterosexual allure as men entered the advertisement's frame.[71]
This also appears to have been the case in New Zealand. Women rarely, if
ever, appeared in advertisements for menswear. Women, however, were informed that to win and hold a man's admiration they had to keep youthful
and that they could achieve this through the use of Max Factor cosmetics.[72]
Men were always watching: 'His eyes are always on your hair', declared an
advertisement for Sheena Shampoo. 'A handsome head of hair is always the
target of admiring masculine eyes.'[73] Men's eyes had to be kept admiring,
and women had to ensure that their appearance was attractive and appealing at all times. This could be achieved through the purchase of products.
Advertisements told of men's desires for 'sparkling white teeth', 'tempting
lips' and light fair hair, which gives '47% more sex appeal'.[74] Brands such as
Icilma cream, Tangee make-up and Savage lipstick, which 'keeps lips excit-
ingly red as long as they need be', were marketed nationally.[75] Femininity

became glamorous, alluring and inextricably linked with consumerism as espoused by Hollywood movie stars and advertising models.

This new femininity was concentrated in the modern office. In 'Smart Clothes for the Business Girl. She Must Dress to Please Women and Men Alike' Lady Chaytor warned that the office worker is 'in the position of having to steer a middle course between looking as though she pays too much attention to dress on the one hand, and running the risk of being a trifle dowdy on the other'.[76] The importance of sexual allure for women was increasingly stressed; dowdiness became unacceptable. As Valerie Steele points out, the twentieth century saw attractiveness in a working woman becoming a more and more desirable attribute.[77] Similar developments occurred in New Zealand. An advertisement for shoes in the *Ladies Mirror* was titled: 'Men quickly notice the difference when women start wearing The Arch Preserver Shoe'; the accompanying illustration showed a businessman entering his office with eyes only for the young immaculately dressed woman in front of his desk, with his busily working typist in the background.[78] The situations vacant column in the *New Zealand Herald* carried a number of advertisements for female workers that listed 'appearance' as one of the requirements, effectively encouraging women to commodify and 'sell' themselves on the basis of their looks. 'Office Girl, smart, wanted, of good appearance, capable of looking after books' was one such request.[79] A girl's appearance was to be treated with care because of its importance to her career: 'Complexions and figures are valuable business assets to the girl who works in an office' working women were advised in 1937. Both had to be maintained through correct diet and exercise.[80] According to 'Charm in the Office', '[w]hen one businessman says to another, "I wish I had a secretary like yours", it's as nice a compliment as could be paid to a girl'. Furthermore, there are 'lots of things besides brains and training and experience that help a girl to get ahead in the workaday world. Their sum total is charm.' The writer defined 'charm' as: 'The way you dress and apply your make-up, your manner of talking, and how you get along with other people'. The article went on to detail the precise manner in which women in the office ought to dress and behave. Clothes should be 'becoming without being flashy or too elaborate', and make-up was to be applied with the object of 'looking as pretty as you can, but not obviously made up'.[81]

Dorothy Dix was scathing about what she considered to be slovenliness in women and bluntly made the point that being attractive would assist a girl in her working life. 'A girl's looks are her capital in these days. They are her letter of introduction, her recommendation . . . if she is sloppy and frowsy, if her hair is uncombed and her hands not manicured . . . she is too hard on the eyes of any man to want to spend his days looking at [her] across a counter or a desk.'[82] 'Trixie the Typiste', in an advertisement for Nugget shoe polish, was allegedly an object of admiration simply because of her bright, shiny shoes. The copy, however, told a different story:

> She fingers the keys
> With the greatest of ease
> And taps out a tune from her notes,
> She's hard to refuse –
> From her head to her shoes
> The boss on her daintiness dotes.[83]

Described in a diminutive manner and register, the dainty typist was valued equally for her attractiveness as for her skill at the typewriter. A 1938 article outlined the importance of 'personal packaging'. Miss Bracket's career was in danger because of her neglect of her appearance until she was rescued by 'the amazing Miss Calderwood' who informed her that her clothes were 'very bad, and you wear them as if you just don't care. Your hair looks as though you didn't care about it either.' She then got right to the point: 'Tell me, are you afraid of the men in the store, or do men just bore you?' Miss Calderwood considered that, to capitalise on their sex, 'women in offices ought to attract men, not repel them'. Under her tutelage, Miss Bracket's story had a happy ending; she became a successful buyer and 'she also got a man'.[84]

But the issue of sex and women's attractiveness increasingly became a problem for women office workers during the late 1920s and 1930s. Although a young woman entering an office had freedoms the shop girl and other female workers did not have, she also faced new tensions owing to her physical proximity to her male co-workers. These types of problems tempered the insistence on attractiveness and led to an emphasis on a particular style of dress and make-up for work. Reasons were given in 'Beauty for the Girl in Business' in 1936: 'There is no individuality in business – you are part of a machine, and must not draw attention to yourself. If your hands are too brilliantly adorned, you will be attracting attention to yourself, and sometimes it may be unwelcome attention.'[85] Advertisements for make-up aimed at young women emphasised the fine line between charm and cheapness. Potential consumers were assured that Tangee lipstick would provide 'lips that appeal to men' but would not give them 'that painted

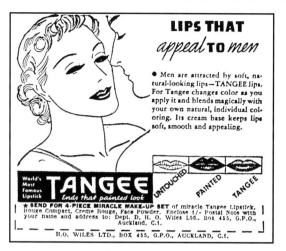

Women are reassured that, by using Tangee lipstick, they will attract men without appearing 'painted' or frivolous.
New Zealand Herald, 10 January 1936.

look'.[86] Instead, a writer in the *Ladies Mirror* in 1931 argued that women who used sex appeal to help them get a job had to anticipate the possibility of negative consequences. She wished that 'the attractive women, who deliberately use sex-appeal . . . would not be so loud in their complaints when too much in that line is expected of them. . . . The use of limited sex-appeal must be something of a gamble, and gamblers must learn to lose gaily.'[87] It was not only danger from men that young women had to guard against, as one article explained. The use of bright colours could distract men from their work, but it could also annoy women superiors who 'are quick to resent clothes that suggest a "vampish" attitude'.[88] If women were too attractive they could cause problems in the office, which was still a male environment, their sexual allure upsetting the professional balance when the situation of men and women working together was still precarious. The masculinity of the office was still soberly suited, while the modern feminine office worker was more and more a sexually desirable object.

In the modernising office of the interwar period, men consolidated their image and power in the business suit. It came to represent a white-collar masculinity that, if dressed right, could ensure success. Just as women could transform themselves through their purchase of cosmetics and beauty products, men could transform themselves through the purchase of a well-cut business suit. Men as well as women participated in the consumer culture presented by department stores and advertising, but their consumption was segregated and carefully constructed to shore up masculinity. Although fashion was not as important for men, having a smart appearance was, and this had to be shopped for. The threat of effeminacy was carefully guarded against by the construction of an acceptable 'safe' masculinity for male shoppers. Women's very existence in the office was viewed as modern. The linkage of femininity with modernity, and especially the modernity of consumption, created tensions for women in the office. The representation of female office workers mirrored the increasing importance placed upon women's sexual attractiveness and their consumption of goods to achieve the right appearance. Women were enjoined to express their femininity in ways that intimated their sexuality but did not disrupt the workplace. Just as men were advised to be careful of their dress but not to be considered effeminate, women had to ensure that they could not be accused of masculinity or cheapness by exhibiting a moderate, compliant but nonetheless fashionable version of femininity through their appearance.

1   Doris McIntosh, 'Dress', *Making New Zealand. Pictorial Surveys of a Century*, 2, 23, 1940; Eve Ebbett, *In True Colonial Fashion: A Lively Look at What New Zealanders Wore*, Wellington, 1977; Jane Malthus, '"Bifurcated and Not Ashamed": Late Nineteenth Century Dress Reformers in New Zealand', *New Zealand Journal of History*, 23, 1, 1989, pp. 32-46; Fiona McKergow, 'Fashion and Femininity: The Sartorial Experiences of Elite and Middle Class Women in New Zealand, 1905-1928', MA research essay, University of Auckland, 1991; Fiona McKergow, 'Bodies at the Beach: A History of Swimwear', *Bearings*, 3, 4, 1991, pp. 16-22; Fiona McKergow, 'Women's Dress in New Zealand 1880-1930', *GRINZ Yearbook*, 1993, pp. 39-51; Sandra Coney, *Standing in the Sunshine: A history of New Zealand women since they won the vote*, Auckland, 1993, pp. 114-15, 150-61; Jane Malthus, 'Adaptation of European Women's Dress in New Zealand in the Colonial Period', PhD thesis, University of Otago, 1997.

2   Gordon Mirams, *Speaking Candidly: films and people in New Zealand*, Hamilton, 1945, p. 32.

3   For example, Kai Jensen, *Whole Men: The Masculine Tradition in New Zealand Literature*, Auckland, 1996, pp. 24-5; Jock Phillips, *A Man's Country? The Image of the Pakeha Male – A History*, revised edn, Auckland, 1996.

4   Elizabeth Wilson, *Adorned in Dreams: Fashion and Modernity*, Berkeley and Los Angeles, 1987; Jennifer Craik, *The Face of Fashion: Cultural Studies in Fashion*, London and New York, 1994; Margaret Maynard, *Fashioned from Penury: Dress as Cultural Practice in Colonial Australia*, Cambridge, 1994; Christopher Breward, *The Culture of Fashion: A New History of Fashionable Dress*, Manchester and New York, 1995.

5   Farid Cheoune, *A History of Men's Fashion*, trans. Deke Dusinberre, Paris, 1993.

6   See, for example, Claudia Brush Kidwell and Valerie Steele, eds, *Men and Women: Dressing the Part*, Washington D.C., 1989.

7   Erik Olssen, 'Towards a New Society', in Geoffrey W. Rice, ed., *The Oxford History of New Zealand*, 2nd edn, Auckland, 1992, p. 254.

8   Danielle Sprecher, 'The Right Appearance: Representations of Fashion, Gender and Modernity in Inter-war New Zealand, 1918–1939', MA thesis, University of Auckland, 1997, pp. 16-29.

9   Tom Brooking, 'Economic Transformation', in Rice, *The Oxford History of New Zealand*, p. 232.

10   E.W. Rogerson, 'Cosy Homes Multiply: A Study of Suburban Expansion in Western Auckland,

1918-31', MA thesis, University of Auckland, 1976, p. 18.

11 Wilson, *Adorned in Dreams*, p. 117.

12 Valerie Steele, 'Dressing For Work', in Kidwell and Steele, *Men and Women*, pp. 64–91.

13 Jo Paoletti, 'Ridicule and Role Models as Factors in American Men's Fashion Change, 1880-1910', *Costume*, 29, 1985; Frank Mort and Peter Thompson, 'Retailing, Commercial Culture and Masculinity in 1950s Britain: The Case of Montague Burton, the "Tailor of Taste" ', *History Workshop Journal*, 38, 1994, pp. 106-27; John Harvey, *Men in Black*, London, 1995; Frank Mort, *Cultures of Consumption: Masculinities and Social Space in Late Twentieth-Century Britain*, London and New York, 1996; David Kuchta, 'The Making of the Self-Made Man: Class, Clothing, and English Masculinity, 1688-1832', in Victoria de Grazia, with Ellen Furlough, ed., *The Sex of Things: Gender and Consumption in Historical Perspective*, Berkeley, 1996, pp. 54-78.

14 Craik, *The Face of Fashion*, pp. 178, 186.

15 Harvey, *Men in Black*, p. 195.

16 Paoletti, 'Ridicule and Role Models', p. 132.

17 Anne Hollander, *Sex and Suits: The Evolution of Modern Dress*, New York, 1995, p. 9.

18 Michael Roper, 'Yesterday's Model: Product Fetishism and the British Company Man, 1945-85', in Michael Roper and John Tosh, eds, *Manful Assertions: Masculinities in Britain since 1800*, London and New York, 1991, p. 195.

19 *Ladies Mirror (Mirror)*, June 1929, p. 66.

20 *New Zealand Draper, Clothier and Boot Retailer (Draper)*, September 1926, pp. 54-5.

21 *New Zealand Herald (NZH)*, 11 January 1926, p. 15.

22 *New Zealand Woman's Weekly (NZWW)*, 8 July 1937, p. 41.

23 *Mirror*, October 1930, p. 61.

24 *Auckland Chamber of Commerce Journal (Commerce Journal)*, September 1932, p. 20.

25 *Commerce Journal*, September 1933, inside front cover.

26 *Commerce Journal*, September 1934, inside back cover.

27 *Commerce Journal*, September 1936, p. 4.

28 *Commerce Journal*, September 1933, p. 2.

29 *Commerce Journal*, July 1935, p. 10.

30 *NZH*, 10 January 1919, p. 2.

31 *NZH*, 14 June 1919, p. 17.

32 Mort and Thompson, 'Retailing, Commercial Culture and Masculinity in 1950s Britain', p. 119.

33 *NZH*, 19 September 1924, p. 14.

34 *NZH*, 8 January 1938, p. 17.

35 *Mirror*, June 1929, p. 66.

36 *Mirror*, November 1928, p. 47.

37 *Mirror*, January 1928, p. 7.

38 Roland Marchand, *Advertising the American Dream: Making Way for Modernity, 1920-1940*, Berkeley, 1985, p. 189.

39 *Draper*, September 1933, p. 34.

40 Jensen, *Whole Men*, p. 40.

41 Susan Porter Benson, *Counter Cultures: Saleswomen, Managers, and Customers in American Department Stores 1890-1940*, Urbana, 1986, p. 75.

42 Benson, *Counter Cultures*, p. 44.

43 *Rydges Retail Merchandising Course*, Sydney, 1937, p. 16, cited in Gail Reekie, 'Impulsive Women, Predicable Men: Psychological Constructions of Sexual Difference in Sales Literature to 1930', *Australian Historical Studies*, 24, 97, 1991, p. 367.

44 *Mirror*, February 1923, p. 25.

45 *NZH*, 27 September 1934, p. 5.

46 *Draper*, May 1928, p. 47.

47 *Draper*, July 1931, pp. 30-1.

48 *Draper*, March 1936, p. 18.

49 See Erik Olssen, 'Women, Work and the Family 1880-1926', in Phillida Bunkle and Beryl Hughes, eds, *Women in New Zealand Society*, Auckland, 1980, pp. 162-6; Shannon R. Brown,

'Female Office Workers in Auckland, 1891-1936', MA thesis, University of Auckland, 1993, pp. 20-4, 154.

50 *Census*, 1921, 'Industries, Occupations and Unemployment', Part VIII, p. 8.

51 Martin Pumphrey, 'The Flapper, the Housewife and the Making of Modernity', *Cultural Studies*, 1, 2, 1987, pp. 179-94; Sally Alexander, 'Becoming a Woman in London in the 1920s and 1930s', in David Feldman and G. Stedman Jones, eds, *Metropolis London: Histories and Representations since 1800*, London, 1989, pp. 245-71; Marilyn Lake, 'Female Desires: The Meaning of World War II', *Australian Historical Studies*, 24, 95, 1990, pp. 267-84; Gail Reekie, 'Decently Dressed? Sexualised Consumerism and the Working Woman's Wardrobe 1919-1923', in Raelene Frances and Bruce Scates, eds, *Women, Work and the Labour Movement in Australia and Aotearoa/New Zealand*, Sydney, 1991, pp. 42-56; Kathy Peiss, 'Making Up, Making Over: Cosmetics, Consumer Culture, and Women's Identity', in de Grazia, *The Sex of Things*, pp. 311-36.

52 *Mirror*, November 1925, p. 69.

53 *Mirror*, April 1926, p. 44.

54 *Optimist*, September 1925, p. 7, Item 60/55, Box 9, Farmers' Trading Company Records, MS 1400, Auckland Institute and Museum (AIM), Auckland.

55 *Commerce Journal*, December 1935, p. 7; *Commerce Journal*, March 1938, inside back cover.

56 *Mirror*, June 1931, p. 9.

57 *NZWW*, 27 February 1936, p. 60.

58 *Draper*, May 1928, p. 7.

59 *NZWW*, 26 January 1933, p. 45.

60 *Farmers' Store News*, August 1937, p. 2, Item 144/55, Box 9, Farmers' Trading Company Records, MS 1400, AIM.

61 *Mirror*, January 1928, p. 7.

62 Reekie, 'Decently Dressed', p. 42.

63 *NZH*, 8 November 1919, Supplement, p. 4.

64 G 1572 1/1, Gordon Burt Collection, Alexander Turnbull Library, Wellington.

65 *NZWW*, 19 July 1934, p. 8.

66 *NZWW*, 21 March 1935, p. 21.

67 *Optimist*, January 1921, p. 7, Item 41/55, Box 9, Farmers' Trading Company Records, MS 1400, AIM.

68 *NZH*, 5 May 1928, Supplement, p. 6.

69 *Mirror*, June 1938, p. 42.

70 *NZWW*, 24 May 1934, p. 33.

71 Lake, 'Female Desires', pp. 272-4.

72 *Mirror*, March 1935, p. 62.

73 *Mirror*, March 1935, p. 67.

74 *Mirror*, October 1935, p. 66; *NZWW*, 17 January 1935, p. 46; *NZWW*, 24 November 1938, p. 73.

75 *NZWW*, 3 March 1938, p. 29.

76 *Mirror*, June 1929, p. 26.

77 Steele, 'Dressing For Work', p. 84.

78 *Mirror*, November 1926, p. iii.

79 *NZH*, 11 May 1928, p. 1.

80 *Mirror*, May 1937, p. 35.

81 *NZWW*, 16 December 1937, p. 40.

82 *NZWW*, 9 June 1938, p. 42.

83 *NZWW*, 25 February 1937, p. 58.

84 *NZWW*, 8 September 1938, p. 26.

85 *NZWW*, 9 April 1936, p. 29.

86 *NZH*, 10 January 1936, p. 3.

87 *Mirror*, December 1931, p. 88.

88 *NZWW*, 16 December 1937, p. 40.

Sweethearts, Soldiers, Happy Families: Gender and the Second World War

Deborah Montgomerie

There are unfortunately few wars where a man can take his wife with him.[1]

The mobilisation of New Zealand citizens during the Second World War was a profoundly gendered process. In particular, women received far more allowance for their private lives than men. While military mobilisation took some account of men's marital and parental status, all men aged 18 to 60 were eligible for industrial conscription, regardless of marital status or fatherhood. In contrast, women were never compelled to join the armed forces and the impact of industrial mobilisation on them was much less severe. Women over the age of 40, and women with children, were not required to register for work of national importance. Many childless women under 40 also found that they could use arguments about the extent of their domestic responsibilities to avoid industrial conscription or mitigate its impact on their lives.[2] Even when men and women worked side by side to contribute to the New Zealand war effort, contemporaries tended to regard their contributions as fundamentally different.

The gaps between men and women's wartime experiences, and the images of happy peacetime families around which those experiences coalesced, in turn shaped understandings of the nature of masculinity, femininity and family in the transition to peace. While most Pakeha believed the nation's only choice was to fight by Britain's side, wartime measures were seldom received with equanimity. In New Zealand, as in the other Allied countries, the period was characterised by a thoroughgoing anxiety about the war's long-term impact on society in general, and on gender relations in particular.[3] Despite the fact that men's lives were disrupted by the war far more than women's, there was a great deal of concern that the war was changing women's priorities. Cartoonists lampooned women in uniforms

163

Male and female experiences and memories of the Second World War were very different and heavily gendered, but the wartime emphasis on heterosexual courtship and socialising reassured people that romance would continue to flourish.
Alexander Turnbull Library, National Library of New Zealand,
Te Puna Matauranga o Aotearoa, C-23001.

and advertisers trotted out comforting images of Mum safeguarding the home front by making steaming cups of cocoa.[4] Humorists joked about married women preoccupied with war work to the extent that 'bachelor' husbands were mending their own clothes and cooking their own meals, single women so busy that only a lucky chap could get a date and post-war households where Mum would relax by the hearth of an evening, smoking her pipe, while Dad laboured in the kitchen resplendent in his apron.[5] These were dystopic satires, not images of a desirable gender order. Utopia was more likely to resemble the expatriate writer John Mulgan's dream of a New Zealand with 'more children in the sands and sunshine, more small farms, gardens, and cottages. Girls would wear bright dresses, men would talk quietly together. . . . They would fill the land and make it a nation.'[6]

The following discussion attempts to capture some of the ways that individual men and women thought and wrote about the war's intervention in their lives. I am deliberately inverting the usual emphasis on women's roles in studies of wartime gender relations by writing more about men than women.[7] Because contemporary ideas about appropriate behaviour for women relied so heavily on reversing what was thought appropriate for men, analysing masculinity will also help us understand femininity.[8]

Not all the materials employed are contemporary to the period. My analysis draws on a large body of sources dating from the 1940s, including private letters, diaries, published accounts, submissions to government and letters from newspapers and magazines. There is also a substantial and growing body of war memoirs published or recorded more recently, evidence of the extent to which the Second World War has occasioned personal and historical reflection on the part of the men and women who lived through it.[9] It is a truism that, in any period, convention inhibits the expression of some ideas while encouraging the expression of others; the post-1945 reflections on the war serve as a useful counterpoint to the contemporary sources. Most notably, the wartime requirement of cheerfulness and stoicism in the face of tragedy has been tempered in the more recent recollections. Strong emotions must be managed in order to be survivable. The passage of time now performs the distancing functions that were assigned to humour and irony in wartime accounts. In other ways, the wartime accounts and the post-war memoirs seem strikingly similar, underlining my point about the longevity of certain ideas, most importantly the emphasis on the family as a vehicle for personal and social rehabilitation. These men and women expected to have different roles in their families but generally agreed on what a family was and on the nature of gender-differentiated roles within families. Idealised images of the family and people's hopes for their own families sustained New Zealand men and women during the war and afterwards provided a way of integrating their different experiences of war. Wartime roles were heavily gendered, but the ideology of the family shared by men and women helped to hold the sexes together.

My goal is to evoke some of the emotional history of the period in order to sketch a set of ideas about romance, family and national defence. There were, of course, no typical experiences. I am endeavouring to use reports on experience as a gateway to a better understanding of the war and the path to peace. I do not mean to suggest that experiences can be reduced to simple catch-phrases or that there is no distinction between the contemporary sources and the post-war commentaries. The following discussion begins by examining key aspects of wartime mobilisation. I then introduce the voices of some of those who lived through the emergency. After using this testimony to evoke the mindset of war, I will further mine it to examine images of rehabilitation and the transition to peace. The conclusion will again return to issues of ideology and the maintenance of the gender order.

Pakeha society was built, among other things, on the belief that gender asymmetry was functional and socially useful, and a related faith in the importance of family-building to the future of the nation. But masculinity, femininity and family are not static; they are dynamic and interlinked social formations that are constantly reinscribed and renegotiated on the shifting terrain of individual desire, social sanction and material possibility. In the nineteenth and twentieth centuries, changes in masculine behaviour and normative images of masculinity have generally been easier to incorporate than challenges to conventional femininity. Men have had more social and political power with which to defend their changing versions of appropriate gender behaviour. They have been expected to be forward-thinking and adaptable and, because of their engagement with public life and the economy, are seen as necessarily more subject to change than women. Women were charged with most of the burdens of maintaining families and ensuring the stability of the gender order. But, paradoxically, women were also seen as unreliable guardians of the gender order, faddish and in danger of being unduly swayed by new ideas and poor advice, particularly after the emergence of an organised women's movement in the latter part of the nineteenth century. Advocates of women's rights frequently faced the accusation that innovations such as votes for women, married women's property rights and female access to higher education would desex women, emasculate men and destabilise society.[10]

New Zealand survived women's suffrage, female education and married women's property legislation, but the spectre of feminist subversion and female dereliction of duty persisted. To cite just a few flashpoints: in the early twentieth century, gender tensions flared in debates over the family wage, women's entitlements to paid work and social security benefits, the propriety of employing married women as teachers, the shortage of domestic servants, women's fitness to serve on juries or join the police force, the implications of allowing women to stand for Parliament, the incidence and criminality of abortion, the morality of contraception and the nature of marriage and parenting. Two central questions drove these debates. First, how different were men and women? Second, how many of those differences could be removed before there was a crisis in the family, and, by extension, a crisis in New Zealand society? The continuing presence of these questions in national discourse is one of the central themes in the history of the nation.

The war provided definite, though temporary answers, to these questions. Men and women were very different, and would make fundamentally different contributions to the winning of the war. And the family? The New Zealand family was not only under threat from the twin enemies of fascism and Asian expansionism, it was also menaced by some of the consequences of wartime mobilisation. Precisely because making war was seen as a profoundly masculine activity, it had the potential to rend great tears in the social fabric by exaggerating the masculine qualities of all its participants, male and female. Whereas much of the interwar debate about gender centred on the dangers of too little separation between the sexes, the wartime debates, though still cognisant of the dangers of the defeminisation of women, were also engaged by the possibility that men might become too different from women to comfortably fit back into civilian society. Men could be overmasculinised by their war experiences, becoming aggressive, anti-social and areligious. Fit for combat, they could become unfit for family life. The best strategy to resist this double threat was to continue to assert the temporary nature of wartime demands on individual character, and the need for war-waging individuals to strive to remain family men and women. The importance of the family and of a sexual division of labour within the family were continually asserted. War-tarnished men and women could be rehabilitated by marriage. Rough and ready soldiers, the prevailing wisdom ran, would be redeemed by loving sweethearts; women who had risked their femininity filling in for men during the national emergency, would be refeminised and refashioned by loving men.

The primary obligation of the male citizen was to defend his country, if necessary, at the cost of life or limb. In the case of New Zealanders in the Second World War this obligation was extended to include the defence of Britain and the Empire, a defence largely undertaken far from either, in Greece, the Middle East, Italy and the Pacific. The military histories of the period rightly emphasise the achievements of New Zealand forces engaging with the enemy on unfamiliar and distant terrain. At a distance of more than 50 years it is easy to lose sight of the significance of the protracted and geographically attenuated nature of the conflict for New Zealand's social history. The war removed large numbers of men from home and family for long periods of time, and no matter how much gloss was placed on the fine character of New Zealand's recruits, it was difficult to completely cover the fact that war service might implicate soldiers in acts of brutality and destruction.[11] Those who were not posted overseas or deployed in combat roles could be coarsened by camp life. Military service, the apex of masculine citizenship, might result in undesirable social impacts if it produced men who could not be reintegrated back into civil society.

Men were classified within the public sphere of citizenship and duty, ranked as soldiers, potential soldiers (underaged boys and fit men held back in reserved occupations), ex-soldiers, failed soldiers (conscientious objectors and the medically unfit) and soldier-substitutes (men past the age of military service and others attempting to fill the gaps in civilian life left by the exodus of military men). Enlistment for the armed services was voluntary until 18 June 1940. Thereafter all Pakeha men aged 16 to 45 were obliged to register for a national reserve force. Those 18 and over underwent a medical and dental examination to determine if they were fit to serve. There were further hierarchies of obligation according to age, ethnicity, marital status and number of children. Call-up commenced with the unmarried. Men married on or before 1 May 1940 were not conscripted until 1942, though they could volunteer for service earlier if they wished. Married men without children were targeted before married fathers, and fathers were ranked according to number of children.[12] Maori men, foreign nationals, the medically unfit and (until March 1942) naturalised British subjects were exempt from compulsory service.[13] By 1942, over 350,000 men – the vast bulk of Pakeha men of military age – had been registered for service. One hundred and sixty thousand volunteers and conscripts served in the military, and approximately 118,000 were posted overseas. Of those sent overseas, 15,000 were wounded. Another 10,000 men received military pensions for psychiatric disorders. Five and a half thousand men did not return at all; the bulk of casualties occurred among troops who fought in Europe and the Middle East. Eight thousand men spent time as prisoners of war.[14]

Male citizens were also required to contribute to the war economy. All men under 60 had to register with the Department of National Service for direction to work of national importance. For men of military age, industrial conscription was integrated into the process of military call-up. Some fit men were held back from the army in reserved occupations. The unfit and those outside the age of military service found themselves labouring under a series of restrictions on their power to choose their job, change jobs, take time off work, refuse overtime or take industrial action. They were soldier-substitutes charged with the responsibility of maintaining essential civilian services and servicing the material needs of the military.

Female citizenship was never militarised, but some women ranked as soldier-substitutes. Women eagerly replaced men in the civilian workforce, though their freedom to do so was severely curtailed after January 1942 with the introduction of a system of industrial conscription that restricted the outflow of women from traditionally female, but nevertheless essential, occupations such as sewing, food processing, hospital domestic work and food service.[15] Under the manpower regulations, childless women aged 18-40 could be required to take paid work in an essential industry or to move to a job with higher official priority. Rural women worked long hours to keep farms going in the absence of fathers, husbands and male employees, assisted after 1942 by 1000 female volunteers organised in a Women's Land Service.[16] The inauguration of women's auxiliaries to the New Zealand armed forces, whose rationale was to ameliorate the military manpower shortage by replacing some men with women, created another class of soldier-substitutes. The women's auxiliaries did not, however, challenge the male monopoly on combat and so-called 'active' military duties. They were relatively small in size, composed entirely of volunteers and primarily employed on clerical and canteen duties. Women continued to relate to the military primarily as the wives, mothers and girlfriends of soldiers, not as soldiers themselves. Femininity was mobilised and nationalised primarily through affective and kin relationships to men on active duty, not through direct enlistment.

The war, despite official rhetoric of equality of sacrifice and erosion of social distinctions, was not a levelling process. It was hierarchical, capricious and inherently unfair, leaving an uneven legacy of coercion, interrupted or involuntary employment and emotional turmoil. The deaths, the wounds, the years of tedium and regimentation represented a massive sacrifice on the part of New Zealand soldiers and their families and inspired a sense of obligation and inadequacy on the part of many. Few could comfort themselves with the thought that they had done 'enough', be it enough to avoid the war, fight it, keep friends and relatives from harm, or heal its hurts. In the wartime hierarchies of masculinity, those who gave their all were, by definition, those who did not survive to see the peace. Who should follow the dead in the roll of honour was contested. Airmen, pilots in particular, carried with them an aura of glamour and technical competence. Infantrymen also had a claim: according to one self-described average New Zealand soldier, 'if ever there was someone to put on a pedestal, it would be the front line infantry soldier'.[17] In both cases, the claims to precedence spoke to the issue of masculinity. The airman and the digger could claim preeminence on the basis of effectiveness in killing the enemy and survival in extraordinary conditions, both hyper-masculine traits that could be troublesome in peacetime.

The services had systems of honours and promotions to rank men's contributions, though official judgments did not always reflect individual soldiers' assessments of the value of the men they served with. Prisoners of war fitted uneasily into the hierarchies, as did male non-combatants. Both groups could be stigmatised as less than active in the prosecution of the war; both could claim extenuating circumstances in defence of their supposed passivity. Maori were widely acknowledged to have put on 'a good show', but whether they had fulfilled Apirana Ngata's hope of paying the price of full citizenship was less than clear.[18] Women's contributions were also difficult to categorise, being either too feminine to be significant or too significant to be appropriately feminine.

Whatever the residual hierarchies of service, it was generally acknowledged that a great debt was owed to servicemen. Although the foremost worry was for the safety of soldiers' bodies, physical survival was not the only issue. Enlistees, their families and the general public were concerned about the psychological and social costs of removing men from their families and exposing them to the rigours of war. The impact of the war on servicemen's long-term material prospects was also a concern, reflecting the popular wisdom that veterans had been ill-served in the aftermath of the First World War. Along with the hierarchies of service and obligation went a sense that, ultimately, the nature of the peace would need to justify the traumas of the war. The dead had to be remembered and returnees offered a life worthy of their comrades' sacrifice. Much of the anxiety about the way that the war was affecting women reflected this concern that veterans should be rewarded by return to a society as unchanged as possible.

Women bore a great deal of the burden of conserving the status quo on the home front. Farms and homes had to be maintained. Marriages had to be nurtured, as did children. Wartime employment was structured by a rigid manpower bureaucracy that consciously aimed to preserve jobs for servicemen and often seemed unresponsive to women's aspirations to earn more money or extend their range of skills. Personal lives were scrutinised against the yardstick of worthiness for the return of 'our boys' and peacetime reconstruction. If the war was won at the expense of the peacetime gender order, the battle to preserve a society fit for New Zealand soldiers to return to would be lost.

War made men and women conscious of their interdependence, even as it placed separate challenges in their paths. Dorothy Findley remembered how her moods used to fluctuate with the war news. Courtship was freighted with uncertainty and worry: 'An engagement ring was not so much a status symbol to be flaunted, as a token of faith and hope that there will in fact be a future'.[19] Keith Elliot was cheered after his return from the Middle East with a Victoria Cross but, public praise aside, remembered, 'My best homecoming gift was the condition in which I found the farm. . . . The war had demanded a great deal of personal sacrifice from my three sisters in their role as land-girls . . . . they had also served, with red and roughened hands and muck covered boots. And had lost none of the grace of womanhood in so doing.'[20]

Elliot's recollection – conventional and earnest – depicts women as heroines of normalcy. Of course, not all women were able to place their lives and their feelings on hold until their men returned. On some topics, the passing of time has not produced candour. The sting of betrayal felt by men who returned to a broken engagement or an unfaithful spouse is seldom commented on in the memoirs but contemporary observers were scathing. In April 1944, a chaplain just back from the Middle East denounced home-front cads, home-breakers and 'other upsetters of morale . . . living on the thrills and frills of war' while brave men fought in their name.[21] The dalliances of absent soldiers were less harshly judged. Woven in with a recognition that the war required men to make extreme sacrifices was an ambivalent sense that it also granted them some licence. Again, few of the post-war memoirs address this issue directly, but occasionally indications of the prevailing double standard surface. Ena Ryan felt the war had to be taken into account when judging soldiers' actions: 'I suppose a lot of people were shocked at the prostitutes, the hookers, but I really don't feel that the people who are not going into battle have any right to criticise the doings of people who are going into battle'.[22] Women lived with the knowledge that, in the words of one artilleryman, 'Bad drink and bad women are always on sale to the man who so desires.'[23]

In keeping with the general uncertainty about the effect of the war on New Zealand society, many individuals experienced the war as a period of considerable personal ambivalence. Margaret Yardley worked as a postie in Timaru. The job was a good one, and had not been available to women before the war, but the war brought more sorrow than opportunity. Her brother was killed in an aircraft accident, and worry about her fiancé made the period 'a teeth grinding and gritting time'. She had always wanted to be a nurse but the manpower authorities would not release her for training. Finally, late in 1943, she was granted permission to go overseas as a voluntary hospital aid. She married her fiancé in Egypt, celebrating with a New Zealand-made cake, Portuguese sherry and a four-day honeymoon in the YWCA. As for many women, her wartime experiences were mixed. The new opportunities were welcome, but they were accompanied by a great deal of anxiety. Her memoir ends equivocally: 'War experiences aged us all and most had difficulties settling down'.[24]

Reticence about the worst aspects of war and a cheerful, almost determinedly humorous stoicism are themes of many of the surviving wartime accounts and post-war reminiscences. Letters, diaries and memoirs all resist images of generic soldiering by distinguishing individual men, emphasising their foibles and the quality of their friendship. Men cemented associations with teasing and affectionate nicknames. Joyce Macdonald nursed a soldier named White: 'but they christened him "Brownie"; heaven knows why! They seemed to have the most amazing choice of names for each other – some, of course, which weren't for my ears!'[25] Eric Barr reported to family friends that, 'I've put on a lot of weight & with my shorts on quite justify my nickname of "Babe". Ken of course is called "Jimmy" after Jimmy Durant [*sic*] the film star with part of his face rather prominent, or else "Blue Nose".'[26] After the war men affectionately recalled the antics of the men they served with, people like Mark Venables' friend Owen Currin, too popular to discipline, 'the humorist of the tent, [who] would try the N.C.O.s out at all times. One day he appeared on parade dressed only in underpants, singlet, boots and lemon squeezer hat!'[27]

The commentary the contemporary sources and the post-war memoirs provide on male friendship reinforces our images of a masculinity defined by homosocial mateship.[28] The conventions of the war itself did not encourage men to acknowledge the extent to which there was a sexual element in these friendships, and despite subsequent changes in attitudes to homosexuality the memoirs are largely silent on this matter. Notwithstanding the gaps in our knowledge, male friendships should not be trivialised, routinely sexualised or treated in simplistic opposition to family and heterosexual relationships. Most men enjoyed male–male socialising in which they did not have to mind their language or watch their manners. Some had same-sex desires, and some were escaping fraught relationships with women. Some expressed their desires in physical ways, others sublimated their feelings in the gestures of mateship. But these were not covert or shamefaced friendships. Men wrote openly and proudly about the fact that they could establish and sustain friendships despite the upheavals of war. In a world where danger was imminent and the future uncertain, it was important to go on caring about individuals. Writing home about their mates was testimony to the continued importance of human connection and individuality in a context in which men were regimented, numbered and classified, and where they could be called upon to do inhuman things. These were ersatz families as well as homosocial communities. Just as a man was justified in fighting to defend his family, he was also justified in acting in defence of his mates. Far from home it was hard to justify violence as national defence, but fellow soldiers could stand in as representatives of the community one was defending. The strength of feeling for fellow soldiers meant that, even when pushed to his limits or tempted to act inappropriately, the Kiwi soldier could still be an object of admiration. Martyn Uren's *Kiwi Saga* describes a corporal who captured the German crew of a Bofors gun:

> This man had left us with a few grim jokes, and his mates had told us confidentially that he was a hard man. But he returned without his jovial grin. Standing up beside the prisoners with a fixed bayonet, he looked grim and savage. I learnt that his best friend had died in his arms from wounds inflicted by the Bofors. I rather admired his restraint.[29]

Family pictures and stories were also important in maintaining soldiers' sense of self and could even be used to close the gap between allied soldiers and their opponents. Alf Voss rose through the ranks to become an intelligence officer with the 21st Battalion and had a high opinion of Kiwi soldiers, but, 'they were sometimes a little too matey. As soon as Kiwis captured a Jerry, they would sit him down, give him a cup of tea and a cigarette and ask, "Where are your [*sic*] from, mate?" Then in a few minutes they'd be showing each other photos of their wives, girlfriends or even their mothers.'[30] Joyce Macdonald remembered how patients in a makeshift army hospital in Italy adopted a 'stray Jerry': '[his] only comment to life in general was to produce a snap of his wife and children, gaze at them with tears rolling down his lined cheeks, muttering "Boomb, boomb". A couple of Cockneys gave him a cigarette while a Kiwi shaved him.'[31]

Pictures were also used to try and close the distance between home and battle front. Keeping up relationships over such great distances and such long periods of time was not a simple matter. The wartime sources convey a sense of the effort involved in a way the more recent memoirs can only gloss over. June Cummings's letters describe how difficult it was to keep up with friends on overseas service when there was so much disjunction between her world and theirs: 'You've no idea how hard it is to write to you over there in all that hell. . . . It rained last night and that heavenly earthy smell you get after rain is intensified tonight by the still, moist atmosphere. The simple things like gardens and flowers remain so fundamentally lovely that it is terrible to imagine what goes on in places were there are no gardens and there are no flowers.'[32] The details of civilian life seemed trivial and insignificant, but what else was there to write about? June queued for film to take photographs to send a friend in the Middle East. She hoped they would ease his worries about his home and his wife: 'they will give you a good idea of how well she has recuperated from the measles & of how the little white house is looking now – & of how your hospitality is to be continued over Christmas'.[33] The pictures have detailed annotations on their reverse: 'that dot on her lapel is her yellow EPS badge & that's one of your stockings you can see down there. Please note the nasturtiums & the size of the hydrangeas for so early in the season.' Another of her friend's wife sitting in her garden is labelled, 'Panorama. It's a pretty grass green frock, patterned in white & when you look closely you can see ducks & jingle bells in the design. There are two pockets in front like this, [drawing].'[34]

Men and women tried to protect themselves and each other from the pain of separation and wartime stress by selectively describing their surroundings, framing their experiences as humorous anecdotes and hinting at, but not dwelling on, trauma. The Neals lived outside Levin during the early years of the war and put a lot of effort into entertaining men stationed at the nearby airbase. The letters the men sent the family convey a quality of determined cheerfulness. An unsigned letter from 1944 explicitly discusses this emotional strategy:

> Though I am afraid I can not plead guilty to always going around with a smile on my face, I know only too well now that a man and a nation are beaten once they lose the ability to smile. Somehow or other a smile drives out all the cantankerous things that make us do and say what in our better moment we wouldn't. I think of all the things I used to grumble about in Levin. Progressively conditions on the stations I was on got worse, until the last show and this one were simply what we ourselves made them. And yet . . . there was nothing really unbearable. I have made up my mind that never again will I grumble about things as they affect me, because invariably they are so much better than I believe they are.[35]

The first page of an undated letter from Cecil Irving is taken up with apologies for not writing sooner. Irving had been posted to Fiji but, 'I was only there a month when I got word that [our] wee child had died so I asked . . . if there was any chance of getting back to N.Z. . . . . I was allowed to come, and believe me I was truly greatfull [*sic*] as my wife was very much broken up when I did get home.'[36] After eight days with his wife Irving had to report back to camp. The letter says little about his son apart from the fact of his death, tailing off into a discussion of his stay in the islands and the weather. It ends with a comment on the state of the war and a glancing, but heartfelt, reflection on his personal loss:

> I wonder what will happen next. The war is getting more serious all the time; so one never knows when I'll have to go overseas again, but I hope it will never be the East, a chap might get heart [*sic*] over there the way they carry on. Well, how are you people doing? How is the little fellow getting on[?] I wish I still had ours to go home to, but things happen.[37]

There was a fine line between indulging in homesickness or self-pity and trying to maintain a sense of connection with people left back in New Zealand. Eric Barr was determined to think about the future in optimistic but not overly wishful ways. A letter written from the Middle East during April 1942 briefly describes parachuting out of a plane under enemy fire before letting himself tentatively envision his return:

> I guess I'll notice a big difference in all the family by the time I get back, especially Robin and Kerry. I hope Robin enjoys the school life. Sorry to hear you have lost all your [Air Force] boys, let's hope some more roll up

shortly. Never know, may be that way myself before the year's out. I consider I've done my fair share over here and want the chance of doing some good with my experience back in N.Z, still there doesn't seem much chance for a while. . . . I would like to be there with you all, but wishful thinking doesn't get one anywhere so I'd better dismiss it.[38]

Remembering home and being remembered at home were important aspects of the emotional economy of war. Music, special places, memories of hospitality and mutual friends were invoked as touchstones of shared pasts and talismans of shared futures. Bill, stationed with the RNZAF in Canada, badgered friends with questions: 'How is the summer in Levin this year? Anything like the one when I was there? How are the boys keeping? O.K. I hope. Have any of you been to Sleepy Hollow lately? Are the boys still coming around to the house – have you seen Bill Simpson lately? Lots of questions, eh!' In closing he added, 'I hope you get this letter – as I don't want you to think I've forgotten you – I'll drop in and see you on the way home soon I hope . . . . p.s. at your next musical gathering sing "Because" and "Beautiful Isle of Somewhere" for me please.'[39] A letter from Gay Gray to her husband Duncan remarked on the eerie coincidence that just as she sat down to write, 'Annie Laurie', their special song, started playing on the radio. The following week, her letter tried to close the geographical distance between them by imagining his physical surroundings: 'Hullo darling – what an awful time you must be having – living like rabbits underground . . . & working hard in all that heat & dust, it must be ghastly'. Fantasising about the future also sustained her sense of connection to her husband: 'All weekend while I was pottering at home I was thinking of all I'd give to have you suddenly transported out of that hateful desert & into the quiet & cool of our little house & what a joy it would be to fuss over you & try & make up for all you are going through. I will darling when you come back home. I promise to make it seem a paradise.'[40]

Official censorship of newspapers and international mails was a fact of wartime life. Bill Gentry, a senior army officer stationed in the Middle East, started discussing serious matters in a letter to his wife on Easter Sunday 1942, then pulled up short: 'Well I suppose there isn't much use in being too serious. You can't say all the things you would like to say; in fact you can't say half of them. I hate the possibility of my ordinary efforts being read even occasionally by the eyes of the censor.'[41] In this situation, where memories and being remembered were crucial to people's emotional and psychological health, small tokens had to stand in for important feelings.

Bill McConnochie wrote back to his fiancée, Bonnie, about an 'awful ca-lamity'. He had lost the gold ring that she had given him. Two weeks later when it reappeared he was jubilant: 'to have it turn up after I had com-pletely given up hope of ever seeing it again was the greatest and most pleasant surprise I have had for years. You have no idea just how lonely that little finger on my left hand felt without your ring on it.'[42]

Yarns and comedies about army life feature prominently in soldiers' accounts of their wartime experiences. Frank Bruno's 1942 collection of vignettes of army life, *Desert Daze*, uses humour to soften the brutality of his subject matter. A number of the stories deal with serious subjects – the long periods of uncertainty waiting to go out again into 'the blue', battles, wounds, fly-blown food – but the material is rendered emotionally palat-able by a combination of ironic distance and comic description of indi-vidual quirks. If flies swarm on your food you can tie a chameleon to your helmet and use it as a captive fly swat. In the desert, 'with bivvy-tents for mattresses; and respirator, anti-gas, for pillows, and the ubiquitous Speed as tea walad, things could have been a damsite worse'. An account of a battle is leavened by stories of 'Deerfoot', the platoon commander who had never been in combat before, and for whom the workings of a compass were 'a Chinese puzzle'.[43]

Self-deprecation and understatement were an important part of this emotional style. According to its author, *Desert Daze* was compiled at the request of fellow 'near-sober First Echelon wife-beaters and debt-dodg-ers'.[44] The ordinariness of the men who fought an extraordinary war was a point of pride. Ted, learning to fly 'lopsided old crates' at Wigram, could praised a fellow airman's skills but not his own: 'Luckily there are a few budding experts here who have already flown solo, including young Ashley. It takes young pups like him to show the way to elderly people like us! Anyway it was a good effort & he's getting on well – not that Ash thinks so. He's too modest!'[45] Again, the importance of humour and friendship comes through. Men were inhibited in praising their own efforts, or talking about their own pain, but they could signal their achievements and emotions ironically or by discussing others.

Francis Jackson's *Passage to Tobruk* was one of the first book-length sol-dier's stories to appear in print. Published in 1943, it is a fiction about 'Mac' MacNeil and 'Jackie' who go to war on a whim, literally deciding their fate with the toss of a coin. The metaphors of romance and family are essential parts of the narrative. The story is framed by two 'weddings'; their farcical enlistment – 'like getting married, but instead of two beautiful brides standing

by our sides, there stood only the solemn Major and the Sergeant complaining of the weather and his gout' – and Mac's marriage to Bobette on
his return from the Middle East, when Jackie, worried by the moony expression on Mac's face, confuses love for 'Dobie's Itch'.[46] In their progress
from one wedding to the other, Mac and Jackie team up with Colin and the
'crazy gang', six mates from Trentham who eat, drink and bunk together,
pool their finances, and entertain each other – just like a family.

There is a didactic insistence in the wartime representations of men at
war on the necessity of harnessing one's emotions. In *Passage to Tobruk* an
interesting reversal takes place. A cablegram transforms Mac and Jackie's
friend, Colin, from an object of love about whom people at home fearfully
wait for news, to a loving subject who must receive tragic news. His wife
has died from pneumonia. Jackie watches as Colin reads the message:

> . . . his hands were shaking. He lifted his head and I could see the tears on
> his cheeks. His eyes were blank in a blanched, expressionless face, and he
> handed the cable to Mac for him to read.
> 'Oh, Colin, I'm sorry, boy,' whispered Mac.
> Colin continued to stare – at some unseen dreams? Then he spoke haltingly:
> 'She was good, and kind. She was loving, and gentle – she never did anyone
> a scrap of harm . . . . I'm the one to blame. I should never have left home and
> left her alone. Now she is gone and there is not much left to fight for.'[47]

Finding something worth fighting for in a world without women and families
was difficult, finding something to live for after the fighting was over even
more so. With the help of the padre and the rest of the 'crazy gang' – even its
renowned 'hard man', 'Stinker', whose impassivity 'had left him as if it had
been torn from him like a mask', Colin pulls himself together to fight in the
battle of Sidi Rezegh but afterwards Mac and Jackie hear he has 'gone a bit
magnoon (mad)', and been invalided home.[48]

War made men more manly but it also exposed their vulnerability. Women
constructed their femininity in relation to the interplay of strength and
weakness in men. In hindsight, Ena Ryan believed that her rather frivolous
pre-war disdain for men was recast by the war:

> We thought that the war was probably going to last for 10 years, it was
> going to be much worse than World War One and so these men thought
> they were going away for a good long time and goodness knows what was
> in front of them . . . . it did have a terrific effect on me. I'd always looked on
> men with rather a beady eye. . . . I changed and I started to realise that men

had terrific pressures put upon them and were really very vulnerable and that it might be a darn good idea to be a little less self-centred and start considering other people for a bit. Now I don't mean that I was the only person who got this feeling. I think it was universal.[49]

Ryan's acknowledgment of the vulnerability of the men who went to war was voiced decades after the war itself had ended. Sources closer to the period suppress this sense of men's fragility, emphasising instead the importance of soldiering on. Joyce Macdonald's 1945 memoir described New Zealand infantrymen as preternaturally pain tolerant and good humoured: 'There was never a murmur or grizzle – every injury was made light of and there was always much good-natured bantering'.[50] She paints a picture of hospitals as zones of female influence, clean and starkly opposed to the dirt of 'Wog'-infested Cairo and the rigours of battle. Ambulatory patients trudged up to her ward to be transformed into clean-shaven paragons ready again for family life:

> For so long they had been treated en masse, just a bunch of numbers .... The orderly and I surveyed our family – a long cold drink all round .... we sponged and cleaned and tidied .... there is no greater satisfaction in the nursing world than to work on a patient made almost unrecognisable by a week's growth and the dust of hundreds of miles, to put him clean and comfortable between cool sheets and hear the muffled voice saying, 'God is this really me – this is sheer heaven!'[51]

This is not a realistic depiction of the experience of nursing men fresh from combat; like little boys, all battle-worn soldiers really needed was to be fed, washed and put to bed. It is a comforting fable about men's resilience and women's capacity to cleanse them of the taint of war.

Women could not compete with men on the battlefield but they could show courage by harnessing their emotions. Nola Riddiford's letters to her sons alternate between telling them how much they are missed and downplaying her anxieties about them.[52] Jessie McClunie was the proud recipient of 'long, uncomplaining letters' from her fiancé, and tried to reply in kind. For two months after the German invasion of Greece, there was no mail. Then, in place of the intimacy and physicality of personal letters and photographs, came curiously disembodied news, 'his name appeared among the missing'. The shock was terrible. Jessie survived by harnessing her emotions, working on her parents' farm and putting her spare time into voluntary war work. For months her letters kept coming back marked

'Return to Sender' or 'Missing believed prisoner-of-war', but her fiancé and the engagement survived the war.[53] Neva Morrison was not so lucky. Devastated by the death of her husband-to-be, she stumbled into work at the local army office where she met 'Howard the Scot'. 'Intolerant to the nth degree', taciturn and 'a woman-hater' embittered by the desertion of his wife, he is not presented as particularly admirable, yet in a curious fashion he becomes a role model. When Neva was posted overseas with the clerical division of the Women's Auxiliary Army Corps, he showed his grudging fondness for her with a handshake and a piece of advice, 'For God's sake, keep your sense of humour or you'll be sunk.' At the war's end Neva was still grieving but was able to reassure Howard that her sense of humour had carried her through: 'Every time I almost lost it, I thought of you'.[54]

War forced men to spend long periods away from their families in the company of other men but that did not necessarily make them hostile to family life. Shortly after Christmas 1939, Bill Gentry, one of New Zealand's very small coterie of career army officers, left his wife Lalla, their five-year-old son and year-old daughter for a posting in Egypt. The couple spent five of the next six years apart. In his letters there is a strong sense of active engagement with the problems of prolonged absence and often moving reflections on the need for a peacetime transformation of soldier into family man and father. Leaving his wife and children produced a chilling sense of dislocation: 'it does not seem to be happening to me at all. Tonight is all unreal and fantastic and I can't bear to think of leaving Lalla and my little children.'[55]

Gentry was a successful officer, working efficiently as General Freyberg's chief of staff in Egypt and later commanding the 9th Infantry Brigade in Italy. He was posted back to New Zealand for a year in May 1943, then returned to overseas duty in July 1944. This was not a man at odds with the life of a soldier, yet his letters return again and again to the theme of separation from his better self, and of temporary sublimation of his identity as father and husband in the business of war. Eight months after their farewell he wrote that he was sorry to hear that his wife still shed tears over their separation: 'I often feel like that too and if I did not have such a lot of work to do I would feel like it so often it would be unendurable. Ours has been such a happy partnership that I for one feel that all the best part of my life is completely dormant. It is only hope that this can't last forever that keeps us going.'[56] The same strategy of empathetic trouble-sharing and longing for the end of the war appeared again in a letter of September 1941:

I am sorry that you have been feeling depressed, my dear. I have a bit too. Two years is an awfully long time and I am just as tired of being a lone unit as you are. It is only half a life this. It isn't even half a life. We live in a mental and spiritual vacuum and are separated from all the things and the few people that make existence worthwhile . . . . I want my wife again; I want my children and my little home and to live an ordinary peaceful life and I don't care how uneventful it is.[57]

Gentry worried about the day-to-day details of his children's development, repeatedly asked for letters about the minutiae of domestic life, urged his wife to spend money on their house and tried not to belittle civilian life, writing in March 1941 while waiting to engage the German army in Greece: 'You seem to be attending a lot of tea and other parties. It must be a help to make the days go. Mine go all too quickly.'[58] He also worried about how the war might be changing his character. On Easter Sunday 1942 he let some of his doubts surface: 'I wonder how you all are. I wonder a lot really and you have no idea how I long to be with you again. I am a very domesticated animal, as you know, at least I was, and no doubt could be again though I must have grown out of some of the more useful domestic habits.'[59] His furlough in New Zealand allowed him to make up for some lost time, but there are hints in the 1944 letters that his year at home was not trouble free: 'I would give a lot for a nice quiet chat in front of the fire. . . . Don't worry about not being [illegible]. I was an awkward husband to live with for that year & ever would be until we can really settle down again & know where we are.'[60]

Domestic happy-ever-afters are important plot devices in many of these narratives' treatment of peace, signalling the successful reintegration of soldiers and sweethearts into civil society. In *Passage to Tobruk* we do not find out what happens to Jackie, but Mac marries pretty Bobette, who becomes 'his world'. Although he 'cannot intrude too frequently, no matter how much they both make me welcome', Jackie accepts Mac's marriage as right and proper, and as a sign of Mac's new maturity. During the last part of his army service Mac's 'personality had registered a complete and lasting change for the better'.[61] Real-life returns were also dominated by hopes for domestic futures and this sense of hope is captured by many of the memoirs. Four years after his capture, Jessie McClunie and her fiancé were re-united in Auckland: 'Smiling a little shyly I hugged him to me. . . . "Ready for that South Island honeymoon, sweetheart?", he asked with a big grin. I laughed up at him, happy beyond words. "We better get married first.'"[62]

There is a self-consciously dreamlike and wistful quality to many of the depictions of women in these writings. Male camaraderie and romantic imaginings could be compatible. In his war memoir, John Blythe, a New Zealand infantryman, recalled sailing for home from Egypt. There was time to cultivate friendships, reflect on the ordeal of war and make plans for the future: 'I found another relative on the ship and we became companions. He was madly in love with a photograph [of a South African woman]. . . . I told him about the girl in the cipher section who was still writing to me, showed him my photographs, and together we dreamed.'[63]

Families had been threatened by the withdrawal of men for military service, but they could also be undermined by their return. Soldier dad and civilian mum had to find a way to live together again in peace. Bracy Gardiner found that marriage to an ex-soldier was emotionally complicated. In the early years after his return, her nightmare-plagued husband slept only four hours each night. Twice she had packed to leave, 'shamefacedly twice I had unpacked, as I remembered my vows and what the men had been through'.[64] Nor did returning soldiers re-enter this world without anxiety, though it is generally only in retrospect that they have been able to publicly admit their fears. During 1945 Allan Yeoman, an army officer, worked at the Rehabilitation Unit in Folkestone, England, repatriating New Zealand soldiers. Looking back on his reasons for taking the job instead of returning home as soon as possible, he identified, 'a simmering unease' that made men – himself included – apprehensive about their return. The chaplain was one of the few people to whom these worries could be confided:

> The padre found himself involved in an unexpected variant of this syndrome. Married men were coming to see him who were terrified of returning home. Most of them had been faithful to their wives, they had corresponded as regularly as circumstances would allow, they had lived for the day that they could go down the gangway to be reunited with their loved ones. But now this longed-for moment was nearly upon them, they could not face it. They felt empty, cold, they felt nothing and it filled them with dread.[65]

How could soldiers' sacrifices be accommodated and assimilated into peacetime society? The conventional answer was quite close to Mulgan's image of a sun-drenched land peopled by happy families. Commenting on the way the people of Kent opened their homes to the New Zealanders, Yeoman philosophised that the social dangers presented by a rapidly demobilised soldiery could be stabilised by 'family life': 'the natural tendency for people who have been deprived [is] to get out on the loose and do things they would later regret. The civilising influence of a good home diverts their demands from the turbulent and the unworthy to the respectable and the decent; and in a family circle they find that their nebulous cravings no longer exist.'[66]

For men who spent time as prisoners of war the return home was often fraught with special difficulty. Some found women difficult to deal with. Bob Anderson, an ex-prisoner of war, returned to his mother and sisters in Port Chalmers, found he had 'nothing to talk to them about, nothing at all',[67] but his comment is not necessarily representative. It is not clear that returned prisoners of war had any more difficulty in relating to women than soldiers who had not been imprisoned. There is, however, more evidence that they were conscious that surviving the war as a prisoner placed them on a different rung of the ladder of martial achievement from soldiers on 'active duty'. The earliest accounts of prison life from ex-prisoners are full of tales of suffering but it is generally a suffering ennobled by struggle to escape captivity. Masculinity, these writers claimed, was reinforced and affirmed in the process of active resistance to imprisonment. Women figure little in these accounts. To quote the title of Colin Armstrong's book written shortly after the war, going to prison camp meant, 'life without ladies'. In the foreword to the book, Victoria Cross winner Colonel L. W. Andrew testified that the author was not the type to 'resign himself to captivity'. Andrew singled out teamwork, comradeship, helpfulness, determination and pride of birth as the qualities that led to Armstrong's eventual escape, presenting him as an exemplar of New Zealand manhood: 'Reading the book, and especially the chapter headed "Kiwis All" one is conscious of one's pride in having served with these men and one feels that while our young nation breeds such men nothing much can go wrong in the future'. Armstrong's account of incessant scheming and eventual escape acknowledges privation uneasily, speaking out only reluctantly against what he sees as the silences required of him. As he says, 'I have gone to some lengths to depict a miserable situation. I have risked the accusation of sensationalism and of seeking sympathy.'[68]

Decades later, ex-POWs could be more open about their difficulties. Many memoirs speak of the dreadful sense of alienation returned POWs felt, but the gendering of that isolation is more complex than a simple opposition between male experience and female chatter. For many of these men, the company of women could provide salve for wounds rubbed raw by the hierarchies of wartime masculinity. In the more recent memoirs, women often feature as allies in the battle to regain masculine self-respect.

The passage of time seems to have allowed ex-POWs to acknowledge the way female sympathy healed rather than emasculated. Claude Thompson, imprisoned by the Japanese in Java and Singapore, wryly noted, 'Looking back, the things that helped me most to rehabilitate myself were my wife Betty, the refusal of Re-Hab to give me a loan and the wonderful friends who helped me.'[69] Allan Yeoman dedicated his book to his wife, his mother who 'waited and knitted and cooked and prayed', family and friends, but the only men explicitly acknowledged are the dead, 'those wonderful fellows who will never tell their stories because they lie forever mute in a foreign land'.[70]

There are suggestions in their memoirs that many ex-POWs felt slighted by the masculine community of their fellow soldiers, rather than by the women in their lives. Harold Smith returned from imprisonment in Germany plagued by nightmares and colitis. He felt deserted, not so much by the woman he married, or women generally, but by society, the army and the government: 'My health was not good but there was no proper medical examination or counselling to help with rehabilitation. I felt most unsettled and it seemed that we returned men were just a seven days' wonder.' His ill health and social unease, which lasted for many years, were, he felt, typical of many prisoners of war. 'Many of us,' he wrote, 'were affected emotionally, experiencing awkwardness in meeting strangers, a strong dislike of crowds and an overpowering desire to be quiet and alone.' Initially he declined a war pension, disliking the dependence it implied. Later, he was rejected for a rehabilitation loan to extend his farm, 'the reason given being that I had rehabilitated myself'.[71]

Evidence given to the 1946 Parliamentary Select Committee on Dominion Population suggests some of the ways in which the iconography of family-building and national service was coalescing in the immediate post-war years. Leigh Hunt, the chairman of the Dominion Settlement and Population Association, suggested that mothers, like demobilised soldiers, be accorded special travel and social privileges 'which no woman no matter how much money she has, can possibly get if she has not a family'. Fathers should be given preference in employment and promotion, mothers honoured as the greatest patriots in the land.[72]

Most of the explicit discussion of gender roles concentrated on motherhood. Witnesses insisted that motherhood was a sign of successful womanhood. Dr P. Lynch, appearing on behalf of the British Medical Association, told the committee that the average woman's health would not be affected by having three or four children, 'and there would probably be increased mental health, the mothers with large families are generally the healthiest and happiest members of the community'. Mrs K. M. Griffen represented the Family Planning Association. She felt that attitudes to large families had become more positive in recent years. 'Young mothers have told me, "Twelve years ago my eldest sister was ashamed to have more than two children. Now I am ashamed if I do not have four or more." There is a different feeling today.' Griffen maintained that the ideal family had five or six children.[73] The silences about fatherhood underline the continued belief in the functional importance of gender asymmetry. Men would work to support large families, mothers would raise the kids.

Masculinity and femininity always comprise multiple parts, but in particular contexts key aspects of these composite identities will be highlighted and amplified. The Second World War provided the context for the amplification of martial aspects of masculinity. At the same time, partly to compensate for the militarisation of masculinity, the supportive, nurturing aspects of femininity were privileged even as women were temporarily replacing men in occupations hitherto barred to them. All men were classed as potential soldiers, all women as potential mothers.

The ideal soldier was usually depicted as a volunteer whose ultimate goal was to reintegrate himself into family/civilian life. There was a larrikin element in the image of the Kiwi soldier, but this boyishness was an important marker of the transitional nature of the military experience. The larrikin soldier, like the schoolboy he resembled, was a nascent family man. Sweethearts, sons, brothers and husbands as well as soldiers, military men's maturity would be finally marked by the transformation of soldiers into fathers. Women, too, might temporarily neglect the family, but the ideal war-working woman was a transient participant in the paid workforce. The real test of the land-girl's or servicewoman's patriotic commitment lay in her willingness to exchange the seductions of men's work for the quieter pleasures of peacetime home-making. Maturity would be marked by the transition from war-working sweetheart to sweet-hearted mother. The ways the men and women who lived through the war have written and spoken about their experience highlight the extent to which gender continuity was maintained, not just because it served the interests of the state, but also because it served the emotional and social needs of individual New Zealanders. Writing the private and psychological dimensions of experience into our social histories of gender is not easy, but it is necessary if we are to understand the elasticity and persistence of gender asymmetry.

Not all men became soldiers, of course, nor did all women become mothers, but the idealisation of these roles was important in quieting social fears about the consequences of wartime mobilisation. The home was seen as a place where a society disrupted by war could be knitted back together, and although women were meant to do most of this work, contemporaries generally agreed this was only fair, given what were seen as men's greater wartime sacrifices. Men and women might risk coarsening themselves by their involvement with a destructive war, but both could be reclaimed through the family. The centrality of heterosexual coupling and family for-mation to images of peace and rehabilitation created a social space in which masculinity and femininity would continue to interact, and a real sense of interdependence and commitment on the part of many individual men and women. Mum and the soldier might not live happily ever after, but they would try to get on.

I would like to thank Raewyn Dalziel and Caroline Daley for their comments on an earlier draft of this essay.

1   John Mulgan, *Report on Experience*, London, 1947, reprinted Wellington, 1967, p. 142.
2   The Schedule of Registration Orders, *Appendices to the Journals of the House of Representatives*, 1946, H-11A, p.133 shows how industrial conscription was applied to women aged 18-40 incrementally over a two-year period from March 1942. Men aged 18 to 50 were eligible for direction to work of national importance from the introduction of the system in March 1942. Men aged 50-59 were included by October 1942 and special registration orders relating to the building industry, engineering and metal trades, and the timber industry meant that men with certain kinds of work experience were eligible for direction up until the age of 70. The argument that the application of industrial conscription to women was shaped by a reluctance to interfere with their domestic duties is elaborated in my essay, 'Man-powering Women: Industrial Conscription during the Second World War', in Barbara Brookes, Charlotte Macdonald and Margaret Tennant, eds, *Women in History 2*, Wellington, 1992, pp. 184-204. A similar set of constraints seem to have guided policy makers in Britain, Canada and Australia. On Britain see Margaret Allen, 'The Domestic Ideal and the Mobilisation of Womanpower in WWII', *Women's Studies International Forum*, 6, 4, 1983, pp. 401-12; on Canada see Ruth Roach Pierson, *They're Still Women After All: the Second World War and Canadian Womanhood*, Toronto, 1986; and on Australia Lynne Davis, 'Minding Children or Minding Machines: Women's Labour and Child Care during the Second World War', *Labour History*, 53, 1987, pp. 86-98.
3   There is an extensive international literature dealing with the impact of the war on gender roles, women's in particular. In the American literature, William Chafe's initially positive assessment of the war as a period in which women's outlook was 'radically transformed ... a watershed in the history of women at work', made in *The American Woman: Her Changing Social, Economic, and Political Roles, 1920 to 1970*, New York, 1972, pp. 135-6, has been scaled back to one in which women's experiences were 'mixed ... a combination of improvements in some areas and persistent discrimination in others', *The Paradox of Change: American Women in the 20th Century*, New York, 1991, p. 121. Seven major books and numerous articles published in the wake of Chafe's 1972 book explore the factors constraining change: Leila Rupp, *Mobilizing Women for War*, Princeton, 1978; Karen Anderson, *Wartime Women: Sex Roles, Family Relations, and the Status of Women During World War II*, Westport, Conn., 1981; Susan Hartmann, *The Home Front and Beyond: American Women in the 1940s*, Boston, 1982; Maureen Honey,

Creating Rosie the Riveter: Class, Gender and Propaganda During World War II, Lincoln, 1984; D'Ann Campbell, *Women at War with America: Private Lives in a Patriotic Era*, Cambridge, 1984; Ruth Milkman, *Gender at Work: The Dynamics of Job Segregation by Sex During World War II*, Urbana, 1987; Sherna Gluck, *Rosie the Riveter Revisited: Women, the War and Social Change*, Boston, 1987. Gretchen Lemke-Santangelo's *Abiding Courage: African American Migrant Women and the East Bay Community*, Chapel Hill, 1996 is the best treatment of African American women though Karen Anderson's 'Last Hired, First Fired: Black Women Workers During World War II', *Journal of American History*, 69, 1982, pp. 82-97 is still useful. Alison Bernstein's *American Indians and World War II: Toward a New Era in Indian Affairs*, Norman, 1991, deals with Native American women in the chapter on the Indian home front. Penny Summerfield's work is central to understanding the experience of women in Britain, in particular her two books *Women Workers in the Second World War: Production and Patriarchy in Conflict*, London, 1984, and *Reconstructing Women's Wartime Lives: Discourse and Subjectivity in Oral Histories of the Second World War*, Manchester, 1998. The collections *Out of the Cage: Women's Experiences in Two World Wars*, edited by Gail Braybon and Penny Summerfield, London, 1987 and *Nationalizing Femininity: Culture, Sexuality, and British Cinema in the Second World War*, edited by Christine Gledhill and Gillian Swanson, Manchester, 1996 are also worth noting. As with Summerfield's monographs, there is a sharp contrast between the empirical social history in the pre-1990 volume and the more reflexive and theoretically sophisticated work published in the post-1990 collection. The Australian literature is more scattered but a good overview can be obtained from Patricia Grimshaw, Marilyn Lake, Ann McGrath and Marian Quartly's, *Creating A Nation, 1788-1990*, Ringwood, Vic., 1994, pp. 255-66. Key readings include Carmel Shute, 'From Balaclavas to Bayonets', in Elizabeth Windschuttle, ed., *Women, Class and History: Feminist Perspectives on Australia 1788-1978*, Sydney, 1980, pp. 353-87; Penelope Johnson, 'Gender, Class and Work: the Council of Action for Equal Pay and the Equal Pay Campaign in Australia During World War II', *Labour History*, 50, May 1986, pp. 132-46; Marilyn Lake, 'Female Desires: the Meaning of World War II', *Australian Historical Studies*, 24, 95, 1990, pp. 267-84 and Kate Darian-Smith, *On the Homefront: Melbourne in Wartime 1939-1945*, Melbourne, 1990.

4   My article 'Reassessing Rosie: World War II, New Zealand Women and the Iconography of Femininity', *Gender & History*, 8, 1, 1996, pp. 108-32, discusses the stereotypical depiction of gender differences in visual images of women in New Zealand's wartime media. Charles Lewis and John Neville's recent article, 'Images of Rosie: A Content Analysis of Women Workers in American Magazine Advertising, 1940-6', *Journalism and Mass Communications Quarterly*, 72, 1, 1999, pp. 216-227, reports that the depiction of homemakers and mothers in magazine advertising (36 percent of all images of women in 1940) declined only slightly during the war to 30 percent in 1943, returning to near pre-war levels by 1946 (33 percent). Images of women wage-earners, 5 percent of their 1940 sample, had increased to 19 percent by 1943 but fell back to 7 percent in 1946, evidence that American advertisers were 'restrained in their use of portrayals of women's new roles in the workforce', p. 223.

5   *New Zealand National Review*, 15 June 1941, p. 16; *Better Business*, June 1943, pp. 39-40.

6   Mulgan, *Report on Experience*, p. 15.

7   On New Zealand women at war see Eve Ebbett's popular history *When the Boys Were Away: New Zealand Women in World War II*, Wellington, 1984, Lauris Edmond's edited collection *Women in Wartime: New Zealand Women Tell Their Story*, Wellington, 1986, Deborah Montgomerie, 'A Personal Affair Between Me and Hitler? Public Attitudes to Women's Paid Work in New Zealand during World War Two', MA thesis, University of Auckland, 1986, Deborah Brosnahan, 'A Woman's Place: Changing Attitudes to the Role of Women in Society During World War II in New Zealand', MA thesis, University of Canterbury, 1987, and my articles 'War and Women: Work and Motherhood', *New Zealand Women's Studies Journal* 3, 2, 1988, pp. 3-16, 'The Limitations of Wartime Change: Women War Workers in New Zealand During World War Two', *New Zealand Journal of History*, 23, 1, 1989, pp. 68-86 and 'Men's Jobs and Women's Work: The New Zealand Women's Land Army in World War II', *Agricultural History*, 63, 3, 1989, pp. 1-14.

8   The history of men as gendered subjects is gradually being written into the historiography of the Second World War. Summerfield's *Reconstructing Women's Wartime Lives* is attentive to the

ways women's ideas about masculinity were implicated in men's ideas about themselves while Clare Wightman's *More than Munitions:Women,Work and the Engineering Industries, 1900-1950*, Harlow, 1999, examines the way that gender explains the experience of both male and female war workers. Margaret Higonnet, et al, eds, *Behind the Lines: Gender and the Two World Wars*, New Haven, 1987, contains some extremely fine essays, the most pertinent here being Sonya Michel's 'American Women and the Discourse of the Democratic Family in World War II'. Joy Damousi and Marilyn Lake's edited collection *Gender and War: Australians at War in the Twentieth Century*, Cambridge, 1995 contains essays about dysfunctional servicemen, Black GIs and male homosexuality but, with the exception of Stephen Garton's piece on repatriation, does not canvass the history of normative masculinity, military or civilian.

9 There are now over 100 published war memoirs ranging in date of publication from Martyn Uren's May 1943 *Kiwi Saga* to a flood of memoirs produced in the 1980s and 1990s when those in their twenties and thirties during the war reached retirement age. In addition to individual memoirs, the list includes a large number of volumes collating the experiences of several people, like Lauris Edmond's edited collection *Women in Wartime*, and less well-known compilations such as the Country Women's Institute's *Wartime Experiences*,Wellington, 1996.

10 See, for example, Margaret Tennant, 'Natural Directions: the New Zealand Movement for Sexual Differentiation in Education During the Early Twentieth Century', *New Zealand Journal of Educational Studies*, 12, 2, 1977, pp. 142-52; Raewyn Dalziel, 'The Colonial Helpmeet: Women's Role and the Vote in Nineteenth-century New Zealand', *New Zealand Journal of History*, 11, 2 1977, pp. 112-23.

11 This side of wartime masculinity is often suppressed in contemporary accounts but surfaces occasionally in calls for women to maintain counterbalancing values, see for example *Press* (Christchurch), 20 November 1944, p. 6.

12 Laurie Barber, *War Memorial:A Chronology of New Zealand and World War II*,Wellington, 1989, p. 65. Men who married between 1 May 1940 and their call-up were not classed as married until the marriage had produced a child.

13 15,744 Maori men voluntarily registered for service before 31 May 1945.

14 Barber, *War Memorial*, pp. 257, 262. Alison Parr, *Silent Casualties: New Zealand's Unspoken Legacy of the Second World War*, North Shore City, 1995, p. 14.

15 Montgomerie, 'Man-powering Women'.

16 Montgomerie, 'Men's Jobs and Women's Work'.

17 E.J. Osborne, *Living it Again*,Waikanae, 1988, p. 7.

18 A. Ngata, *The Price of Citizenship*,Wellington, 1943.

19 Bracy Gardiner, ed., *It Wasn't Easy. Memoirs of Wartime Women of the South*, Invercargill, 1990, p. 34.

20 Keith Elliot with Rona Adshead, *From Cowshed to Dog Collar*,Wellington, 1967, p. 123.

21 *New Zealand Herald*, 4 April 1944, p. 4.

22 Anna Rogers, ed., *The War Years: New Zealanders Remember 1939-1945*,Wellington, 1989, p. 55.

23 Martyn Uren, *Kiwi Saga: Memoirs of a New Zealand Artilleryman*, 5th edn, Auckland, 1943, p. 44. The flyleaf of the fifth edition lists two previous Middle East editions of May 1943, and two New Zealand editions in July and September 1943.

24 *Wartime Experiences:A Collection of Short Stories from Members of the Country Women's Institute*, Blenheim, 1996, p. 110.

25 Joyce Macdonald, *Away from Home: the Story of a Nursing Sister in the Middle East*, Christchurch, 1945, p. 13.

26 Eric W. Barr to Neal family, 5 April [?1942], Neal family papers, ms papers 1494, Alexander Turnbull Library, Wellington, (ATL).

27 Mark Venables, *My Quiet War*, Auckland, 1982-3, p.12.

28 Chapter 4 of Jock Phillips, *A Man's Country?:The Image of the Pakeha Male – A History*, Auckland, revised ed. 1996, is the best historical treatment of relationships between New Zealand soldiers. See also John McLeod, *Myth and Reality: the New Zealand Soldier in World War II*, Auckland, 1986. Much work remains to be done to document the history of gay and lesbian experiences in New Zealand during this period. Allan Bérubé's *Coming Out Under Fire: Gay Men and Women in World War Two*, NewYork, 1990, details the struggles of homosexuals and lesbians in

the American military and has some good material on gay and lesbian civilians. Leisa Meyer's *Creating G.I. Jane: Sexuality and Power in the Women's Army Corps during World War II*, New York, 1996 is a compelling analysis of the way that assumptions about heterosexuality and the persecution of homosexuality and lesbianism shaped the integration of women into the American army. On Australia see Garry Wotherspoon's 'Comrades-in-arms: World War II and Male Homosexuality in Australia', in Damousi and Lake, eds, *Gender and War.*

29 Uren, *Kiwi Saga*, p. 162.

30   Lawrence Watt, *Mates and Mayhem: Frontline Kiwis Remember,* Auckland, 1996, p. 141.

31 Macdonald, *Away from Home*, p. 162.

32   June Cummings to Duncan Gray, 3 December 1941, George Duncan Dunbar Gray papers, ms papers 2086, folder 3, ATL.

33 June Cummings to Duncan Gray, 16 December 1941, Gray papers, folder 3, ATL.

34 Misc. photographs, Gray papers, folder 4, ATL.

35 Letter (last page missing) from a soldier stationed in the Pacific to Neal family, 18 April 1944, Neal family papers, ATL.

36 Cecil Irving to Neal family, n.d., Claudelands base, Hamilton, Neal family papers, ATL.

37 *Ibid.*

38 Eric Barr to Neal family, 21 April 1942, Neal family papers, ATL.

39 Bill to Neal family, 20 February 1942, Neal family papers, ms papers 1494, ATL.

40 Gay Gray to Duncan Gray, 25 October 1941, 3 November 1941, Gray papers, folder 1, ATL.

41 Sally Mathieson, ed., *Bill Gentry's War 1939-45,* Palmerston North, p. 133.

42 Bill McConnochie to Bonnie Elliot, 28 September 1944, 10 October 1944, quoted in C.E. Grubb, ed., *A Long Time Away: the Wartime Experiences of WW2 Fighter Pilot F/O W.G. McConnochie, D.F.C.*, Alexandra, 1995, p. 184.

43 Frank Bruno, *Desert Daze*, Auckland, 1944, pp. 59-60, 69.

44 Bruno, *Desert Daze*, p. 3.

45 Ted to Neal family, Taieri, 16 March 1942, Neal family papers, ATL.

46 Francis Jackson, *Passage to Tobruk*, Wellington, 1943, p. 12.

47 Jackson, *Passage to Tobruk*, p. 92.

48 *Ibid.*, p. 143.

49 Rogers, *The War Years*, p. 48.

50 Macdonald, *Away From Home,* pp. 12, 65.

51 *Ibid.*, pp. 11-12.

52 Riddiford family papers, ms 5714, folder 066, ATL .

53 Country Women's Institute, *Wartime Experiences*, pp. 24-6.

54 Neva Clarke McKenna, *Angel in God's Office: My Wartime Diaries,* North Shore City, 1996, pp. 17, 20, 173.

55 Diary entry, 25 December 1939, quoted in Mathieson, *Bill Gentry*, p. 11.

56 Bill Gentry to Lalla Gentry, 31 August 1940, Gentry papers, ms papers 5525-8, ATL.

57 Bill Gentry to Lalla Gentry, 25 September 1941, Gentry papers, ATL.

58 Bill Gentry to Lalla Gentry, 25 March 1941, Gentry papers, ATL.

59 Bill Gentry to Lalla Gentry, Easter Sunday 1942, Gentry papers, ATL.

60 Bill Gentry to Lalla Gentry, [date torn] 1944, Gentry papers, ATL. Mathieson's selection from this letter is heavily edited.

61 Jackson, *Passage to Tobruk*, p. 142.

62 Country Women's Institute, *Wartime Experiences*, pp. 24-6.

63 John Blythe, *Soldiering On: A Soldier's War in North Africa and Italy*, Auckland, 1989, p. 182.

64 Gardiner, *It Wasn't Easy*, p. 13.

65 Allan Yeoman, *The Long Road to Freedom*, Auckland, 1991, pp. 184-5.

66 *Ibid.*, p. 186.

67 David McGill, ed., *P.O.W. The Untold Stories of New Zealanders as Prisoners of War*, Lower Hutt, 1987, p. 152.

68 Colin Armstrong, *Life Without Ladies*, Christchurch, 1947, pp. 3-4, 28.

69 Claude Thompson, *Into the Sun*, Warkworth, 1996, p. 156.

70 Yeoman, *Long Road to Freedom*, p. vi.

71 Harold Smith, *Memories of World War II: Experiences of a Junior Officer, Greece, Crete, Egypt, Libya and POW*, Pokeno, 1996, pp. 130-1. Contemporary evidence of uncaptured soldiers' attitudes to their captured fellows is sparse, but in Gentry's wartime letters there is some evidence of impatience towards ex-POWs that speaks to the issue of hierarchies of masculine sacrifice. Gentry felt that POWs expected too much mollycoddling, 'All of these ex PWs have a curious psychology owing to being shut up so long. They seem to want a lot of sympathy though of course their lot has been much easier & less dangerous than that of any equivalent soldier even though it has been infinitely more boring.' Bill Gentry to Lalla Gentry, [date torn] November 1944, Gentry papers, ATL.

72 Verbatim Evidence, Dominion Population Select Committee, Legislative Series 1/1946/1 National Archives, Wellington, p. 10.

73 *Ibid.*, pp. 83, 248.

The Man in the Grey Flannel Suit: White-Collar Masculinity in Post-War New Zealand

Frazer Andrewes

In the mid-twentieth century, the growth of powerful bureaucratic and organisational structures and the increasing employment of men in white-collar occupations dictated a reconfiguration in the representation of New Zealand masculinity. Taken at face value, white-collar work seemed to share few characteristics with New Zealand's traditional and more convention-ally 'muscular' images of masculinity, and was in fact antithetical to settler mythologies that stressed the worth of manual labour and the benefits of a rural life. As the sociologist Michael Roper has stated, business, the world of the white-collar worker, does not instantly equate with common defini-tions of masculinity.[1] However, the post-war period saw a subtle shift in the way white-collar work was realised, as the nature of work patterns and the ordering of society changed. Images of white-collar men attempted to convey a sense of powerful masculinity, of control and ability. This chapter aims to assess how these stereotypically passive and sedentary occupations could be represented as embodying traits of strong and assertive masculinity.

During the period immediately after the Second World War, and par-ticularly after the last vestiges of wartime rationing were removed in 1950, New Zealand experienced a hitherto unknown level of prosperity and eco-nomic growth. Fundamental economic and infrastructural changes affected the balance of society. New Zealand was rapidly developing an urbanised, consumer culture; statistics indicate a society rapidly embracing post-war prosperity.[2]

Consumerism developed hand-in-hand with suburbanisation and the reification of the family. In this period New Zealand's consumption of commodities was greater than ever before. The ownership of material goods was a visible indicator of status and it also served to define gender

In the post-war years male invincibility in business was literally represented by the images of smartly dressed men. Newsview, July 1953, Auckland Museum.

identities. Men could gain prestige from the ownership of a certain type of car, and the number of household appliances a family possessed attested to the man's capabilities as a breadwinner and technocrat. The number of cars licensed in the country more than doubled between 1945 and 1960, and the production of household appliances, particularly radios, washing machines and refrigerators, advanced rapidly.[3] Electricity consumption rose as more users were connected, and telephones became increasingly common. Many formerly gravel roads were sealed, considerable expense was laid out for the construction of highways, and the country's first motorways, where men could take their symbols of masculine achievement for a spin, were constructed.

But consumer culture had a potentially deleterious effect on men and on the public image of their masculinity. In order to purchase the expanding number of goods available, and keep up with the Joneses next door, people increasingly turned to hire purchase or other forms of short-term credit. A limited survey showed that, at the end of 1955, £9,663,000 was owed under hire purchase and that, by the end of 1960, this amount had increased to almost £15,000,000.[4] New Zealand was becoming a nation of debtors, and indebtedness was a slur on the masculine ability to earn enough money to purchase household goods. An alternative to debt was for women to continue to work outside the home after marriage. Whatever strategy was adopted, indebtedness or a working wife questioned the male's success as breadwinner, and undermined one of the central functions of domestic man.

White-collar breadwinners perhaps faced this contradiction more than other men. White-collar work struggled to define itself as manly in the face of increasing numbers of women entering the tertiary sector in both public administration and private enterprise.[5] When compared with other more obvious constructions of physical masculinity in 1950s culture (particularly images of military and sporting masculinity), the largely sedentary and passive images of business may seem to claim little kinship. Yet parallels can be drawn. As David Morgan conjectures, '[p]ictures of stockbrokers, bishops or dons might not seem as embodied as images of sportsmen or warriors, but if we fail to see their bodies in these cases this may be because of a prior framework of understanding that links men, bodies and action'.[6] In fact, despite the strength of images of muscular manhood, images of white-collar masculinity operated within a public discourse of surprising and, ultimately, powerful fluidity.

One of the most significant ways of expressing masculinity in any context is through the exercise and control of power. The masculine imagery of blue-collar work largely relied on strength and collectivity. The masculinity of white-collar work, as defined in the 1950s, was a much more complex creation. At one level it incorporated familiar elements of 'traditional' masculine stereotypes. For example, the journal of the Chambers of Commerce of New Zealand illustrated the cover of their first issue of 1947 with the torso of a man, clearly white-collar, as he was depicted wearing a tie, rolling his sleeves up over muscled and sinewy forearms. There are obvious parallels between this image and iconographical representations of working-class men. To reinforce the muscular tone of the picture it was militaristically captioned 'Operation 1947'.[7] On other occasions, businessmen were equated with the 'pioneers' of New Zealand's past. As the president of the Associated Chambers of Commerce stressed, '[i]t was the pioneer business man in this country who developed its export industries, and found the markets without which New Zealand would be a backward and underdeveloped nation'.[8] But these formed only part of the overall representation, and were subsumed into a more sophisticated image of manliness, one that both responded to and reacted against a hegemonic conception of manly endeavour and the looming threat of feminisation of the white-collar workplace.

The difficulties men had in defining white-collar work as masculine led to an ambivalent and sometimes hostile attitude towards women workers. One area where such antagonism became evident was in the debate surrounding equal pay for public employees. Here men faced the double challenge of women working in the same white-collar jobs, and, particularly in the post-war period, pushing for equal pay. Aside from expressions of outrage at the prospect of (as they saw it) an eroded living standard, a common reaction was for men to hide behind belittling and depreciating humour.[9] A protest by various women's groups to the government during 1956 prompted the publication of a piece of facetious doggerel in a major daily newspaper:

> . . . Sir, I'm afraid this Outrage to Womanhood
> Isn't going to do the Government any Good.
> Let's back down, before the Amazonian Horde
> Converges on the Capital with Fire and Sword
> And Umbrellas levelled, and seizes the Reins
> Of Government, or as Much of it remains!
> Give them their equal Pay, if that will appease them,
> The ladies (Bless 'em) — why,
> ANYTHING to please them![10]

The Amazonian horde took until 1960 to achieve equal pay in the government sector, but long before that sociologists and other writers in New Zealand and other industrial societies were concerning themselves with the role of the male manager and his masculinity. In 1951, the American sociologist C.Wright Mills attempted to analyse the new and burgeoning white-collar class against the 'old middle class', by looking much more systematically at the systems that governed the lives of these people.[11] In Britain, Roy Lewis and Rosemary Stewart endeavoured to assess the character of the businessman at a time when the British Labour government was attempting to implement widespread nationalisation.[12] Of all these works, William Whyte's treatise on the organisation man pushed boundaries the furthest by shifting the focus away from the place of work and analysing the life environment, assessing not just the impact of new jobs, but also that of suburbanisation and consumerism.[13] New Zealand did not have a comparable sociological literature, but articles in periodicals such as *New Zealand Commerce* and *Management* indicate that the world of white-collar work, the science of management and the life of the executive were occupying the minds of more and more people.[14] New Zealand's white-collar executives imbibed the works of such management gurus as Lyndall Urwick and Peter Drucker, both of whom strove to define the optimum style of managerial success.[15]

This chapter will use two different source bases to investigate the construction of white-collar masculinity. The first of these is advertising material, specifically that depicting the white-collar worker predominantly, though not always, in the office environment. The second category of sources are the articles on white-collar work and particularly the work of the business executive published during the late 1940s and 1950s. In their desire to best articulate and define the businessman and his role, these sources say much about prevailing attitudes to gender and white-collar occupations.

Roland Marchand has commented that in early- and mid-twentieth-century advertising the businessman often played the part of generic man, far outnumbering depictions of men in other occupations.[16] In the post-war years, this could have been a reflection of structural changes occurring in the economy, and it also conforms to the image of an increasingly urbanised society. Businessmen were often depicted in a dialogue with modernity. Advertisements asserted the control of businessmen over their surroundings, and their mastery of technology. Control of people's lives, generally employees and particularly female secretaries, correlated with the businessman's

Using the right shaving cream promised success in business and in love.
Newsview, March 1953, Auckland Museum.

control over his physical surroundings. Although advertising from the pre-war period had also made this link, in 1950s New Zealand these images had growing resonance. In an increasingly consumerist, urbanised and industrialised society, control of technology and control of people equated with considerable power. Advertising is a medium designed to entice the prospective consumer into becoming an actual consumer, and is therefore primarily selling a product. But advertisements also carry with them definite social messages, sometimes as an intentional ploy on the part of the advertising agency, and sometimes inadvertently or subconsciously. As the Marxist social analyst Judith Williamson has stated, '[a]dvertisements are selling us something else besides consumer goods: in providing us with a structure in which we, and those goods, are interchangeable, they are selling us ourselves'.[17] Because of this function, advertisements are useful in a gender analysis since they depict an idealised version of the gendered self and the way cultural expectations of gender operate.

The most prominent metaphor of white-collar masculinity used in the advertising of the 1950s was that of the confident and successful businessman, at one with his work and with his life. The common image was of a smartly groomed man, neither a youth nor very old, who embodied the physical traits that defined a 'manly' man. The businessman always wore a suit and tie, was tall, well-built but slim, with square shoulders and an open, strong-jawed face. The figure of the white-collar man was clearly associated with an urban and strongly middle-class culture, but its ubiquity as an image in public literature, and the increasing relevance of urban society in the post-war years, made it strongly representative of masculinity and not simply of class hegemony and power. By the post-war period, the masculine image of the white-collar worker was more useful than other common exemplars of masculinity, including traditional blue-collar images of physical strength and the bonds of common fellowship. Blue-collar work, particularly its union iconography, has resolutely advanced an image of virile and potent masculinity.[18] The blending of this manly imagery with the more abstract notion of financial power, leadership and the ubiquity of the public image made the white-collar man an important and culturally relevant symbol of masculinity.

One of the most distinctive indicators of masculinity in advertising copy was the way a man looked. Success in business was often conflated with personal appearance, or the tailoring of one's clothes. Rainster rainwear advertisements pictured a tall, dignified, almost aristocratic gentleman, generally at leisure, but with an air of supreme confidence in himself. He was, 'The important man. He tops off his success with the top-coat of success.'[19] Another advertisement featuring the same man had as its caption, '"Broad shoulders" that "can take it"'.[20] The reference was to the waterproofing of the raincoat's shoulders, but the copywriter's intention was to highlight the masculinity of its wearer. Advertisers even equated active success with items of clothing that were hidden from the world's view. Jockey underwear claimed that they were 'built [a suitably manly description] for the man of action' and provided 'maximum masculine comfort'. The illustration of Jockey's man of action showed a smartly dressed businessman with briefcase firmly clasped and arms (but nothing else) swinging, a broad smile on his face. This is an image of confident white-collar masculinity, with the world literally at its feet.[21] Some advertisements mixed business success and success with women to create a definitively manly persona. An advertisement for Palmolive shaving cream pictured a smiling, suit-clad man with a young woman draped decorously around his neck, and the caption 'Look Successful ... Be Successful ... '.[22] The ambiguity about whether the man's success is in love or in business (or both) is intentional. In a less ambiguous statement, Palmolive even went so far as to list the occupations of those successful men who used its products around the border of an advertisement; the majority were white-collar: lawyers, accountants, bankers, salesmen, insurance agents and executives.[23]

The link between appearance and employment was not just a marketing ploy dreamed up by the advertising agencies. Various articles on and by businessmen stressed the importance of maintaining a manly appearance in the business world. An American case, quoted in a New Zealand magazine, commented that:

> [the] most vivid example of the marriage of outstanding appearance and success is displayed by members of the Young Presidents' Organisation, all men under forty years of age who have reached the top of the business world in a hurry. In a recent survey it was found that 140 of the young titans who had skyrocketed to success owned an average of 14.3 suits apiece and bought three or four new suits a year. Every one of them stressed the importance of personal appearance. They averaged 29 shirts, 30 pairs of socks, 10 pairs of shoes, four hats, two overcoats, and 1.5 raincoats.

The article also stressed that '[f]or a top-ranking executive, a general manager or secretary, a large wardrobe may be a necessity, a part of his job.'[24] Such excessive concentration on clothing and appearance might on the surface seem unmanly or effeminate, but the emblem of the suit and its cultural meaning for men at this time render its implications for manliness more obvious. As Frank Mort and Peter Thompson have written, '[m]oving beyond the advertising image, it is clear that for many . . . initiation into the culture of the suit was part of a broader initiation rite into manhood. . . . [The] purchase of "the suit" was a public sign of full male status. It was always approached with seriousness and forethought. The assumption of this adult persona conferred privileges as well as the burden of responsibility.'[25] A suit conferred on its wearer the distinction of white-collar masculinity. Often what was meant by appearance had broader significance than simply external aesthetic appeal. As one businessman stated, summing up those qualities he looked for when recruiting new people, '[a]ppearance is [a] factor, meaning personality, dress, speech. These things are important in any kind of work, and they must be counted in. Your grooming, the way you carry yourself, your ability to express your thoughts clearly, to make firm answers, these all add up to appearance, and are very important.'[26]

But while appearance and grooming were obviously important factors in both gaining employment and then maintaining a forceful, manly image, the key to success was knowing where and when to draw the fashion line. An article on group discussion leaders in a New Zealand management periodical ended with a list of dos and don'ts for prospective leaders. Some of the recommendations focused on personal appearance, advising that the

This advertisement makes a powerful link between military and corporate leadership.
Whether in a suit or a uniform, powerful men shared a common masculinity.
New Zealand Commerce, June 1956, Auckland Museum.

leader should 'be as well dressed as any member of his group but not no-
ticeably better than average' and that he should 'avoid excessive grooming'.[27]
Businessmen should adopt manly personae, but avoid becoming either too
manly or, more worryingly, too effeminate. Another concern was that a
man might be too conspicuous if he were too well dressed and would
therefore flaunt the boundaries of the egalitarianism on which New Zealand prided itself. A series of advertisements run for Invincible suits epitomised
the masculine style deemed proper for businessmen. One advertisement
placed a smartly dressed man in front of a city vista redolent of both sophistication and, in the lines of its buildings, business power.[28] Later
advertisements reduced the scale but focused more closely on the person
and how the suit enhanced him. 'Whether in business or in love, to be well-
dressed is to be confident – and confidence brings success', declared one
advertisement.[29] The final image was of sexual attraction and business power
made tangible, as an attractive woman gently touched the man on the shoulder and praised him for his smartness. 'And it isn't only SHE who will
notice it. The well-groomed, well-dressed man is the one the Boss will
naturally send to see important people. You start with a big advantage, both
in social and business life. Clothes cannot make the man, but an Invincible
Suit will make the *most* out of you.'[30] In effect, the advertisement claims to
make men who (in their new clothes) will be invincible in both love and
business.[31]

But the iconography of white-collar masculinity was more involved than a simple appeal to the man's external appearance. A common signifier of masculine strength was the pursuit, capture and exercise of power in various forms. The power commanded by white-collar workers, and particularly executives, is more abstract than common representations of masculine strength. The strong arm of labour and the iron and steel imagery of military prowess are more concrete in nature, but no more powerful than executive strength. Copy writers, illustrators and authors drew on both traditions to indicate masculinity in general, but the composite picture of the executive or the manager transcended these images. Authors often spoke of the executive in terms that emphasised the holistic aspect of the profession. 'Because of its generality of scope, because it involves working with every other type of person, because it is heavy with variety and responsibility, executive work uses the whole man as few other professions do. . . . Measuring executive ability means measuring the whole man, − not physically, to be sure, but as a human personality.'[32] The inference of such a statement was that because executive work used the whole man, the executive is more of a man. Another author, dealing with the question of what the job of an executive actually entailed, came to a similar conclusion about its appeal to the 'well-rounded' man. 'Now it seems to me that there are three important aspects of any executive job. Firstly practical; secondly psychological; and thirdly philosophical. . . . The top executive should spend but an essential minimum of time on the study of purely practical results, but rather ensure, with a knowledge of the philosophy of the business, that the right psychological atmosphere exists in which good practical results can mature.'[33] The ability to effectively control such diversity of talent was construed as power.

The world of white-collar work was intensely hierarchical. Business magazines devoted considerable space to questions of executive success and the definition and distillation of those qualities that marked a businessman as a leader. It is the question of leadership where the parallel between organisational masculinity and military masculinity was most closely drawn, and where business became a battleground of hostile take overs, covert operations and corporate raiders, where only men with leadership skills could successfully negotiate to a position of strength. An article on executive selection procedures commented on the considerable interest shown by management groups in wartime developments in officer selection procedures, and how some institutions even toyed with the idea of including a practical (physical) section in managerial selection.[34] Even advertising made the powerful link between military and corporate leadership. A DB Lager advertisement pictured a well-

Planned
Packaging
makes money
in your
Factory too

A package planned by experts does more than sell itself to the customer. Factors such as convenience, economy in use, packing-rate, storage-saving and so on, are all considered before the container goes into production. By tackling these problems at the outset, overhead costs are cut, handling time is reduced, money saved . . . before your product leaves the packing room.

WHY CARDBOARD MAKES THE BEST CONTAINER

Cardboard plays a part in packaging for almost every type of product. Boxes or cartons are light, yet strong. Being collapsible, they occupy a minimum of valuable storage space. They're suitable for packing and protecting heavy solids, powder or breakables. And yet the unit cost of cardboard containers is, in almost every case, far below that of any other packaging material !

THE RIGHT WAY TO PLAN PACKAGING

The only sure way of getting good packaging for your product is to discuss the matter with your boxmaker right from the start. His experience will be of the greatest help in producing a container that cuts costs, protects the product, and at the same time, presents it to the customer in the best possible manner. If packaging in any form is your immediate problem, call in your boxmaker now.

ISSUED IN THE INTERESTS OF BETTER PACKAGING
BY B. J. BALL (N.Z.) LTD., PAPER MERCHANTS
Sole Agents for WHAKATANE BOARD MILLS LTD.

The confident businessman in control of his life and his employees. Note that the workers have their backs to the window, while the boss looks out into the wider world. New Zealand Commerce, July 1952, Auckland Museum.

dressed businessman greeting three handsome and decorated officers in what appeared to be a gentlemen's club. The caption, 'A man is known by the company he keeps', reinforced the sense of fraternity among the men, a sense that they all shared common manly qualities.[35]

Leaders were required to display characteristics that set them apart from other men. As one author put it, '[l]eadership can make common men into uncommon men.'[36] A New Zealand admiral and high commissioner to Australia during the 1950s contributed an article to an administrative periodical in which he attempted to essentialise those qualities of leadership he deemed necessary in the successful executive. One of the most important, to his mind, was courage: 'No craven commander can be a leader of men. Particularly I refer to moral courage which is more difficult to display than physical courage. If both are present so much the better. . . . I cannot believe that these qualities would not help those in command of the community. The man who will be physically brave in an emergency and who will fight for a principle for his organization is surely a likely leader.'[37] Other authors stressed different qualities of leadership. Some saw 'judgement, savoir faire, insight, fairmindedness' as the most vital factors; others concluded that character and personality were of equal importance.[38] What is clear is that the sum of these parts added up to a man of supernormal traits who embodied masculine stereotypes of rationality, mental agility and courage. One commentator even went as far as to accord cosmic significance to the role of the strong leader: '[I]t is significant that where there is an imaginative and bold leader at the top, good executives appear to emerge and develop throughout the organisation almost of their own accord, like planets condensing from clouds of inter-stellar dust'.[39]

In the advertising of the period, white-collar workers were depicted 'getting on with the job' in much the same way as their pioneer forebears were reputed to have done. Although the working environment had diminished in size (from the bush to the office), advertisements transformed the businessman into a far more effective and efficient worker. Many post-war advertisements featured businessmen engaged in a narrative with modernity. Technology, and the businessman's control of it, was a common indicator of masculine capabilities. Michael Roper has considered the phenomenon he describes as 'product fetishism', in which industrial managers made a 'psychic investment' in the goods they produced, and in some cases even eroticised the product or the technology by which it was produced.[40] This level of analysis was gained through interviews with company managers. Unfortunately, advertisements do not describe in such detail the innermost feelings and desires of the executives themselves. They do, however, glorify technology and, in so doing, reinforce not only the modernity and efficiency of the company, but also make a clear connection with masculine power. The post-war period was one of technological boom and optimism. As Andrew Wernick writes, in these years 'elements of an older patriarchal techno-worship were strongly reinforced, and in the advertising of the time its themes and images came dramatically to the fore'.[41]

Roland Marchand has commented on the visual clichés of the white-collar businessman employed in advertising tableaux during the twenties and thirties. The basic tenets seem to have survived through the fifties and, it could be claimed, exist in basically the same form in modern advertising copy. What Marchand describes as the tableau of 'master of all he surveys' was a common device in articulating prestige, power and command.[42] Advertising illustrations made the businessman master of his own domain, a figure in control of his life. An advertisement for, of all things, cardboard packaging, depicted an executive watching a production line of male workers busily filling cardboard boxes. Behind the workers stretches a large, seem-ingly endless, expanse of window symbolising, perhaps, the prospects await-ing them in the marketplace: it is significant that only the executive looks through the window, while the workers have their backs turned to it. The executive seems supremely confident, his arm gesturing to the scene, taking control of both the workers and the production process. Beside him a younger man, similarly suited, regards him approvingly.[43] The businessman's win-dow was a much used device for conveying images of power and command. An advertisement for air-conditioning units pictures a cool, poised execu-tive, a small smile on his face, adjusting the controls of his McAlpine air conditioner, positioned within his easy reach. He epitomises the confident businessman, his large desk uncluttered apart from an impressively large stamp, blotter and pen set. But most importantly, the air conditioner is set into a huge, apparently boundless, window. Through the window can be seen the hazy outline of large, industrial structures.[44] The businessman has, as the advertisement explains, control of the weather at his fingertips, just as he has control of his corporation viewed through the office window.

While a panoramic view and the aura of control this conjured up were important metaphors for manly business, the control of technology, and the ease with which one controlled it, were most firmly tied into the discourse of modernity. The most ubiquitous of these technological symbols was the telephone, a humble enough medium in the present age of fax, electronic mail and Internet, but at the time the most rapidly growing form of com-munication in New Zealand.[45] The telephone was a link to the world, a conduit that could help to expand the businessman's power and that of his company. Some advertisements linked confidence and success with the tele-phone. In 1950, New Zealand National Airways Corporation (NAC) ran an advertisement that emphasised the businessman as a master of all forms of technology. An executive is shown seated at his desk, the phone raised in one hand, almost as if it were displayed to the viewer, and a set of aeroplane tickets in the other. This businessman is at ease not only with the telephone, but also with the still relatively uncommon medium of domestic air travel, two ways by which distances could be shortened and business done more rapidly.[46] Conversely, inability to use technology correctly was a symbol of business failure. In an advertisement selling internal telephone systems, an irate managing director, one fist raised in the air, the other grasping the telephone, roars into it 'What . . . Hunt's line still busy . . . . But I must contact him urgently!'[47] The message was quite clear. The ability to use technology properly conveyed to the businessman an aura of rational, masculine control. Failure to do so not only meant potential lost business, but also reduced the businessman to fits of irrational temper, even hysteria. The answer to such problems, according to the Standard Telephones and Cables company, was to install an intercom system which, as a graphic explained, would place the manager at the heart of his organisation with his finger literally on the intercom button, metaphorically on the pulse.

Much as they mastered technology, businessmen in advertisements exercised seemingly effortless control over the women in their employment. It is, however, difficult to gauge whether such confidence was actually the case in white-collar work. Men faced the post-war period with some confusion and uncertainty about their place in it. This was despite the overbearing emphasis the period placed on delineating very clear roles for males and females. An advertisement encouraging young people to begin saving for their future made these distinctions perfectly obvious. A young man and a young woman stand side-by-side and stare dreamily skyward, each contemplating future desires. The man has a fully equipped workshop in mind, and the woman a modern, pristine kitchen, packed with the latest appliances. The copy alerts her to the fact that saving would enable her to be more independent in years to come, 'and a great help to your future husband when you start planning your dream home'.[48]

Regardless of such blithe reassurances of correct gender prescriptions, nagging uncertainty meant that men had to try to reinvent themselves in the face of what they perceived to be a loss of manly identity. C. Wright Mills commented at length on this sense of malaise and status panic among American white-collar workers, and the way in which these men tried to prove they had not lost or diluted their masculinity. He saw the solution opted for by most American white-collar men as being a kind of justified conformity. 'To be compatible with the top men is to act like them, to think like them: to be of and for them – or at least to display oneself to them in such a way as to create that impression.'[49] The way in which men in New Zealand attempted such a reinvention, however, seemed to rely more on the categorisation of themselves as other than women. Confusion over the apparent contradictions of life manifested itself in the relations between men and women and, more relevant to the scope of this topic, the way men represented women. Concrete examples of status panic were not readily in evidence in either the periodical literature or advertising copy, but there was a proliferation of images that sought to undermine the impact and presence of women in the world of masculine white-collar work.

*Remington used images of male power and female
deference to sell typewriters.*
New Zealand Commerce, December 1955,
Auckland Museum.

The most common interaction between men and women portrayed in advertising was between the male executive and his female secretary. As discussed above, businessmen, and especially those whose companies produced consumer goods, often fetishised their products. In advertisements, these same companies transferred this fetish onto the figure of the purchaser, picturing the businessman gloating over various types of office machinery. Much of this office equipment (typewriters, accounting machines, 'computers') was not the province of the businessman himself but was for the use of his female secretary, 'typiste' or receptionist. Advertisers often incorporated the secretary into the advertisement's visuals. Rosemary Pringle asserts that the most common representation of the secretary until the 1960s was as the deferential and ladylike 'office wife', and the distinctions between wife and secretary seemed at times to blur quite significantly.[50] An article in the popular New Zealand monthly, *The Mirror*, reported on a British businesswoman, Mrs Evelyn Gordon, who had conducted a survey of executives who had married their secretaries. The article stressed the qualities bosses looked for in a wife, and how neatly they measured up to the qualities of a good secretary: efficiency, enthusiasm and a charming personality. As Gordon stated, '[i]f a woman has the qualities to be a first-class secretary then the same qualities will also make her a first-class wife.'[51] Highlighting the similarity between wives and secretaries diffused some of the fear the white-collar men felt about women in their profession. Women workers could be more easily accepted if their function in the office was equated with housework and the supportive role of the wife. As Pringle points out, however, the 1950s were characterised by a qualitative change in the representation of secretaries. In the advertising copy of this period the image of the sexually charged secretary was far more prevalent than the safer image of the office wife.[52] Such depictions brought a heightened awareness of masculine prestige by placing businessmen in a position of power over a symbol of attractive and illicit sexuality. In this way men could, in fantasy at least, break from the bonds of domesticity which, in previous representations, had followed them into the office.

Advertisements objectified the figure of the secretary and, by placing a sexually attractive figure beside the office equipment, charged it with erotic meaning. In all the images, men were given the dominant place, the position of power over their female employees, mastering both the technology and its operator. An advertisement for Remington typewriters, claimed by the copywriters as 'usually bought by a man, used by a woman, and judged by both', pictures an expanded view of two of the keys, one lower that the other. On the top key is drawn the figure of a man, one hand in pocket, the other pointing down to the lower key on which his secretary sits, looking up at him intently, a dictation pad on her knee.[53] Another advertisement placed the reader in the position of choosing between two secretaries, one a conservatively dressed, sternly efficient woman, the other an attractive, vivacious girl. The copy claimed that making a choice was hardly fair, but '"RV" Office Equipment is finished in attractive Grey Hammerglaze; soft ... neutral ... an ideal setting for the blondest blonde, cutest brunette'.[54] Regardless of whether the message of the advertisement is to buy office equipment to suit your secretary, or hire a secretary to suit your office equipment, the commodification of women as an office accessory is vividly apparent.

Often the advertisements worked by playing to the male gaze as, in a reversal of traditional gender stereotypes, women were depicted as active and men as passive.[55] But no subversive intent can be read into these advertisements since male passivity was employed only so that the man could gaze upon the secretary at his leisure. An advertisement for a dictation machine (claiming to 'create' the perfect secretary) showed a young and attractive typist looking coyly over her shoulder at a group of six male executives, all staring at her in admiration.[56] One business machine company claimed, pictorially, that purchase of their machines could reinvigorate the businessman and renew his confidence and assurance. In one picture, a dazed executive sat head in hand, surrounded by reams of paper, but, after the purchase of a new accounting machine, he was able, in the second picture, to recover his suave and manly demeanour as he stood gazing at one of the women in the typing pool using it.[57] Several advertisements employed the device of the unseen male gaze, the businessman watching as the women worked. One claimed a woman to be a 'virtuoso at the keyboard', showing only her back, seated at the typewriter.[58] A more ominous advertisement depicted a woman working a large and complicated computer, watched from some distance by the figures of two men, headless and incognito, framing the scene.[59] Such representations place all the power with the men. Although they were depicted as passive (and despite the fact that it was the woman who was operating the equipment), their gaze intimated control and surveillance, as well as the possession and objectification of the female operator and the machine.

Women constituted one of the biggest threats to a stable construction of masculinity in the minds of white-collar men, even those managers and executives unlikely to face direct competition from women for their jobs. A common male fear was that women were encroaching on male occupations, particularly in the white-collar sector. An article published one year after the war's end claimed that men were 'invading' women's jobs because women no longer wanted to do what was regarded as traditionally women's work. The article's author expressed astonishment at the fact that women refused to return to the work they had done before their direction to essential industries during the war, and stated that higher wages and more interesting, less monotonous, jobs were the major reasons for their refusal to do 'traditional' work. The tone of the article was clearly one of concern that women, by their obstinacy, were demasculinising male workers and forcing them into a situation where their position as breadwinners was under threat. 'With this attitude of mind predominating throughout New Zealand it is not strange that factories hitherto almost exclusively staffed by women and girls find themselves unable to get sufficient workers and resort must be had to men.'[60] Women were seen as having a detrimental effect on several levels, forcing male wage labour into 'feminine' occupations and, by feminising white-collar work, further increasing the ambiguity of the masculinity of such employment. In subtle and not so subtle ways, advertisers and authors chipped away at the credibility of women as white-collar workers, relying largely on objectifying images, belittling humour and supposedly informed debate.

But even those advertisers who accepted that women were carving out a place for themselves in the business world refused to let women contend on an equal footing with men. In the late 1940s, the Bank of New Zealand ran a series of advertisements highlighting their services for the business community. One such advertisement depicted the 'business woman', but the accompanying text and its meaning were subtly different from the accompanying text for the 'business man'. The businesswoman banked with the BNZ because she had need of 'experienced guidance' and because she found the bank manager 'courteous and helpful'.[61] The businessman, however, used the BNZ because he needed to 'consult my Bank Manager at every opportunity' and because he appreciated the 'confidential service' he received.[62] He consulted, she received guidance. The advertisement, while nodding in the direction of career women, still indicated that women were considered subservient to both their business peers and their male bank managers. An advertisement for the New Zealand Insurance Company suggested similar inequities. Above the caption 'Important meeting of directors', a husband and wife sit at home before their fire.[63] The advertisement claims that the man and his wife are the directors of the most important company in the world, namely their family, and that security for their future is an important consideration for both. But the image belies the words, as the woman is portrayed in a role more fitting to a secretary than a director. Her husband, in a large armchair, leans forward, holding his glasses in one hand, and gesturing with a sheaf of papers in the other. His wife, seated in a much smaller chair, smiles back at him, continuing her knitting as she does so. The advertisement, directed at husbands not wives, firmly places him as the director, the decision-maker. If his wife had been depicted with a dictation pad rather than a pair of knitting needles, she would neatly reverse the more common advertising dichotomy; whereas the secretary was often the 'office wife', in this picture the wife was transformed into the 'home secretary'.

While secretaries were depicted as performing useful, if at times gratuitously decorative, functions, other women had no place in a businessman's world. An article attempting to justify different wage rates for men and women claimed that in general 'women are less ambitious than men'. An employer, the article's author postulated, was concerned 'with the potential talent of his staff, so that he can fill more responsible positions. . . . [H]e will look to his male employees for such talent, for a multitude of reasons. . . .

[H]ow many business deals are settled over a glass of scotch in clubs from which women are debarred? Again, how many male workers would willingly accept directions, or censure, from a female executive?'[64] Clearly not that particular author. In one 'humorous' article, a correspondent explained that a new wife could be a fiscal advantage. '[I]n New Zealand the best day [for marriage] is March 31. This is because the [tax] exemption in respect of a wife is allowable irrespective of the duration of the marriage in the income year. In other words, even though you have supported your wife for only a couple of hours you can take a full year's exemption for her.' And if, surprisingly, such a marriage did not work out, 'try to [divorce your wife] on April 1 – or April 2 if you are superstitious. The point is that the exemption for a wife extends in respect of a taxpayer – other than an absentee – who at any time during the year was a married man. So why support your wife for more days than are necessary?'[65]

The tenor of articles written about management and white-collar work indicated a hard-nosed, sometimes technical, always masculine environment. The language presupposed that most of the readers would be men, and that most of the people concerned with management and white-collar work would also be men. Statistics clearly indicate this to be false but, in the powerful realm of public imagery, control lay with men. Women – wives and secretaries – were marginalised, regardless of their actual impact on the work environment, and articles and advertisements stressed the dangers of women mixing in the white-collar environment. An article in *New Zealand Commerce,* designed to alert businessmen to the problems of dealing with women, portrayed them as potentially hazardous and disruptive in the office environment if not treated differently from male employees. The article was a litany of sex stereotypes, with women characterised as overemotional, illogical, conformist and hard-working only if suitably encouraged. The author placed working women into three categories: 'The career woman [who] feels she can handle her job like a man', 'The old maid [who] substitutes her job for the average woman's life-purpose' and 'the married woman [who] stays on the job because of family needs'. The overriding emphasis of the article was to stress that the male supervisor needed to tread warily to avoid the unpleasant consequences of a misplaced word or action. 'In all three types, problem situations will appear from time to time if you work with women. The most frightening experience you are likely to come up against is the flood of tears let loose without any warning. . . . Finally keep in mind the fact that some women use tears as a deliberate weapon. Better not yield. Whatever happens, you have to maintain your standards – undiluted by tears.'[66]

The danger for men lay, according to the article, in losing hold of the essentially masculine traits of rationality and emotional control in the face of irrationality and emotional excess. To yield would be to compromise one's masculinity.

The businessman became an archetypically masculine image in the 1950s, with good reason. As the structure of society and the economy altered, the tertiary sector and business became increasingly important. In a rapidly suburbanising society, the utility of the white-collar man as a masculine signifier increased. I have argued that the way in which the image of white-collar masculinity was constructed incorporated images of more traditional masculine traits, especially those found in blue-collar or labour imagery and in militaristic metaphors, but transcended these by creating a more nuanced and ultimately more forceful portrait of manliness. At the core of this image was power, the control over people and over production, the mastery of financial resources and technology. Importantly, masculinity was also defined in contrast with femininity. The advertising images of white-collar masculinity were subtle, but the nature of men's control directly over women's lives was quite clear: wives and secretaries were there to serve the needs of the businessmen, and advertisements celebrated the mastery these men had over women. Women were marginalised, but they were placed firmly where men could voyeuristically gaze on them at work. In the 1950s the suit was re-encoded, and reinforced, as a sign of masculine power and achievement. White-collar manliness did not necessarily supplant more stereotypical forms, but it did represent a significant change in the way masculinity was formulated. It also lends support to the notion that we cannot view the 1950s as having been categorised by a single, hegemonic conception of how masculinity was constructed.

I would like to gratefully acknowledge the assistance of Barry Reay, Caroline Daley and Deborah Montgomerie in the formulation and preparation of this chapter.

1   Michael Roper, *Masculinity and the British Organization Man since 1945*, Oxford, 1994, p. 19
2   New Zealand's gross national product jumped from £399,400,000 in 1945 to £1,233,300,000 by 1960. *New Zealand Official Yearbook* (*NZOYB*), 1961, p. 744.
3   The number of washing machines increased from 38,804 in 1952-53 to a peak of 57,376 in 1954-55, and the number of refrigerators increased from 36,114 in 1952-53 to 71,538 in 1955-56. Radio production increased from 56,480 in 1952-53 to 120,867 in 1959-60. *NZOYB*, 1957, p. 644; 1961, p. 528.
4   *NZOYB*, 1961, p. 631.
5   Graeme Dunstall, 'The Social Pattern', in Geoffrey W. Rice, ed., *The Oxford History of New Zealand*, 2nd edn, Auckland, 1992, pp. 460-61.

6   David Morgan, 'You Too Can Have a Body Like Mine: Reflections on the Male Body and Masculinities', in Sue Scott and David Morgan, eds, *Body Matters: Essays on the Sociology of the Body*, London, 1993, p. 71.

7   *New Zealand Commerce*, January 1947, p. 1.

8   'New Zealand Still Needs Pioneers', *ibid.*, April 1955, p. 5.

9   See Margaret Corner, *No Easy Victory: Towards Equal Pay for Women in the Government Service, 1890-1960*, Wellington, 1988. For further information on the equal pay issue see Bert Roth, *Remedy For Present Evils: A History of the New Zealand Public Service Association from 1890*, Wellington, 1987.

10 Corner, *No Easy Victory*, p. 56.

11 C. Wright Mills, *White Collar: The American Middle Classes*, New York, 1951.

12 Roy Lewis and Rosemary Stewart, *The Boss: The Life and Times of the British Business Man*, London, 1958.

13 William H. Whyte, *The Organization Man*, Harmondsworth, 1969. This work was originally published in the United States in 1956.

14 *New Zealand Commerce* began publication shortly after the end of the war, *Management* began in the mid 1950s.

15 Both men wrote influential works on management which became essential reading for post-war executives. For examples of Urwick's writings see *The Elements of Administration*, 2nd edn, London, 1947, and *Leadership in the Twentieth Century*, London, 1957; for Drucker see *Concept of the Corporation*, New York, 1946 and *The Practice of Management*, London, 1955.

16 Roland Marchand, *Advertising the American Dream: Making Way for Modernity, 1920-1940*, Berkeley, 1985, p. 189.

17 Judith Williamson, *Decoding Advertisements: Ideology and Meaning in Advertising*, London, 1978, p. 13.

18 There are several works detailing the imagery of labour in various countries. Three of these for, respectively, Great Britain, Australia and New Zealand are John Gorman, *Banner Bright: An illustrated history of the banners of the British trade union movement*, London, 1973; Ann Stephen and Andrew Reeves, *Badges of Labour, Banners of Pride: Aspects of Working Class Celebration*, Sydney, 1985; Gregory Burke and Ann Calhoun, eds, *Art and Organised Labour: Images of working life and trade union life in New Zealand*, Wellington, 1990. While all these works document the iconography of the union movement in some detail, none make anything but the most marginal comment on the sometimes desperately masculinist imagery displayed. For a far more gender-conscious treatment of the imagery of the working classes, see Barbara Melosh, *Engendering Culture: Manhood and Womanhood in New Deal Public Art and Theater*, Washington, 1991.

19 *New Zealand Herald (NZH)*, 7 June 1956, p. 9.

20 *Ibid.*, 9 August 1956, p. 6.

21 *Ibid.*, 17 August 1956, p. 17.

22 *Newsview*, March 1953, p. 62.

23 *Ibid.*, February 1952, p. 81.

24 'Can your appearance affect your job?', *The Mirror*, November 1959, p. 32.

25 Frank Mort and Peter Thompson, 'Retailing, Commercial Culture and Masculinity in 1950s Britain: the case of Montague Burton, the "Tailor of Taste"', *History Workshop Journal*, 38, 1994, p. 119. For an extended consideration of the gendered nature of style and consumption see Frank Mort, *Cultures of Consumption: Masculinities and Social Space in late Twentieth-Century Britain*, London, 1996, and for a detailed discussion of the cultural and sexual significance of suits see Anne Hollander, *Sex and Suits*, New York, 1994.

26 'Is There Room at the Top?', *The Mirror*, November 1959, p. 35.

27 R. D. Greenwood, 'Group Discussion Leaders' Manual', *Management Review*, November 1950, p. 12.

28 *Newsview*, March 1950, inside front cover.

29 *Ibid.*, August 1951, inside front cover.

30 *Ibid.*, July 1953, inside front cover.

31 In New Zealand's male culture the word 'invincible' conjured up images of strength and masculinity, namely the 1924 All Black team known as the 'Invincibles', the epitome of rugged heroism.

32 R. S. Parker, 'Measuring Executive Ability', *New Zealand Journal of Public Administration*, XV, 1, 1952, p. 18.

33 A. D. Granger, 'The Job of the Chief Executive', *Management*, November 1957, p. 30.

34 J. R. Jennings, 'Recent Developments in Selection Procedures for Executive Positions', *Management Review*, February 1951, pp. 20-3.

35 *New Zealand Commerce*, July 1956, p. 30.

36 J. D. Hounsell, 'Personnel Management Concerns the Office, Too . . . ', *Management*, January 1959, p. 46.

37 Sir John Collins, 'Leadership', *New Zealand Journal of Public Administration*, March 1959, p. 8.

38 R. S. Parker, 'The Wider Aspects of Management', *Management Review*, November 1950, p. 6.

39 Granger, 'The Job of the Chief Executive', p. 35.

40 Roper, *Masculinity and the British Organization Man*, pp. 132-5.

41 Andrew Wernick, *Promotional Culture: Advertising, ideology and symbolic expression*, London, 1991, p. 54.

42 Marchand, *Advertising the American Dream*, p. 238.

43 *New Zealand Commerce*, VIII, 1, July 1952, p. 22.

44 *Management*, IV, 7, October 1958, p. 48.

45 The number of telephones per 100 of population increased from 17.2 in 1949 to 27.6 in 1959. NZOYB, 1950, p. 270; 1961, p. 374.

46 *New Zealand Commerce*, May 1950, p. 8.

47 *Ibid.*, November 1950, p. 4.

48 *NZH*, 21 September 1956, p. 19.

49 C. Wright Mills, *The Power Elite*, New York, 1956, p. 141. For a more recent and equally provocative analysis of the breadwinner ethic and masculine re-fashioning, see Barbara Ehrenreich, *The Hearts of Men: American Dreams and the Flight From Commitment*, New York, 1983.

50 Rosemary Pringle, *Secretaries Talk: Sexuality, Power and Work*, Sydney, 1988, pp. 6-12. As C. Wright Mills in his discussion of the modern office of the fifties suggested, many executives had two 'wives'. He writes, '[the private secretary] takes care of his appointments, his daily schedule, his check book – is, in short, justifiably called his office wife', Mills, *White Collar*, p. 207. Michael Roper also makes the point that the secondary nature of the work performed by wives and secretaries, and the limited control they have over where and when it is done, indicates commonality by reflecting their lack of social power. Roper, *Masculinity*, p. 162.

51 George Calhoun, 'How to Marry Your Boss', *The Mirror*, May 1959, pp. 12-13.

52 Pringle, *Secretaries Talk*, pp. 12-13.

53 *The Mirror*, December 1955, p. 33.

54 *Management*, November 1958, p. 12.

55 For a lucid and succinct treatment of the theory of the male gaze, see Ros Ballaster, Margaret Beetham, Elizabeth Frazer and Sandra Hebron, *Women's Worlds: Ideology, Femininity and the Woman's Magazine*, London, 1991, pp. 36-8.

56 *Management*, July 1960, p. 20.

57 *New Zealand Commerce*, July 1954, p. 12.

58 *Ibid.*, September 1956, p. 10.

59 *Management*, September 1958, p. 12.

60 'Men "Invade" Women's Jobs', *New Zealand Commerce*, October 1946, p. 11.

61 *Ibid.*, September 1949, p. 50

62 *Ibid.*, August 1949, p. 50.

63 *Ibid.*, July 1956, p. 2.

64 Thersites, 'Equal Pay for Women: What Does it Mean for Business?', *New Zealand Commerce*, July 1957, p. 17.

65 'The Best Time to Shoot Mother-In-Law', *New Zealand Commerce*, December 1952, p. 1.

66 'What you need to know when you deal with women', *New Zealand Commerce*, May 1954, pp. 47-8.

Men, Women and Leisure Since the Second World War

Jock Phillips

Let us begin with two events, both of which took place over 40 years ago at one of Dunedin's most sacred places, Carisbrook. The first occasion was the afternoon of Tuesday, 26 January 1954. Queen Elizabeth II, at that stage a young glamorous mother, very much the Princess Diana of her age, had come to see a sports meeting. Thirty-three thousand other people were there. Some had come to see the sports, but most to see the Queen. They came in family groups – Mum, Dad and the kids – all wrapped up in their rugs, and carrying their thermos flasks, for there was a distinct chill in the air. The entertainment involved both men and women – men in pipe bands and wood-chopping contests, women in three teams dancing the reel o' Tulloch alongside five teams of marching girls. The highpoint was when Yvette Williams, Dunedin's favourite daughter, attempted to break the world long jump record. The Queen reportedly joined the crowd in uttering a long drawn-out 'Oh' when a no-jump robbed the heroine of the record. It was all good family fun.[1]

The second event occurred two and a half years later on Saturday, 14 July 1956. The occasion was the year's first rugby test between the Springboks and the All Blacks. This time the crowd was larger – 39,300 – and it was predominantly male. A few had slept outside waiting for the gates to open; others had arrived early in the morning and brought along their camping stoves to cook up breakfast. A younger generation of males was present, but most were to be found, dressed in uniform, sitting in the special schoolboys' enclosure. Those on the terrace were standing in muddy slush and the ground was soon strewn with rubbish and empty bottles. Spectators used interesting examples of Kiwi ingenuity to cope with the difficulties – hosepipes for urination, wooden clogs to give more height. Despite such efforts, most did not see any of the game's three tries, their view blocked by

*Speight's 'The Last Ewe' campaign relied on stereotypes of the 'Southern Man'
to advertise beer.*
Courtesy of Speight's Brewery, Dunedin.

screaming fans in front. The occasional fight broke out; one pair went for each other with seating planks. One hundred and fifty members of the crowd required first aid. Nor were injuries to be found only on the terraces. On the field, the price of New Zealand's 10-6 victory was as follows: Irwin – severe rib injury putting him out for the season; Archer – rib injury; Dixon – bruising to the ribs requiring hospital treatment; McIntosh – stitches for an eye injury; Buxton – stitches for an eye injury. The Springboks got off comparatively lightly: Du Preez broke a leg, and Ackerman damaged a leg cartilage. The general conclusion was that it was 'a hard game'. Afterwards the Kiwi celebrations filled the pubs to overflowing, with jugs being passed to those forced to wait outside.[2]

Leisure in the 1950s is not the major focus of this article, which concentrates upon changes since 1970, but these two scenes do establish two different patterns of the 'Southern Man' – and for that matter the 'Southern Woman' – at play.[3] They provide a model against which later changes can be measured. The Springbok test scenario suggests that one pattern of leisure in the post-war period revolved around gender separation. Men found leisure enjoyments within a male culture that existed quite separate from the world of women. At its heart was the classic troika of rugby, racing and beer. While the men were off at Carisbrook and the pub, the women were at home bottling jam, knitting jerseys, looking after the kids or, if they were single, they may well have been at the movies. Other impressionistic evidence reinforces this perception of a strong pattern of gender segregation in 1950s leisure. The newspapers and weekly papers of the period divided themselves into the women's pages that dealt with recipes, knitting patterns and tales of Hollywood starlets; while the sports pages focused almost exclusively on male sports. Novels and non-fiction accounts of the period reinforce this impression of separate leisure-time roles.[4] Some oral history accounts suggest that even when men and women shared the same leisure occasion, they occupied different social and physical space. Pamela King, for example, recalled that when men and women in Golden Bay came along to the local dances, the men would retreat outside to the keg perched on the back of a truck.[5]

This portrait of 1950s leisure raises a question. Does such a pattern of segregation still apply or has it largely disappeared as men's exclusive spaces – the pub, the bank at the rugby ground – have been 'invaded' or transformed, and alternative forms of leisure have emerged, individualistic, often cultural in form, which have integrated more of the play of men and women?

215

The scenario of the Queen's visit suggests quite another pattern. Here we have a scene of men and women enjoying a leisure occasion together. From this perspective we can see the 1950s as a great age of family fun, in which men and women married young – he settling down as the 'family man', she as the good 'Kiwi housewife' – and together entertained their kids with Sunday drives, holidays at the beach and winter evenings around the open fire playing 'Happy Families', not to mention family outings to see the Queen. This model of gender integration in leisure immediately raises the question of its relationship with the first pattern of gender segregation; and it also leaves us with a historical issue: have these family-based forms of leisure declined subsequently? With fewer men and women living in long-term monogamous relationships and both men and women discovering an individualistic self-indulgence in leisure, has the extent of play shared by men and women in the family diminished?

At its crudest level, then, our question is: are New Zealand men and women today spending more or less of their leisure time together? Or, more precisely, do the two patterns of the 1950s – gender-separate leisure and family leisure – still survive or have the patterns become more mixed and complex?

The early 1970s is the first period when we can really move beyond impressionistic data to some useable figures. Although New Zealand has long collected good census data, the leisure habits of men and women were not among the questions explored. But in that period two factors helped provide answers. Local authorities began to examine their provision of leisure facilities (whether parks or libraries or swimming pools) more scientifically. At the same time sociology, which had arrived in New Zealand universities on any scale only in the 1960s, began to provide a cohort of recent graduates skilled in social survey techniques. The result was a series of statistical surveys on New Zealanders' leisure habits. The work produced does have grave problems, as one would expect from a young social science. To quote Mairi Jorgensen in her excellent 1974 overview essay on the series of surveys: 'It is immediately obvious that the information is limited, patchy, and seldom conclusive. We know more about sports recreation than arts or entertainment, about young people than about middle-aged or old people, about Pakehas than Maori or Islanders.'[6] We might add that class and occupational analysis is wholly absent.

With these problems in mind, let us nevertheless see what the surveys tell us. One of the first really useful studies looked at recreation patterns in Auckland in 1971.[7] As can be seen from Table 1, the results showed that in outdoor team sports, indoor sports (which included such activities as squash, darts, snooker, table tennis) and water-based sports, men had, on average, twice the number of activities as women. Further, this figure does not show just how separate men and women's activities were, because there were some sports, such as rugby or league, which were almost exclusively male, and others, such as netball or marching, which were exclusively female. Even in those sports that both played, such as hockey and cricket, the two sexes did not play together. On the other hand, in the four less physical forms of recreation – personal grooming, social activities (which meant activities like youth clubs and dancing), the arts and hobbies – women had a clear numerical dominance over men in the number of their activities. Again the raw figures understate the extent of separation. For example, the hobbies included dressmaking and cooking classes, which were overwhelmingly female, and woodwork and metalwork, which were equally strongly male.

Table 1: Auckland recreation patterns, 1971: mean activities per person

Categories	Males	Females
Outdoor team sports	.40	.20
Outdoor recreation (horse riding, tramping, etc.)	.16	.09
Outdoor individual sports	.21	.14
Indoor sports	.51	.24
Water-based sports	.44	.23
Personal grooming and keep fit	.05	.15
Social activities	.16	.19
Arts	.37	.50
Hobbies	.53	.59

(Source: Community Activities Section, Auckland Regional Authority,
Recreation Patterns in Auckland, Auckland, 1971)

The suggestion in these figures of demarcated recreational patterns in the early 1970s seems at first confirmed by the most extensive survey of the period, the 1974–75 *New Zealand Recreation Survey*.[8] Respondents were asked to indicate from a list of options which activities they had been involved in 'more than once or twice' over the previous year. The list revealed a fascinatingly respectable view of recreation – watching television, going to the pub, or having sex were not options. In a 1979 survey, strong gender contrasts were revealed by those options which were considered (see Table 2): 33 per cent of men had taken part in rugby over the previous year, but only 7 per cent of women; the same proportion (33 per cent) of men had watched sport, compared with 21 per cent of women. Reflecting men's pub-going habits, which were not surveyed, 30 per cent of men had played billiards, snooker or pool, but only 6 per cent of women.

Table 2: Involvement level by sex in cultural and selected other activities, 1979 (%)

	Males	Females	Total
Cultural			
Listening to records	33	39	36
Cinema, theatre	20	25	22
Music	17	24	20
Visiting parks, gardens, zoos	14	21	18
Visiting museums/galleries	11	16	14
Dancing	8	16	12
Seeing cultural activities	7	14	11
Musical instruments	11	13	12
Painting/sketching	8	11	9
Drama/opera	5	9	7
Maori arts and crafts	3	5	4
Ballet	1	5	3
Selected other activities			
Reading	35	53	44
Gardening	37	44	40
Swimming	34	36	35
Cooking, baking	8	49	29
Visiting, entertaining friends	22	36	29
Sewing	2	55	28
Watching sport	33	21	27
Picnics, barbecues, hangis	22	30	26
Dining out	21	28	25
Rugby union	33	7	20
Walking for pleasure	13	26	20
Billiards, snooker, pool	30	6	18
Religion	14	22	18

(Source: David Tait, *New Zealanders and the Arts: Results from a Survey of Attendance and Interest Patterns in the Performing and Visual Arts*, Wellington, 1983, p. 5. The table is based on results of the *New Zealand Recreation Survey* undertaken in 1979)

Turning to women's recreational habits, we find that the contrasts were even stronger: 55 per cent of women had sewed over the past year, but only 2 per cent of men; 49 per cent had cooked or baked, only 8 per cent of men; 36 per cent had visited or entertained friends, 22 per cent of men. These were all home-based activities and some of them, such as sewing or cooking, clearly blurred the distinction between work and play. These contrasts of men and women's leisure were not simply a reflection of different cultures; they partly reflected clear inequalities of power and access to resources. Men, with much greater earning power than women, could afford to go to the pub and play billiards. They had time because women were at home looking after the children. Married women, by contrast, financially dependent upon men and unable to purchase free time, were forced to fit their recreations around their family duties.

But this is not a full explanation for the differences. Women attended more cultural activities outside the home, such as going to the cinema and theatre or visiting museums, than men. The same was true of church-going, if this can be classed as a leisure activity. Cultural definitions of gender-appropriate interests, as well as economic determinism, continued to influence the way men and women filled their leisure time. These figures, then, seem to bear out the stereotype that, at least up to the 1970s, adult men spent much of their leisure time with their mates watching or playing sport and going to the pub, while women found their recreations at home or in cultural centres. The contrasts appear even stronger if the preferred recreations are examined. Three-quarters of the men named a sport as one of their three preferences, as compared with half of the women. Fifty-eight per cent of women named a cultural activity, and 45 per cent of males.[9] Clearly men and women did spend some of their leisure in largely gender-segregated environments.

On the other hand, it seems probable they did not spend *all* their recreation time in this situation. If we look again at the 1979 survey, we discover that, despite the strong gender contrasts in some activities, the four most popular activities overall were, in order, reading, gardening, listening to records and swimming. In all four pursuits, women were slightly more active than men were but not (apart from reading) significantly so; and all four (including reading) were among men's most popular leisure-time enjoyments. Reading, gardening and listening to records are, of course, home-based pursuits – and we must remember that the survey did not include watching television or having sex (also activities usually enjoyed in the home).

Other surveys of the period pointed to the importance of the car as a second site for family-based recreation, and often the car led the family to water. Studies in Palmerston North in 1969, in Hamilton in 1971, in Christchurch in 1973 and in the Wellington region in 1974, all showed how important driving to picnics or to the beach was for both men and women.[10] In the Palmerston North study, driving was the most popular recreation for men: in Hamilton 82 per cent of trips were by family groups, 41 per cent to water-based enjoyments such as swimming or boating, and 26 per cent to scenic attractions. In other words, whether it was the Sunday drive to a beauty spot, summer holidays at the beach, listening to music, or watching television at home, men were enjoying some leisure time alongside their wives and often their children.

Of course, because men and women acknowledged their participation in the same activities and occupied broadly the same space, it did not necessarily mean that they did them together or shared the same roles. Within the home, both men and women enjoyed reading, but it may be that he read rugby memoirs and she read novels. Although both claimed to enjoy gardening, it may have been that he mowed the lawn and looked after the vegetables while she tended the flowers. Although both men and women enjoyed water sports, it is plausible that he went surfing while she took the children to the suburban pool. When it came to setting off in the car, which both sexes claimed as such a popular recreation, he may have been likely to drive while she played 'I spy' with the kids. Once the family had reached the motor camp for their holidays, she was often left to guard the tent and cook the meals while he went off fishing with his mates (for sea-fishing is among the most exclusively male of all activities). Of such important nuances the statistics do not talk and we are left with impression and memory. James K. Baxter, for instance, wrote of National Mum taking down the family photos, while Labour Dad in Grunt Grotto 'sits and reads the sporting page'.[11] Nevertheless despite the frustrating lack of precision in the evidence, we can reasonably confidently conclude that, in the 1970s, the two models of leisure we posited from the 1950s still survived. Alongside a series of activities that were highly gendered by occasion and space – very crudely, sports for men and culture for women – there was also a set of enjoyments that revolved around the family as a collective unit. Even within the family, men and women often carried out gendered roles, so perhaps we can refine our patterns further into leisure that is gendered by exclusion and leisure that is gendered by the dynamics of relationships.[12]

These two leisure styles seem to have been strongly demarcated. They were partly distinguished by life cycle and this was especially the case for men. The late teens and early twenties were a period when both men and women were physically active. Sport was important to both genders, although their sporting interests were very different. In the 1974–75 recreation survey, 36 per cent of men under 25 were involved in rugby, 35 per cent of women of that age were involved in netball (see Table 3). But even at that age the home-based activities had already assumed great importance for women. Of the top six activities for women under 25, five were home-based: sewing, cooking, reading, listening to records and knitting. There were only two such activities among young men's top six involvements (records and reading), and in both cases the numbers were lower for men. Young males' interest in the pub was reflected in the fact that 39 per cent of men under 25 participated in billiards or snooker. These were not among young women's top 40 activities. Gender separation, therefore, was especially strong among the young and unmarried.

Table 3: Involvement in activities by gender and age (at least 30%)

MEN				WOMEN			
Under 25	**%**	**25–49**	**%**	**Under 25**	**%**	**25–49**	**%**
Swimming	46	Gardening	45	Swimming	59	Knitting	60
Listening to records	42	House maintenance	38	Sewing	59	Sewing	59
Billiards/snooker	39	Reading	34	Cooking	53	Gardening	51
Rugby union	36	Listening to records	34	Reading	53	Reading	50
Watching sport	34	Watching sport	32	Listening to records	53	Cooking/baking	48
Reading	34	Fishing, salt water	32	Knitting	44	Picnics, barbecues	41
Fishing, salt water	32	Swimming	32	Cinema, theatre	37	Visiting, entertaining friends	41
		Billiards/snooker	31	Netball	35	Listening to records	40
		Picnics/barbecues	30	Visiting, entertaining friends	33	Dining out	38
		Rugby union	30	Picnics, barbecues	31	Swimming	34

(Source: David Tait, *New Zealand Recreation Survey 1974–75,* Wellington, 1984, pp. 16-17)

Marriage itself did not immediately diminish the separate spheres. Its effect appears to have been rather to diminish women's leisure options and confine them rather more to the home. Blokes continued to go off to rugby and the pub. It was the coming of children that changed things. Fathers spent more of their time around the home or taking the family to the beach. In the 25- to 49-year-old age group the first four activities for men in the 1974-75 recreation survey were all home-based: gardening, house maintenance, reading and listening to records. True, these were rather different home-based pursuits from those that topped women's activities at a similar age – knitting and sewing were the two favourites – but the dominance of the family man in this age group was clear. The figures suggest that, as the children grew up and left the home, so home-based interests remained important for both men and women, but slightly changed their character. Gardening and reading grew in favour, but activities carried out for, or with, children declined, such as swimming for men or sewing for women.

If life cycle demarcated exclusive leisure from family leisure, time was another factor. The most obvious example up to 1967 was six o'clock closing, which allowed the male an hour of frantic boozing with his mates before he headed off home to Mum and the kids. But that was only one division. Days of the week demarcated gendered leisure from family leisure. Saturdays were for team sports and the pub, where men could be boys while women stayed at home and were mums. Sunday was family day, when the family went off to the church or (more likely) set off on the Sunday drive.[13] Holidays, too, tended to be family times.

The figures on which these views are based are necessarily crude, and obliterate particularity. We know little about how Maori and Pakeha patterns of leisure differed, or whether there were important differences of class or even distinctions between town and country. We are left with broad generalisations which must be treated as norms and which do not account for many individual differences. Even in the 1950s and 1960s, there were men in New Zealand who stayed home and found enjoyment in cooking, while their spouses went off to play team sports. But at the level of generalisation, the figures do reveal a pattern. At least up to the 1970s, there were certain time periods and age groups when men and women expressed themselves in highly gendered leisured activities. At other times and periods of the life cycle (especially as parents) men and women shared family fun, even if they played rather different roles.

What has happened since that time? Is this still the norm? Have the leisure interests of men and women grown together or further apart?

We must note first that there have been considerable changes in the traditionally exclusive male interests of rugby, racing and beer. The first major change came in 1967 when six o'clock closing was defeated in a referendum. The result initiated a transformation in the physical environment of hotel drinking, as carpets and easy chairs and distinctive decors – sometimes with a historical flavour, sometimes vaguely ethnic – were introduced. The ambience was altered from a crowded uncouth watering place with a lavatorial atmosphere, attractive only to boorish males, into a more spacious and relaxed environment with tables, comfortable chairs, perhaps food to eat or a band to listen to. All of this was designed to encourage people to stay longer and to attract women. In place of the old inner-city dives, new pubs were opened in the suburbs. The suburbs were where families were found, and it became easier for husbands and wives to drink together. In the late 1980s there was another development, as urban pleasures re-emerged in the form of extravagantly decorated bars with flamboyant names designed to suggest international sophistication. The old inner-city haunts of working-class men became the late-night abodes of the young, the affluent, and the trendy – middle-class groups that included as many women as men. The liberalisation of liquor laws and the spread of a restaurant culture also mean that 'eating out' was often the occasion when alcohol was consumed; and again this was a leisure pursuit that attracted as many, if not more, women than men.

As the sites for drinking changed and became more attractive to women, so did the drinks. Until the mid-1970s, beer, that drink of the hard man, was still consumed in large and increasing quantities. But thereafter average beer consumption began to drop, while wine consumption showed a significant increase. In 1971 the average New Zealand adult drank 237 bottles of beer and 13 bottles of wine. Twenty years later, the average beer consumption had dropped to 188 bottles, while the number of bottles of wine drunk per capita had more than doubled to 29.[14] A greater range of export quality and 'natural' beers appeared on the market. This was liquor to be savoured rather than quaffed at blinding speed. All these changes have served to break down the male exclusivity of pubs and alcohol drinking. Although about 70 per cent of alcohol is still consumed by males, things are changing. The number of women abstaining from alcohol has dropped from 20 per cent in 1969 to 15 per cent in 1995 (the figure for men is 11 per cent).[15] Although the beer advertisements continue to pitch themselves at an aggressively macho market, it is significant that among the younger age group the consumption of alcohol by young women is now virtually the same as for young men. A recent Alcohol Liquor Advisory Council (ALAC) study of those aged 14 to 18 suggested that men and women had very similar patterns of drinking. Thirty-four per cent of both males and females were identified as heavy drinkers.[16] This should not necessarily be regarded as a huge step forward in the liberation of women, but it does suggest that drinking, as a leisure occupation, is becoming less of a male pursuit than it once was.

Gambling, too, is less exclusively male. Betting was never entirely a male pursuit – community 'Housie' attracted numbers of women – and even gambling on horses was not a male monopoly. But in the 1974–75 recreation survey there was a significant difference between the number of men and women who had attended the races – 19 per cent of men 50 and over as against 11 per cent of women. Significantly, even in 1974–75 the number of males involved in horse-racing was less among younger men – only 13 per cent of men aged 25–49 went to the races, and it was not among the top 40 activities of those under 25.[17] Since then there has been a declining interest in horse-racing and betting on horses generally. In 1979, in constant 1996 dollars $1,700 million was spent on horse betting. By 1996 the figure had dropped to just over $1,000 million. In contrast, the forms of gambling that had increased were those equally attractive to women as men – Lotto (which by 1996 was taking in over $600 million), gaming machines ($1,314 million) and the casinos (which creamed off an astonishing $1,453 million).[18]

Sport, too, has seen subtle changes that have started to challenge its gender exclusivity. Rugby was traditionally the very core of the male culture in New Zealand. Followed by men, participated in by men, it also encouraged in spectators and players alike an aggressively male character type.[19] Since the 1970s, the game has undergone a number of revolutions. The 1981 Springbok Tour was one catalyst. Although the protests against that tour were primarily about race, those who marched also spoke of other concerns, such as the overdominant place of rugby in the national identity. Women, especially, voiced criticisms of the nature of the rugby culture. Among the answers to a questionnaire distributed to anti-tour protesters in 1981 were some revealing comments: from a 66-year-old woman, 'Loathe Rugby a primitive game'; or a 30-year-old mother, 'I have for years resented the dominance that rugby has in the homes, schools and society in general. Its [sic] time that a few other values took over from bloody rugby'; or a 28-year-old female editor, 'I was brought up in North Canterbury (Alec [sic] Wylie country) and I detest the way rugby males relate to women'.[20]

The game's administrators slowly began to respond to such sentiments, not to diminish the place of rugby in the New Zealand ethos, but to transform its values and image so that the game might appeal to a wider family audience. Increasingly, too, they were motivated by commercial concerns as the game went professional and there was a need to market rugby to the widest possible audience. So rugby administrators put less energy into maximising participation – into ensuring that every male had his initiation in the scrum – and more into making the game an appealing spectator sport. A World Cup was introduced in 1987, full professional rugby followed in 1995 and the rules were changed to ensure more fluid and entertaining play. The old bullocking cauliflower-eared locks who had once been the heroes were replaced by fleet-footed backs with golden hair or Polynesian features. Colin Meads, 'Pine-tree' of the King Country, was eclipsed by South Auckland's Jonah Lomu with his Walkman and his McDonald's advertising contract.

It is difficult to prove that all these changes have increased the game's following among women, but women now play the game where once they did not. In a season notable for the failure of the All Blacks, the 1998 success of the Black Ferns in winning the women's World Championship brought brief media attention to women's participation in the game. Many more women now watch rugby. Television New Zealand claimed that 54 per cent of female viewers over the age of five watched the Super 12 semi-final between the Blues and the Highlanders in 1998. The figure for males was 61 per cent. A quarter of the Canterbury Rugby Supporters Club in that year was female.[21] Other changes suggest a different clientele at rugby games. Where once most of the spectators crowded onto the uncouth and distinctly macho ambience of the bank, now most of the grounds have seats. The increasing numbers of Sunday games is also suggestive of rugby's entry into this traditionally family day. The game is becoming family entertainment, not an exclusive male zone. The numbers of men actually playing the game have fallen. The most spectacular growth in sports participation by contrast has come in touch rugby, which by 1997 had 75,000 participants.[22] Perhaps this is because of its less violent character or perhaps it is precisely because touch has encouraged involvement by women as well as men.

While rugby has become less exclusively male in its following, netball has become less exclusively female. Here again the other gender – in this case male – are starting to play. More significant is the increased following of the game among a television audience of both sexes and all ages. When it comes to watching sport, the 1991 *Life in New Zealand Survey* suggested that a remarkably similar number of New Zealand men and women did so at least once a week (20 per cent of men, 17 per cent of women). Interestingly, the contrasts were much stronger when people were asked to name their favourite leisure activity.[23] Perhaps we should not exaggerate the changes here. At least in terms of participation, the contrasts remain strong: in the 1991 survey, 15 per cent of males aged 19 to 24 played rugby, but only 2 per cent of women; 13 per cent of women of that age played netball, but only 3 per cent of men.[24]

In some ways, the most significant change in sporting recreation in New Zealand over the past 25 years is the relative decline of team sports and the growth of individualistic physical activity. Some of this has come in individualistic sports – cycling, golf, canoeing, sailing, diving, skiing, swimming, tennis – and some in individualistic recreation such as tramping and walking or fitness classes. In general, these are recreations that span both genders. Of course the gender balance does vary considerably from one recreation to another: aerobics or fitness classes show a marked female dominance; boating, surfing, and diving remain predominantly male. In 1991, 23 per cent of men participated in snooker or pool, but only 6 per cent of women. But in those individualistic activities that attract the largest following – swimming, walking and cycling – the participation rates of men and women were, by 1991, extremely even.[25] The men and women seen jogging around our cities in the evenings do represent a new unisex recreational pattern.

Another major change that has occurred in New Zealand and has helped to integrate the leisure of men and women is the increasing importance of urban culture. There are two key factors in this change. One is the simple fact that our cities have grown and now hold a large proportion of our population. In 1951, under a third of New Zealand's population lived in cities of over 100,000; in 1996, over one half (53 per cent) did so. In that year more than a million people were living in Auckland. Big cities breed specialised amenities for cultural life: museums, theatres, galleries, coffee shops. People look to the city as much as to the beach or the bush or the sportsground for their leisure-time highs. They start to think of the city as a place of fun, as well as of work. City leisure is commercialised leisure and is intended to appeal to as many people as possible. So urban enjoyments tend not to be gender specific. In 1991, about 20 per cent of both men and women ate out at least once a week.[26] The unisex café culture emerges as the male beer culture disappears.

A second key factor in the emergence of this urban culture is the educational transformation of New Zealand. At the end of the Second World War

there were fewer than 10,000 people in this country with university degrees. Today there are over 50,000 in university every year and there are
over 200,000 people with degrees. These are people whose education has
encouraged them to think about issues and to enjoy cultural as well as
physical pursuits. They often have professional jobs and their self-definition
and aspirations have more to do with urban and financial success than physical
strength. These people have provided a new audience for the cultural amenities of the city.

The city has also bred a new acceptance of sexual variety. In the traditional New Zealand value system homophobia had kept men suspicious of
any 'poofterish' activity, such as going to concerts or flower gardening or
recreational cooking. When homosexual law reform became a major political issue in 1985, the polls showed a strong contrast between the city and
the province; and when the city won and the law was changed, it is arguable
that homophobia and the fear of being thought 'effeminate' gradually disappeared.

Such social changes served particularly to legitimise cultural interests
among men. In the 1974–75 recreation survey, every cultural activity showed
a dominance of interest among women. Even with respect to reading there
was a gender difference of 53 per cent to 35 per cent.[27] By the late 1970s,
the seeds of change were apparent. A survey conducted in 1979 found that,
among people under the age of 35, men were no less inclined to attend
performances or exhibitions than were women of that age, whereas among
the older age group there was a difference of 10 per cent. Indeed, of those
under the age of 25 more men than women actually attended a performance or exhibition.[28] Equally significant were two additional findings of
this study: that among men under the age of 45 the rate of male attendance
at exhibitions or performances was much higher in the city than in rural
areas; and that there was a huge contrast between those with university
qualifications and those without. Eighty-five per cent of people with university degrees attended a performance or exhibition whereas only 40 per
cent of those without School Certificate did so. The implication of these
figures was clear: cities and higher education are associated with a new taste
for cultural recreations, especially among men.[29] By 1991, the *Life in New
Zealand Survey* showed that there was a striking similarity of use of cultural
facilities by both men and women. Of those aged 15 or over, 8 per cent of
males had been to an art gallery in the past four weeks, 11 per cent of
women; 12 per cent of males had gone to a concert, 13 per cent of women;
7 per cent of men had visited a museum, 9 per cent of women. As might be

expected, the numbers were greater and the balance of gender more even among the tertiary-educated.[30] Cultural recreation was no longer the preserve of women.

The final important change that has affected the gender balance of leisure in New Zealand over the past generation is the transformation of the family. In the 1950s and 1960s, most adult New Zealand women were based in the home as wives and mothers, and so their leisure usually took place around the home. This made it difficult for many women to distinguish between work and play. Was knitting a jersey for young Johnnie or baking a birthday cake for Mary work or play? Over the past 50 years there has been a series of revolutions in the New Zealand family system. First, women have delayed marriage and further delayed child rearing. They have not automatically rushed into setting up their own family soon after leaving school. In 1976, the average age for first marriage for women was just over 22 years. By 1995, the figure had risen to almost 27 years.[31] Women now had at least 10 years after leaving school in which to develop their own lives as individuals. They were not necessarily family-bound. This fact was signalled by the declining size of households in New Zealand. In the 1991 census, 21.1 per cent of dwellings had only one person living in them; and 31.9 per cent contained only two.[32] In other words, over half of all dwellings contained two people or fewer. Some in small households were elderly, a few were solo parents, but the figures also pointed to numbers of women and men who did not have major family responsibilities and were freer to participate in leisure outside the family environment.

Second, and equally as important even for those with family responsibilities, increasing numbers of women were in paid employment. In 1961 under 20 per cent (18.7 per cent in fact) of adult women were in the full-time workforce. By 1996 the rate had risen to 35.8 per cent and another 20.4 per cent were working part-time. In other words, over 56 per cent of adult women were in the workforce. The comparative figure for men was only 66.7 per cent. Even more dramatically, in 1951 fewer than 10 per cent of married women were working full-time; 40 years later the figure was approaching 50 per cent.[33] In leaving home to go to work, women developed a much stronger sense of the difference between work and play. Increasingly they had raised expectations about leisure as relief from work and of course they possessed additional independent incomes to afford leisure pursuits. Delayed marriage and child bearing gave them more opportunity to develop their own leisure interests. Often they could afford to buy a car, which gave them opportunities to follow interests outside the home, opportunities that were once denied the housewife stuck in the distant suburbs. Even for women with dependent children, a revived feminist movement helped to spread the idea that mothers, no less than paid workers, needed time out from their daily toil.

The result of these changes for women was that home-based leisure such as knitting or sewing declined, but women's outside leisure interests, both physical and cultural, grew. Again, the figures bear out these trends. The 1991 *Life in New Zealand* survey found that of women in full-time work, 30 per cent took part in a high level of physical activity, which was only 3 per cent less than the male figure.[34] Inequalities of power and resources had by no means disappeared. The 'double shift', under which women in paid employment were also seen as having primary responsibility for housework and child care, necessarily limited women's recreational opportunities. A woman's earnings often went to supplement the family income rather than to buy leisure-time enjoyments for herself. Men on average spent $574 on their leisure activities each year; women spent only $309. Difficulties in affording the costs of travel, equipment or club subscriptions continued to limit women's leisure opportunities.[35]

The changes in the family also affected men and their leisure patterns. With their partners often heavily involved in paid work, men were forced to take on additional family responsibilities, and they necessarily spent more of their time outside the job in family concerns. By 1991, among men aged 25 to 44, 29 per cent were participating in physical activity with their children and 42 per cent with their spouse. Forty-one per cent gave as their reason for doing physical activity, 'To do things with family'.[36] When asked about their leisure, 11 per cent of males cited 'family activities' compared with 12 per cent of women, and almost exactly the same number of men and women claimed that playing with children was their favourite leisure activity.[37] It is not clear whether this represents a dramatic increase in family recreation from the 1950s and 1960s, but it certainly represents a rather different form of family recreation. In the early period, family leisure tended to mean the whole family. On Sundays the husband would join his wife and kids in outings together. Increasingly as both partners work, there is a tendency for men to look after the kids one day, and women the next. Perhaps one day they might park the children with friends and enjoy a break together. Furthermore, the strong demarcations that divided personal leisure from family leisure weakened. Once New Zealand men tended to spend Saturday with the boys and Sunday with Mum and the kids. Now the man is as likely to spend Saturday shopping with his wife and kids and perhaps go to the footie on Sunday. He is as likely to be a solo Dad taking one child to a family restaurant as he is taking the whole family on a Sunday drive to the bush. The introduction of Sunday shopping, the spread of shopping malls and the phenomenal increase in fast-food eating places all represent and facilitate a new kind of leisure in which New Zealanders, both men and women, are at one time looking after the family's needs and enjoying some recreational fun.

The extent of these changes should not be exaggerated. I do not want to suggest that we have reached an egalitarian nirvana in which men and women share family responsibilities and child care and each has time to follow their own leisure interests. It is clear that in the hours away from the job, women continue to spend far more time than men on housework. In 1991, men in full-time work spent 7.3 hours a week on housework; women spent 11.7 hours. Men had four extra hours a week to enjoy themselves. Among part-timers, the difference was even greater: men 7.8 hours a week, women 16.9 hours.[38] Men working part-time were spending their additional non-working time in leisure activities whereas women were occupying much of it in housework.

It is also true that the extent to which women, and indeed men, are able to take time off from both work and family to follow their own interests varies greatly according to income and stage of the life cycle. Some can afford to purchase child care; others cannot. Retired men and women, if fit and financial, have much greater freedom to share their leisure interests.

And when men and women do choose to pursue their own independent leisure-time activities, they still often make slightly different choices – women go to fitness classes significantly more often; men to golf. In the 1991 *Life in New Zealand Survey*, some revealing differences showed up about the motivation for leisure activities: 42 per cent of women took part in physical activity in order to control their weight; only 28 per cent of men gave this as their reason. Equally revealingly, 27 per cent of men took part in order to compete against others, but only 12 per cent of women. Around the house leisure time also remained gendered. In 1991, about twice as many men as women were active in house renovations and chopping firewood and they were more likely to clean the car and mow the lawns; women remained more likely to cook and sew.[39]

Yet the trends were towards greater similarity between men and women in patterns of leisure. In the 1991 census of volunteers, there were actually slightly more men than women working in the arts and cultural areas (although the numbers were very similar), and although in sports coaching and administration the numbers still clearly favoured men, the participation of women was considerable.[40] At school, the gap between the percentage of boys and girls playing sport is closing. Whereas in 1991 76 per cent of boys played at least one sport and 65 per cent of girls, by 1996 the respective figures were 80 per cent and 77 per cent, a reduction in the gap from 11 per cent to 3 per cent.[41]

Let me pull all of this together. In the period up to the early 1970s, patterns of leisure for men and women were very different. Women found it much more difficult than men to have time out away from the family home, and when they did so their interests were distinct from men's. They were more active in cultural matters, less active in sports and when they did participate in sport it tended to be with their own gender in netball or hockey. Women's most popular relaxations were at home in cooking and knitting and gardening. Men, by contrast, had a number of sites of largely exclusive male enjoyments, at the rugby ground, at the pub, in the TAB. They did participate in family leisure – going to the beach for a Sunday drive – but they often played distinct and appropriately masculine roles within the family, and family time was strictly demarcated from work time and blokes' time. It tended to occur after the pubs were closed and on Sunday.

These patterns have not entirely collapsed, but radical changes in our leisure patterns have occurred. Women have had more time, money and leisure – power, in other words – to participate in activities outside the home. Women have joined men in the pubs and wine bars of the cities, they have developed shared interests with men both in the old sports like rugby and in new individualistic ones such as jogging; and men in turn have discovered the culture of the city. More of these independent recreations are unisex. In the home, both men and women still take much leisure with the family, but for men it is less a demarcated time or space and less often involves the entire family unit. The trip to McDonald's with Dad is now as common as the family drive to the beach.

One should not conclude that the worlds of men and women in New Zealand are now becoming one. It is, rather, that exclusive gendered cultures are declining and men and women in New Zealand are facing a greater diversity of options together. In part, this increase in choice for all is a reflection of a more diverse society – a development that takes us beyond the bounds of this essay into discussions of New Zealand's more varied ethnic mix, contrasts of big city and small community and increasing ranges of incomes and lifestyles. But it is also because the changes described have gradually undermined the extreme gendering of New Zealand society. In play as in work, women are now taking part as once they did not; while men are discovering that drinking beer and watching rugby are no longer the compulsory prerequisites to being a Kiwi male.

1   *Otago Daily Times*, 27 January 1954, p. 1; *Dominion*, 27 January 1954, p. 10.

2   *Evening Post*, 16 July 1956, p. 8; *Otago Daily Times*, 14 July 1956, pp. 1, 9; *ibid.*, 16 July 1956, pp. 1, 5, 8; *Dominion*, 16 July 1956, p. 11.

3   On the idea of the 'Southern Man' and its use by Speight's to advertise their beer, see Robin Law, 'Masculinity, place and beer advertising in New Zealand: the Southern Man campaign', *New Zealand Geographer*, 53, 2, 1997, pp. 22-8.

4   Robert Chapman, 'Fiction and the Social Pattern', *Landfall*, 29, 1953, pp. 26-58; Leslie M. Hall, 'Women and Men in New Zealand', *Landfall*, 45, 1958, pp. 47, 49, 51.

5   Nelson Golden Bay Oral History Study, 'Interview with Pamela King', side 3, in Oral History Centre, Alexander Turnbull Library, Wellington.

6   Mairi Jorgensen, *Recreation and Leisure: A Bibliography and Review of the New Zealand Literature*, Wellington, 1974, p. 41.

7   Community Activities Section, Auckland Regional Authority, *Recreation Patterns in Auckland*, Auckland, 1971.

8   David Tait, *New Zealand Recreation Survey 1974-75*, Wellington, 1984.

9   *Ibid.*, p. 20.

10 Palmerston North City Corporation, *Trends in Recreation Preference: Report no. 13*, Palmerston North, 1969; Hamilton City Council, *Study of Regional Recreation Activity*, Hamilton, 1971; E. R. Henderson and J. Stacpoole, *Regional Recreation Conservation Study, Part 1*, Wellington, 1974; A. M. Neighbour, *Outdoor Recreation in Christchurch – A Survey of Activity Patterns*, Christchurch, 1973.

11 James K. Baxter, 'Ballad of Calvary Street', in *Selected Poems*, Auckland, 1982, p. 42.

12 I thank Deborah Montgomerie for this point.

13 Tait, *Recreation Survey*, p. 60.

14 *New Zealand Official Year Book* (NZOYB), 1993, p. 151.

15 Sally Casswell, 'Alcohol Consumption by Women', *Australia and New Zealand Journal of Sociology*, 19, 1, 1983, pp. 146-52; 1995 figures supplied by ALAC.

16 ALAC, *Youth and Alcohol Survey Overview*, Wellington, 1997.

17 Tait, *Recreation Survey*, p. 16.

18 *NZOYB*, 1997, p. 328.

19 Jock Phillips, *A Man's Country? The Image of the Pakeha Male – A History*, revised edn, Auckland, 1996, pp. 82-130.

20 Peter King and Jock Phillips, 'A Social Analysis of the Springbok Tour Protestors', in David Mackay et al., eds, *Counting the Cost: The 1981 Springbok Tour in Wellington*, Wellington, 1982, p. 12. See also John Nauright and David Black, '"Hitting Them Where It Hurts": Springbok-All Black Rugby, Masculine National Identity and Counter-Hegemonic Struggle, 1959-1992', in John Nauright and Timothy J. L. Chandler, eds, *Making Men: Rugby and Masculine Identity*, London, 1996, pp. 205-26.

21 *Sunday Star-Times*, 31 May 1998, p. C4.

22 *Sunday Star-Times*, 12 October 1997, p. B11.

23 Grant Cushman et al., *Life in New Zealand Survey*, IV, Wellington, 1991, pp. 52, 12.

24 Will Hopkins et al., *Life in New Zealand Survey*, III, Wellington, 1991, p. 32.

25 *Ibid.*, pp. 28, 32, 34.

26 Cushman et al., *Life in New Zealand*, IV, p. 52.

27 Tait, *Recreation Survey*, pp. 13, 14, 20.

28 David Tait, *New Zealanders and the Arts: Results From a Survey of Attendance and Interest Patterns*

in the Performing and Visual Arts, Wellington, 1983, pp. 12, 13.

29 *Ibid.*, pp. 39, 45.

30 Cushman et al., *Life in New Zealand*, IV, pp. 22, 23.

31 *NZOYB*, 1997, p. 115.

32 *NZOYB*, 1993, p. 86.

33 The actual figures were 9.7 per cent and 45.8 per cent. See Statistics New Zealand, *All About Women in New Zealand*, Wellington, 1993, p. 82.

34 Hopkins et al., *Life in New Zealand*, III, p. 14.

35 Cushman et al., *Life in New Zealand*, IV, pp. 104, 118.

36 Hopkins et al., *Life in New Zealand,* III, pp. 38, 48.

37 Cushman et al., *Life in New Zealand*, IV, pp. 6, 12.

38 Hopkins et al., *Life in New Zealand,* III, p. 24.

39 *Ibid.*, pp. 20-1.

40 Hillary Commission for Recreation and Sport, *The Business of Sport and Leisure: The Economic and Social Impact of Sport and Leisure in New Zealand*, Wellington, 1993, p. 58.

41 *NZOYB*, 1997, p. 318.

This 1974 cartoon jokes about the implications of 'second wave' feminism for men. Broadsheet, July 1974.

'When Dad Was a Woman': Gender Relations in the 1970s

Barbara Brookes

A photograph records two young people with long hair, sitting naked on a beach, looking confidently and optimistically out on the world. The year is 1974 and they are committed to a new vision of gender relations where women and men would share work and child care. The man's long hair perhaps signifies rebellion and a willingness to explore a feminine side of the self. The woman's long hair is harder to read: it perhaps signifies nature, although what is natural is under review. Underneath the story of the free-flowing hair lay a larger subtext: an exploration of the nature of women and men, a pushing of the boundaries to explode understood conceptions of masculinity and femininity. Despite apparent nonchalance, the matter was deeply serious. The world was to be reordered by removing traditional expectations of women and men and seeing what would result. Fathers could be mothers and mothers could be fathers; rigidity of roles would give way to a flowering of opportunities for the next generation. The world was to be turned upside down.

There were many young men with long hair in New Zealand in the 1970s but only a few who made the journey into a feminine self. For most it was a surface change following the international fashion led by rock musicians, quickly abandoned as careers required conformity to older modes of masculine appearance. But for some men and their partners, the subjects of this chapter, the journey went deeper: it was a commitment (or stumbling steps) to pursuing an idea of equality and, most of all, to trying to work out what equality meant. Did it mean looking alike (the men's long hair was often accompanied by beards), did it mean sharing the housework, did it mean working together; what extent of social reorganisation was necessary and, importantly, what did it mean for concepts of marriage and family? The meaning of equality was a contested notion and, in the working out, it held unanticipated, and sometimes personally devastating, consequences.

A number of women who were active in the women's liberation move-ment have written about its impact on their lives.[1] The stories of their male partners are less well known. This chapter attempts to address the changes in gender relations wrought by the resurgence of feminism in the 1970s. At that time, the language of gender roles was predominant, implying that, by changing behaviour, relationships between women and men would be trans-formed. Yet behavioural change was not a simple endeavour in a world where the social power available to people with male and female gender identities was unequal. In 1971, the Minister of Finance, Robert Muldoon, stated confidently, 'could we contemplate the situation where a woman getting equal pay is the breadwinner, and the husband stays home and looks after the children? I don't think we could.'[2] Support for the status quo was strong.

Feminists, by questioning received wisdom about male and female roles, set out to undermine the traditional order of things. They sought to bring about a change in consciousness, including an understanding that, rather than being natural, masculinity and femininity were performed in relation to each other. I am interested in this change in consciousness and in examining the disjunction between theory and practice as couples tried to incorporate new feminist ideas into their everyday living. In order to do so, I have charted the journeys of four Pakeha men whose lives were deeply touched by feminism in that decade. My aim is to put their stories into the wider context of the transformation of expectations of gender in 1970s New Zealand.[3]

In a postscript to his 1973 examination of the position of women, W. B. Sutch agreed with Germaine Greer that women themselves could impede the advance of feminism by clinging 'to the so-called "feminine role"'. But, he continued:

> An even bigger problem is the men. They, too, have been conditioned to their role as the lords of creation. This arrogance and sense of superiority exists in some degree in almost every man. The conditioning that induces it is deep and very lasting. While it remains neither women nor men will be free.[4]

According to Sutch, men and women were conditioned from infancy by a system of child raising based on a vision of men as providers and women as nurturers: a system that stunted the potentialities of both.

The model of relations between the sexes that my four interviewees —

Bob, Chris, James and Adam (all born in the 1940s) – grew up with was not dissimilar to that of most of their contemporaries in post-Second World War New Zealand when less than 10 per cent of married women were involved in the paid labour force.[5] Their mothers did not work in paid employment; with the exception of one woman plagued by mental illness, they devoted themselves to their children and their husbands' careers, and spent substantial amounts of time in voluntary work for the church and the community. Their fathers were the family breadwinners. James and Adam, however, were unusual in that their mothers had university degrees. Bob's mother had completed both Associate and Licentiate qualifications of Trinity College, London, in piano and violin, eventually having to decline a scholarship to study the violin in England because of her family circumstances. For all of the men, there was a sense that their mothers had 'talents which weren't used'.[6]

Bob related his sympathy for feminism directly to the influence of his mother:

> . . . more important for me than my awareness of her wasted talents was my sharing of her passion. It was possible to love, and to feel passionately about people, plants, and technical matters. It was possible to do this while hauling the washing or sitting by the river. This was a powerful person and this was a woman.

A nurturing of respect for women could prove to be as important as any non-traditional roles mothers might have.

These four men were part of the élite and mostly male group who studied at university in the 1960s. All four were attracted to anti-military causes, in the first instance, the Campaign for Nuclear Disarmament. As Bob put it, remembering his participation in the 1962 Featherston to Wellington anti-nuclear march, there was an 'awareness of polarisation' from a 'rigid caricature of masculinity on one hand and something different on the other hand'. Once men who had opposed war were regarded as shirking 'their responsibility towards society' by rejecting the male prerogative of taking up arms.[7] Men who chose not to play rugby might also have their masculinity thrown into question. The anti-apartheid movement, however, provided scope for a critique of the macho culture of rugby. The vague awareness of a different type of masculinity which Bob expressed might be reinforced by intellectual interests, in literature, in oriental philosophy, or in history.

By the mid-1960s, Committees on Vietnam were being organised in the main centres to oppose New Zealand's involvement in the Vietnam War. Young people were increasingly involved in new styles of protest, such as 'teach-ins' and mass demonstrations. The movement, Roberto Rabel has argued, 'led many to question the kind of society New Zealand was and what its role in the world should be'.[8] Although there were women involved in both the peace movement and the Vietnam protests, the questioning of societal values did not extend to women's rights. There was a limited vocabulary to discuss any types of relationships between the sexes and a fear that, should certain things be expressed, anarchy would result. This fear lay behind the 1967 decision to limit the viewing of the film version of James Joyce's *Ulysses* to audiences segregated by sex. Molly Bloom's soliloquy expressing sexual desire was thought likely to ignite uncontrollable passions.[9]

If heterosexual desire had to be expressed within controlled bounds, there was scarcely space at all for homosexual imaginings. Lesbianism was not something Adam, pursuing a master's degree in the mid-1960s, had heard of, though he succeeded in communicating the basics of what he imagined male homosexual behaviour to be to a horrified girlfriend. In 1965 four magazines, including *Modern Adonis* and *Male Classics*, were banned in New Zealand on the grounds that they 'intended to attract and promote homosexuality'.[10] The boundaries of sexual behaviour were tightly circumscribed, although the limits were being pushed. Increasing numbers of married women were working, the illegitimacy rate was rising to unprecedented levels and the contraceptive pill offered women new opportunities to experiment with their sexuality.

Two of my respondents fit a common profile of life events in the 1960s. Bob was typical in his age cohort in that he married at 24 in 1964. Unlike most of their peers, however, the couple delayed child bearing for four years. Chris's partner was one of the 50 per cent of 16–19-year-olds who were pregnant before marriage. Chris, at 20, 'wanted to do the decent thing', and married his 16-year-old lover at the end of 1968. Bound together by the impending child, the couple was shattered by the infant's subsequent death at only one year old. Later, in a 'very sixties' arrangement, Chris and his partner attempted to set up a household with another couple, in an open marriage arrangement. They pooled their possessions and tried to overcome 'old-fashioned' values such as jealousy. The continual intensity of debate and the emotional and sexual tensions were exhausting. Chris eventually left the foursome and found sanctuary working at a hospital where experiencing the disintegration of others' lives helped put his own into perspective.

Pursuit of advanced degrees meant postponement of personal entangle-ments for Adam and James and exposure to radical politics in the United States. 'Race was the big issue,' Adam recalled of his arrival in the Southern United States in 1965. And recognition of one type of oppression based on race was quickly followed by another, that of subjugation based on sex. James recalled reading Betty Friedan's *The Feminine Mystique*, first published in 1963, which argued that American culture did not 'permit women to accept or gratify their basic need to grow and fulfil their potentialities as human beings'.[11] In the same way in which Norman Mailer argued that Americans' fascination with the Negro was a way of getting out from under their own culture, feminism, for James, represented a 'way of getting out from under'.

In the United States, Adam and James entered into relationships with women who became interested in feminist literature and increasingly active in the women's movement. These women represented new forms of rebel-lion for New Zealand-raised men: urban sophistication and political icono-clasm. Both women were intellectuals, in pursuit of higher degrees, and both had been pregnant. For one woman, raised as a Catholic, pregnancy had meant an early and unsatisfactory marriage. Adam recalled that it was reading Kate Millett's *Sexual Politics* which led his partner into feminism. James's partner had had an earlier pregnancy that had been aborted under appalling circumstances, an event that radicalised her and began a long and energetic commitment to feminism.

In the late 1960s and early 1970s in American student circles, James recalled, 'everything that had been an established principle of life was up for question'. But the marriage contract itself, as yet, remained unexamined, even if the ceremonies were unconventional. Both men studying in the United States married there. For Adam, the civil ceremony was undertaken at a convenient moment, before friends arrived, while James and his partner had an outdoor celebration, James in purple flares, with the Beatles' 'Here Comes the Sun' playing. Marriage marked a commitment thought to be for life, even if the models of relationships parents provided 'no longer fit with the times and individual circumstances', or in fact were the epitome of what one was rebelling against.[12]

What did marriage mean? One strike for independence for women was retaining their own names. James's wife never considered abandoning her name for that of her husband. The women pursuing advanced degrees as-sumed that they would continue their academic careers and both took up teaching appointments, supporting their husbands while the men finished theses. But role models for egalitarian marriages in the sense of shared wage-earning and domestic responsibility were few. James recalled the 'disjuncture between what you thought ideologically should happen and what you emotionally felt'. Because these men had grown up in households where fathers were unquestioningly dominant, there was no guide to follow and the meaning of equality had to be hammered out intellectually and emotionally, often in a hostile climate.

Men embarking on relationships with feminist women in the 1970s found themselves in uncharted territory. The traditional male prerogative of taking the initiative in most aspects of relationships had to be abandoned, and this was both challenging and confusing. Chris met a feminist who 'had a completely different idea of what a male/female relationship was about'. This woman regarded herself as proactive in making decisions, whether about having sex or where one went for the evening. No longer was the man expected to be in control, and feminists had arguments to back up their positions. Acceptance of the intellectual premises of feminism came quickly for some men 'but it was very, very hard to actually start acting and believing this in terms of your personal life'.[13] Giving up control was perhaps the hardest part, having grown up with the belief that men were 'inherently superior'.[14] It was also difficult to adjust to a relationship in which time apart, such as separate holidays, was as valued as time together, in a culture where most women acquiesced to 'male demands, male patterns and male careers' and where the symbol of domestic happiness was shared leisure:

> Friday nights I used to find particularly bad because, always, after a hard week, I felt like relaxing and my idea of relaxing was to go over to her place, play music, and fall into bed. Her idea of relaxing was to have time to herself.

It was 'difficult to handle, continually having to squash myself, trying to retrain and focus myself on what was the best thing to do rather than on what my gut instinct wanted to do'.[15]

Men committed to equality chose to demonstrate their commitment in different ways. Chris typed out his partner's library school bibliography on equal pay 'as a political statement. She couldn't type. Neither could I but I felt as a male I had to support this somehow. So I typed it out with two fingers, 30 pages.' Such gestures of support were easier than fundamental decisions about the future, where men might derive support from the wider society's positive associations of power and control with masculinity. In particular, the question of equality in career aspirations created tensions between couples.

Chris and his partner completed library school and faced the question of career moves:

> then came the big decision. We both were qualified, we both wanted to seek jobs, we both wanted careers, who was going to go where? And if we wanted to keep the relationship that meant one person had to follow the other . . . we hesitantly debated this problem and again there was something in me as a male that felt somehow that I should have the first choice . . . that if I found a good job she should . . . acquiesce and find a job somewhere with me and we never really reached agreement on that.

Chris's problem was solved by accident: by chance the couple ended up with jobs in the same city. The solution to this problem for James and his partner lay in applying to share one job in a university department in 1973, a request that proved too radical for the university. The compromise offered by the university was very much a reflection of the times, giving James a full-time job and his partner a third of a job, and the option to organise the teaching as they wished. The couple was such a novelty that they were the subjects of a television interview on their domestic arrangements. James recalled being aware at the time that people were interested in finding models of new ways of living. Adam's wife accompanied him to New Zealand when he took up a job and did some part-time teaching while finishing her doctoral thesis. Bob and his wife worked in the same city, although she worked part-time after their first child was born. In these two latter cases, decisions about careers had an impact on the relationship at a later point.

Did equality mean doing everything together? James and his partner taught together which, in the end, he became 'a real strain being in the situation of living with someone and going to work with them. It was too much. It was unreasonable.' Brought together by intellectual interests, the two academic couples continued to pursue them jointly, but with varying levels of intensity. The nature of these men's employment, however, allowed them flexible use of their time that was denied men with rigid working hours.

Adam had cared for his wife's two children while she worked in North America and on return to New Zealand continued to do the bulk of his academic work at home, allowing attention to household matters. Bob believed that his wife did more around the house because of the nature of his full-time employment. Domesticity, for these educated women, was not enough. 'The physical structure of women', wrote Christine Wren, 'no more suits them to washing floors, cooking, cleaning toilets or for that matter looking [after] children than the equivalent parts of the male.'[16] To feminists, roles were not inherent in biology but constructed; it was possible to take them apart and reorder them. But there was tension in translating theory into practice. Women who were good cooks were reluctant to abandon their kitchens to the hands of less competent partners. Men had to learn 'that if the house was a tip it was as much their responsibility as their partners'.[17] Women 'had to cope with breaking traditional bonds' by demanding partners take an equal share in domestic and family life. What one regarded as equal might be interpreted by the other as too much, causing resentment if well-meaning partners felt their efforts were unappreciated. 'It was difficult working out what the boundaries were, [when it] was fair to be assertive, and coming to grips with what you could intellectually see was legitimate but what emotionally you found hard to take.'[18]

The lack of parental leave meant the decision to have children impacted on careers. James and his partner realised that, in order for her to be able to continue her commitment to her job, she would have to give birth when university classes were not in session. They managed to plan their first child's birth for November and the second's for February. James attended fathers' classes at the hospital in 1975:

> All these men were very gauche and embarrassed about the situation. They realised that it was a modern thing to be there but they felt uncomfortable, particularly in a room full of blokes, about showing that they were comfortable about being there. And I remember we went round and had a tour round all the various parts of the hospital and went to the premature ward and saw this little baby and one bloke said 'Oh, he doesn't look like an All Black front row does he?' And the whole place cracked up . . . the edge of tension exploded.

Six years earlier in Dunedin, Bob attended antenatal classes and his son's birth, by no means a universal practice at that point. He found the pre-birth involvement enjoyable and an important emotional preparation for parenthood. Adam also attended the birth of his children. From the outset, raising children was to be a shared experience. All the men with children attempted to share the routine child-care tasks in a way that their fathers never had. Such intimate relations with children were demanding but also intensely enjoyable, an experience, James recalled, 'that humanises you and gives you a sense of proportion'.

Men's groups formed in order to examine what the commitment to equality meant. The one Bob belonged to in 1970 was 'loose, with no ideological position' and did not last long. Chris and Adam did not belong to such a group. James joined a men's group in Wellington in 1973–74, made up of middle-class professional men married to feminist women:

> We were all basically supportive of the idea [of feminism] but realised that actually it needed a good deal of talking through and mutual support and trying to work out what an appropriate role for men was that didn't sort of make you a complete wimp and when it was legitimate to say you had rights too. Morally you were on the wrong foot and so . . . it took a lot of working out. It was really helpful to share things with other people.

The couples who began exploring the meanings of equality found that the issues multiplied the closer they looked. Departures from the masculine norm were often tentative. The tendency to combine long hair with beards perhaps expressed a desire to maintain and express masculinity within the context of a reappraised femininity and limited changes in men's behaviour.

There was optimism that collective institutions could be created to counter the 'military-industrial complex'.[19] Being 'alternative' encapsulated various commitments to ecology, to conservation and to self-help: 'There was a strong sense that you were creating a new way of doing things'.[20] Food co-operatives were formed to cut out middlemen and 'beat the system'.[21] It took energy and commitment to get to the vegetable market early in the morning and then distribute the food to others. While Bob remembered the good fresh produce, for Adam, from a 'book family' with little experience of business, the co-op 'was bit of a grind': 'The buyers would go in . . . and cabbages were cheap, and they'd come back with a box of cabbages, and get really pissed off if people wouldn't want cabbages'. And within the co-op there were struggles between women and men over decision-making, Chris recalled, 'as much as in any other social grouping'.

Energy also went into setting up alternative preschools, when existing playcentres and kindergartens were found to be lacking. A collective organisation pooled funds to buy a house for a preschool:

> We wanted to do something with a group of people and there was a feeling that if we started this thing up it would be something we were all equally involved in in some way. And it was, there was quite a spirit of everyone being involved in different ways, from practical ways to planning what the kids would be doing and actually going along and being there with the children.[22]

Such child-care alternatives aimed to foster fluidity in sex roles and less authoritarian relations between adults and children. Much energy was put into trying to create different ways of living that avoided hierarchy and competitiveness. And 'each activity . . . generated its own larger community'.[23] The cohesiveness of these alternative communities meant that the men involved never had to justify the extent of their involvement in the domestic sphere. Bob believed the 'Kiwi joker' who disdained child care and the domestic sphere 'existed more in mythology than reality', but then he 'usually moved in circles with teachers and people who are professionally pretty interested in children and in the importance of children'.

There was less protection from criticism for Chris who, with his partner, set up house with a group of feminist women (some of whom initially had reservations about a male in the household), including a lesbian couple. Up to this point Chris had had little exposure to the gay community:

> I remember sometime shortly after we moved in . . . the first physical shock of seeing two women behaving intimately towards each other in an obvious sexual way. . . . Part of me said that's good and another part of me said that's not right. . . . But eventually it became more the norm.

Members of the wider feminist group associated with the household were involved in relating sexual fantasies for a New Zealand edition of *Forum* – a soft-porn magazine – a matter which they saw as 'part and package of liberating their sexuality, being able to talk about these things openly'. There was an excitement for women in being able to talk about sex in a way that had previously been prohibited for 'nice' girls. Soon feminist talk focused more on exploitative male sexuality and lobbying began for amendment of the 1977 Evidence Act to make the sexual history of rape victims irrelevant in the trials of accused rapists.

For some women, the logic of feminism was clear: sleeping with men meant sleeping with the enemy. And for some the enemy was cast, for strategic reasons, as less than human. Acknowledging the humanity of the 'enemy' could complicate political commitments and undermine efforts at social change.[24] Bob found 'the thread attacking men . . . a bit scary, and [it] made me feel a bit defensive'. He recalled a close friend's distress when his wife left him for a lesbian lover:

> His distress was because he loved his wife, not because she left him for a woman. For some time when he rang his wife and the lover answered the phone, she would call out to his wife that 'the mutant' wanted to speak to her.

Such hostility to men seemed to Bob 'quite incompatible with the template of passionate feminism set in my mind by my experiences with my mother'. In his view, the theoretical advances being made were not being matched by practical developments in relationships.

Adam recalled a lesbian member of his wife's feminist group treating him as if he had little right to exist in his own household. He noted two tensions within feminism in the mid-1970s. One was feminist women's recognition of the middle-class nature of their movement and their desire to reach out to working-class women. The other was 'that living with a man was to some extent inconsistent with or incompatible' with feminism, which had a 'sub-lesbian theme'. A lesbian woman's expressed desire for a man's partner could be 'disconcerting' and the critique of marriage 'destabilising'.

Marriage was certainly under the microscope. A Dunedin Collective for Women member reported 'shattering news'. She had learnt at the first national women's liberation conference that 'legally *a woman must provide domestic labour to her husband*'.[25] 'It may be', another member wrote, 'that the institution of marriage as it exists is not objectively a very healthy one for a woman.'[26] According to another article, it was a 'total institution' akin to a prison or a psychiatric institution, serving to 'reinforce isolation of married women, dependency, loss of self esteem'. Unlike prisoners and asylum inmates, however, women could be seen as complicit in their own incarceration: 'the role of a wife is largely bound by custom as opposed to authority and therefore it is within woman's power to change it'.[27]

The critique of marriage and commitment to collectivity led, in some quarters, to sexual experimentation and a 'feeling that marriage wasn't all that valuable'.[28] By the mid-1970s, 'living together' outside marriage had become much more common, signalling an important attitudinal change.[29] Possessiveness in relationships could be seen as a patriarchal plot that kept women tied to one man. For some this meant there was 'not the same exclusive commitment to marriage and the relationship'.[30] Intellectually, the idea that one had a primary partner and that that partner might have affairs with others seemed sustainable but emotionally, 'when it came to the crunch, it was very difficult to deal with'.[31] Some couples coped with sexual experimentation; for others it led to an unravelling of the relationship. These unravellings had serious consequences because of another issue brought to the fore by feminism: that of shared child raising.

Bob and Adam were divorced in the 1970s and faced the trauma of separation from their children. Both had been very involved with their children and, when their wives wanted to live in different places, they did not want their children to go. They had, in Bob's words, deep emotional bonds:

> because if you're involved with your children right from pre-birth, you're aware of them developing in the womb, and you're preparing and fantasising about them right from that stage, then you have a very strong commitment to your children and it's an emotional commitment.

Bob, unusually for the time, was granted care of his children. A few other fathers who had invested time in their children were also awarded care of their children when the matter came to court. In one respondent's view, they were better at raising their children than feminists of that generation because they were less conflicted about their role encompassing both parenting and working.[32] The decision to award 'custody' to men might be seen as a logical outcome of equality but it was not anticipated by feminist women. In Fern Mercier's words, '[t]he cost of grounding ideals in reality is high, and we and our children paid dearly'.[33]

From James's perspective, 'doing that hard work on personal changes was more important than passing laws'. One of the important legal changes was the 1976 Matrimonial Property Act which, for the first time, recognised the contribution made to marriage by a non-earning spouse. Speaking in support of the bill, Dr A. M. Finlay argued that 'We in this country have a long heritage of viewing [matrimonial property] through male eyes, starting from the position where the woman had no rights at all'.[34] In a small but important way, feminists of the 1970s began dismantling this heritage and forced men to see the world through women's eyes.

For some men, trying to view the world through women's eyes was a way of getting out from the constraints of New Zealand male culture, and it became part of a larger critique of a society in which the All Blacks were regarded as the epitome of manliness. With hindsight, the belief that male and female roles were completely interchangeable seems to Bob to have been 'naïve'. Yet at the time that belief was extremely liberating and opened up all sorts of possibilities about how to live, as well as high expectations of personal happiness. The latter foundered as relationships fell apart, but all the men interviewed see their particular circumstances, rather than the assumptions of feminism, as responsible for placing their relationships in jeopardy. Holding two autonomous individuals together despite their different trajectories no longer seemed essential when individual needs could be better met apart.

★   ★   ★

The result of women's liberation, an anonymous 1970s pamphlet warned, would be the destruction of 'marriages, families and homes'. The antidote to this 'Diabolical Doctrine' lay in women establishing 'MAN (head) of the home'. 'God doesn't want a masculine woman, neither does he want a Feminine Man.' A masculine woman was one who took up traditionally male occupations, had 'great power and influence' and lost 'natural affection'.[35] Feminism dethroned men from their position as 'lords of creation' and a few men, my four respondents included, tried to establish relationships of equality. But if a 'masculine' woman's way to advance appeared clear, through fulfilling employment and equal pay, the path for 'feminine' men was not so obvious. Feminism allowed women to expand the vocabulary of the feminine identity and the history of women's oppression gave their claims moral authority. Women entered public bars, wore trousers, lifted weights and entered non-traditional occupations such as fire fighting. In contrast, men who accepted the feminist cultural critique were required to question the basis of their identity, the power and control they had traditionally exercised.

Men were to give up power, but just when did self-abnegation stop? Was it for this generation of men to give up all their ambitions in order to hold relationships together? None of the men took this path. Individual rights were held in tension with responsibilities and a new commitment to sharing domestic tasks and, as with any untried route, there were unexpected outcomes. Those committed to feminism in the 1970s opened up paths of possibility for the future and, for some of them, there was no turning back.

I would argue that the patterns of respect for women's abilities and ambitions that men developed in personal relationships were an essential underpinning for working alongside women in public life. The small understandings hammered out between couples pursuing equality had large implications for women in the workplace. In the 1970s greater numbers of women moved into medicine, law, university teaching and non-traditional occupations. The feminist claim that women should be accorded equality made it possible to demand new standards of behaviour. Unwanted sexual attention at work, for example, could now be named sexual harassment. And, in the long term, women's right to bodily integrity was asserted in the legal prohibition against rape in marriage.

'One came out of that whole period', James believes, 'with quite high expectations of happiness.' And for this highly selected and unrepresentative group of men happiness in personal relationships remains modelled on a vision of equality, even if what that means in personal relationships is still contested:

you've got to [be involved with] someone who is as interested in life and as fulfilled in life as you are otherwise it is necessarily an unequal thing and in the end it's not satisfying. I'm absolutely convinced of that, I have no doubts.[36]

Chris, who briefly returned to being the provider and decision-maker within a traditional relationship, found unexpected difficulties:

despite the comfort I felt slipping back into a relationship where I was expected to be in control, I still didn't find that very easy. I found it easier being on terms with someone . . . I could treat as an equal. . . . The other kind of relationship I now find . . . I can't take. I want someone . . . I can really relate to as a friend. . . . If you see someone as inferior you don't treat them as a friend, you treat them as an object.

Feminism promised to change both men and women, and for Bob, Chris, James and Adam, openness to change provided them with new sources of satisfaction in their lives. These men were a privileged, but also an adventurous, few. They did not go all the way, as some did, and experiment with role reversal by becoming house husbands. They have abandoned long hair and flares and perhaps the optimism that a new society can be readily achieved by force of will. But they have not jettisoned the idea of equality between the sexes, literally brought home to them in the 1970s. The five-year-old daughter who looked at the photograph of her long-haired parents and commented 'That's when Dad was a woman' was well aware that an era had passed. The legacy of that era will be played out in her life and those of her contemporaries.

Thanks to Megan Cook and Dorothy Page, who made very useful comments on an early draft of this essay.

1   Maud Cahill and Christine Dann, eds, *Changing Our Lives: Women Working in the Women's Liberation Movement, 1970-1990*, Wellington, 1991.
2   Cited in Sandra Coney, 'The Role of Women in New Zealand Society. A Submission to the Select Committee on Women's Rights by Auckland Women's Liberation', Kathleen Johnson papers, MS papers 4580, f.8, Alexander Turnbull Library (ATL), Wellington.
3   I am grateful to the four men who agreed to be interviewed. The author carried out the interviews and pseudonyms have been used.
4   Dorothy Page directed me to Sutch's contemporary view. W. B. Sutch, *Women with a Cause*, Wellington, 1973, p. 231.
5   In 1951 9.7 per cent of married women were in paid employment. Department of Statistics, *All About Women in New Zealand*, Wellington, 1993, p. 217.
6   Adam, interviewed in Dunedin, 31 October 1997. In 1969 29.6 per cent of university graduates were women. Department of Statistics, *Profile of Women: A Statistical Comparison of Females and Males in New Zealand*, Wellington, 1985, p. 24.

7   Lex Johnston quoted in David Grant, *Out in the Cold: Pacifists and Conscientious Objectors in New Zealand during World War II*, Auckland, 1986, p. 123.
8   Roberto G. Rabel, 'The Vietnam Antiwar Movement in New Zealand', *Peace and Change,* 17, 1, 1992, p. 27.
9   See, for example, the review of *Ulysses* in the *Listener,* 16 June 1967, p. 25.
10 Stuart Perry, *The Indecent Publications Tribunal: A Social Experiment*, Christchurch, 1965, p. 117.
11 Betty Friedan, *The Feminine Mystique*, Harmondsworth, 1963, p. 68.
12 Adam, interviewed in Dunedin, 31 October 1997.
13 Chris, interviewed in Wellington, 6 November 1997.
14 Chris, interviewed in Wellington, 6 November 1997.
15 Chris, interviewed in Wellington, 6 November 1997.
16 Christine Wren, *The Synthetic Woman in a Plastic World*, Wellington, 1972, p. 1.
17 James, interviewed in Wellington, 6 November 1997.
18 James, interviewed in Wellington, 6 November 1997.
19 James, interviewed in Wellington, 6 November 1997.
20 Adam, interviewed in Dunedin, 31 October 1997.
21 Bob, interviewed in Dunedin, 30 October 1997.
22 Bob, interviewed in Dunedin, 30 October 1997.
23 Adam, interviewed in Dunedin, 31 October 1997.
24 'In many radical movements, left and right,' Cass Sunstein has written, 'those who seek social change portray themselves as more than human, while they portray their enemies as less than human or as fundamentally other than human. . . . Of course there are strategic and other reasons for speaking in these ways. Acknowledgment that, for example, members of the Nazi party were also human beings may complicate and in that way undermine our effort to understand what the Holocaust was all about. . . . Such an acknowledgment may lead to a kind of distorting evenhandedness and easy sentimentality that make social change and looking at reality hard to accomplish.' Cited in a review of Stephen Macedo, ed., *Reassessing the Sixties*, by Francis Rocca, 'The decade of radical disaster', *Times Literary Supplement*, 1 August 1997, p. 12.
25 *Woman,* 4, 9 April 1972, p. 1.
26 *Woman,* 5, 23 April 1972, p. 2.
27 *Woman,* 14, 15 September 1972, p. 4.
28 Bob, interviewed in Dunedin, 30 October 1997.
29 Chris, interviewed in Wellington, 6 November 1997.
30 Bob, interviewed in Dunedin, 30 October 1997.
31 Chris, interviewed in Wellington, 6 November 1997.
32 James, interviewed in Wellington, 6 November 1997.
33 Fern Mercier, 'An Odyssey', in Cahill and Dann, eds, *Changing our Lives*, p. 51.
34 *NZPD*, 408, 9 December 1976, p. 4723.
35 Undated, single sheet, Kathleen Johnson, MS papers 4580, f.7, ATL.
36 James, interviewed in Wellington, 6 November 1997.

CONTRIBUTORS

Frazer Andrewes is a PhD candidate in the Department of History, University of Melbourne, Australia. Having completed his MA at the University of Auckland on the representation of masculinities in post-war New Zealand culture, he is currently undertaking research into the experiences of modernity in Australia during the 1930s.

Barbara Brookes is a senior lecturer in history at the University of Otago. Her research interests have focused on the history of women and the history of medicine. She is the author of *Abortion in England, 1900-1967* (Croom Helm, 1988) and a co-editor of two volumes of essays on the History of Women in New Zealand. She is currently working on an overview history of women in New Zealand and has recently edited a volume of essays on 'The Idea of the Home in New Zealand' (forthcoming, Bridget Williams Books, 1999).

Caroline Daley is a lecturer in history at the University of Auckland where she teaches twentieth-century New Zealand social and gender history. She became interested in the gendered history of leisure while working on her book, *Girls & Women, Men & Boys: Gender in Taradale 1886-1930* (Auckland University Press, 1999). She is now working on a book-length study of gender and leisure in twentieth-century New Zealand.

Bronwyn Dalley is a senior historian at the Historical Branch, Department of Internal Affairs. Her chapter in this volume was researched and written during her tenure at the Stout Research Centre as the J.D. Stout Fellow in New Zealand Cultural Studies. It is part of a larger study on gender, culture and sexuality in New Zealand urban centres between 1869 and 1929.

Tim Frank was born in Auckland in 1962, and is married with four children. He is presently researching New Zealand fathers and fatherhood in the early twentieth century for his PhD at the University of Auckland.

Charlotte Macdonald teaches in the History Department at Victoria University. Her published works include *Women in History: Essays on European Women in New Zealand History* and *Women in History 2*, both edited with Barbara Brookes and Margaret Tennant (Allen & Unwin, 1986; Bridget Williams Books, 1992); *The Book of New Zealand Women/Ko Kui Ma te Kaupapa*, edited with Merimeri Penfold and Bridget Williams (Bridget Williams Books, 1991), *The Vote, the Pill and the Demon Drink* (Bridget Williams Books, 1993) and '*My Hand Will Write What My Heart Dictates*', with Frances Porter (AUP/BWB, 1996).

Deborah Montgomerie is a lecturer in history at the University of Auckland. After completing a master's degree at Auckland University she worked as a researcher for the Waitangi Tribunal. In 1989 she went to the United States on a Fulbright scholarship, receiving a PhD in American history from Duke University in 1993. She is currently working on a book provisionally titled, 'The Women's War: New Zealand Women 1939–45'.

Erik Olssen, FRSNZ, has been Professor of History at the University of Otago since 1984. He has published several books, among them *The Red Feds* (Oxford University Press, 1988) and *Building the New World* (Auckland University Press, 1995) and over 60 papers, including several essays on the history of women and the history of the family in New Zealand. He is also director of the Caversham Project, one of the largest social-history projects in the world.

Jock Phillips is acting general manager, Heritage Group in the Department of Internal Affairs. He came to the department in 1989 as the nation's Chief Historian following 16 years teaching American and New Zealand History at Victoria University of Wellington, where he was the founding director of the Stout Research Centre for the study of New Zealand society, history and culture. From 1993 to 1998, he also served as the conceptual leader for the history exhibitions at Te Papa, the new Museum of New Zealand. He has published 10 books on New Zealand history, of which the best known is *A Man's Country?*

Danielle Sprecher graduated in 1997 with an MA (Hons) in history from the University of Auckland. Her chapter in this book is based on work from her MA thesis, which was concerned with representations of gender and fashion in the interwar period in New Zealand.

INDEX